# SOLD

## — TO THE —
## HIGHEST BIDDER

# DANIEL M. FRIEDENBERG

★

# SOLD

## —— TO THE ——
# HIGHEST BIDDER

*The Presidency from
Dwight D. Eisenhower to George W. Bush*

★

## FOREWORD BY HOWARD ZINN

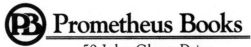 **Prometheus Books**

59 John Glenn Drive
Amherst, New York 14228-2197

Published 2002 by Prometheus Books

Inquiries should be addressed to
Prometheus Books
59 John Glenn Drive
Amherst, New York 14228–2197
VOICE: 716–691–0133, ext. 207
FAX: 716–564–2711
WWW.PROMETHEUSBOOKS.COM

06 05 04 03 02    5 4 3 2 1

Library of Congress Cataloging-in-Publication Data

Friedenberg, Daniel M.
    Sold to the highest bidder : the presidency from Dwight D. Eisenhower to George W. Bush / Daniel M. Friedenberg ; foreword by Howard Zinn.
        p. cm.
    Includes bibliographical references and index.
    ISBN 1–57392–923–9 (alk. paper)
    1. Presidents—United States. 2. Democracy—United States. 3. Income distribution—United States. 4. United States—Politics and government—1945–1989. 5. United States—Politics and government—1989– I. Title: Presidency from Dwight D. Eisenhower to George W. Bush. II. Title.

JK511 .F75 2001
973.92'092'2—dc21

2001049202

# CONTENTS

★

# LIST OF ILLUSTRATIONS

---★---

★

"He [the king of Brobdingnag] then desired to know, what arts were practiced in electing those whom I called Commoners. Whether a stranger with a strong purse, might not influence the vulgar voters. . . . How it came to pass, that people were so violently bent upon getting into this assembly . . . that his Majesty seemed to doubt it might possibly not be always sincere: and he desired to know, whether such zealous gentlemen could have any views of refunding themselves for the charges and trouble they were at. . . ."

Jonathan Swift, *Gulliver's Travels*, "A Voyage to Brobdingnag"

# FOREWORD
## *Howard Zinn*

I t has been a persistent theme in the history of political philosophy, from Plato onward, that wealth has a crucial effect on any
system of government. Plato did not believe in democracy, but he
understood that the possession of wealth by the leaders of a society
would have a detrimental effect. In his *Republic*, his philosopher
kings would live austere lives, to avoid their corruption: ". . . none of
them [the guardians who are rulers of the state] should have any
property of his own beyond what is absolutely necessary."

In our own time, we find that this requirement, even if fulfilled,
would be insufficient to ensure honest and good government,
because the president of the United States, even if he is not affluent
himself, may be surrounded by people of wealth whose interests he
is expected to serve. Plato's assumption was utopian, "that our aim
in founding the State was not the disproportionate happiness of any
one class, but the greatest happiness of the whole."

Jean-Jacques Rousseau, in his *Discourse on the Origin of Inequality*,
did not describe a Platonic utopian state, but described the reality he
saw in modern society, that governments were established for the
benefit of the wealthy class, and that

> . . . society and laws which gave new fetters to the weak and new
> forces to the rich, irretrievably destroyed natural liberty, established

11

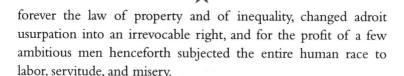

forever the law of property and of inequality, changed adroit usurpation into an irrevocable right, and for the profit of a few ambitious men henceforth subjected the entire human race to labor, servitude, and misery.

Across the Channel from Rousseau, Adam Smith was describing the nature of government much more honestly than those today who see Smith as the hero of the "free enterprise" philosophy. In a lecture in the 1760s he said: "Laws and governments may be considered in this and indeed in every case as a combination of the rich to oppress the poor, and preserve to themselves the inequality of the goods which would otherwise be soon destroyed by the attacks of the poor, who if not hindered by the government would soon reduce the others to an equality with themselves by open violence."

Such a statement could not be made so bluntly to people as literate as the Americans, who had just won their struggle for independence against England, a large number of them having read Tom Paine's *Common Sense* and the outpouring of popular pamphlets that accompanied the revolutionary struggle. So when James Madison was setting forth the political philosophy behind the Constitution in the Federalist Paper #10 (designed to persuade New Yorkers to ratify the new document), he made the same point, more indirectly, but unmistakably.

Madison noted that societies were divided into what he called "factions," based on who owned property and who did not. This would breed conflict, and a strong government would be needed to control that conflict. And the faction that most needed to be controlled, he said, was "a majority faction" (a statement that should trouble those who think the Founding Fathers wanted a democracy).

The framers of the Constitution had fresh in their minds Shays's Rebellion, the revolt of farmers in western Massachusetts against the moneyed power that controlled the state legislature. It would be good, Madison said, to have a strong central government whose power covered all the states, because then "[a] rage for

⋆

paper money, for an abolition of debts, for an equal division of property, or for any other improper or wicked project, will be less apt to pervade the whole body of the Union than a particular member of it."

The government that was put in place by the Constitution fulfilled that aim. It would, over the next two centuries and beyond, by its domestic and foreign policies, maintain the dominant position of the wealthy in society. Its legislation would be class legislation: tariffs for the manufacturers; subsidies for the railroads, the oil companies, and other giant corporations; armed forces to clear out the Indians, to open the West to enterprise, and to disperse rebellious workers who went out on strike.

The chief executive would preside over all that. Only in rare instances, when popular movements grew powerful enough to threaten the system, as in the 1930s and 1960s, would the president sponsor legislation on behalf of minorities, the poor, the unemployed, the homeless, the farmers, and the workers. After the decline of the social movements of the 1960s, the government, whether Republican or Democrat, would revert to its normal stance, maintaining economic injustice at home and using its military power abroad in the interest of corporate wealth.

There is a simplistic test of democracy which asserts that the more people vote, in what is called a "free election," the more democratic the society is likely to be. But when huge sums of money enter the electoral process, determine who are to be the candidates, and create a dependency of those elected on the wealthy interests who made their election possible, democracy has been corrupted. When the means of communication in a society become concentrated in fewer and fewer hands, so that the information given to the public is now controlled, elections can no longer be said to be free.

These assertions demand that historical evidence be brought forth to support them. Daniel M. Friedenberg supplies that evidence powerfully, persuasively, and colorfully, as he describes and dissects the policies of the American presidents of the last half century.

If he had exposed the power of the moneyed interests over the presidency in the case of one individual, it might be dismissed as an aberration from the norm. When that power is shown to persist again and again, in the administrations of ten presidents, the accusation cannot be dismissed. This book thus performs an immensely valuable service for democracy in America. It is patriotic in the best sense of that term.

# INTRODUCTION

*"Government is not reason, it is not eloquence—it is force."*
George Washington

*"So that in the first place, I put for a generall inclination of all mankind, a perpetuall and restlesse desire of Power after power, that ceaseth only in Death."*
Thomas Hobbes, *Leviathan*, part 1, chap. 11

The writer André Gide agreed with most of his fellow Frenchmen in supporting the Vichy puppet government set up by Nazi Germany during World War II. He then wondered if he was right because, he noted in his wartime diary, the majority was usually wrong. This skeptical view, the opposite of the populist *vox populi vox Dei*—the voice of the people is the voice of God[1]—has some roots in truth. Two obvious examples come to mind. The great majority of the Spanish people backed the Inquisition, which was only abolished there by Napoleon; a more recent case is the enthusiasm of most Germans, among the most cultured people in Europe, for Hitler.

One could take a reverse view of the quality of American presidents to the extension of the franchise. When blacks, women, and the poor could not vote, Washington, the two Adams, Jefferson, Madison, and Monroe were elected. After the victory of the so-called common man with Andrew Jackson, both the presidents and the quality of their cabinets declined to such an extent that, following Lincoln, even educated persons can barely remember the names of our chief executives during the rest of the nineteenth century.

This is not an argument for a return to monopoly control by

propertied white Protestant males. However, it does show that a larger electorate does not of itself mean better candidates. A misinformed majority can be worse than an informed minority.

The essential point is that the quality of candidates elected in modern times depends not so much on more votes or more communication—whether through newspapers, magazines, radio, television, or the Internet—but on the pressures brought to bear through huge sums to distort and lie, as well as to blot out contrary views. That such spin may even be sincere in some cases is irrelevant: The belief that the top monied class should rule society can be genuine and indeed was embraced by many honest men throughout American history. But this belief cannot be stated, for, as the early political party leaders of the Federalists learned, it does not win elections. The aim, therefore, is to convey the opposite view, that the ordinary citizen rules, in order to retain power. This is the source of the corruption of communication as well as the cynicism of both the candidates and the general public.

We have no Conservative and Labor parties, with clearly defined views, in our country as there are in Europe.[2] We have, rather, a froth of candidates put up by private interests, very often contributing money to both parties. It is the money of these interests—or the personal fortunes of the candidates themselves—that buys the media, and it is the media that, except in times of extreme crisis such as the election of Franklin D. Roosevelt, elect candidates. Our communication thus is less education and more miseducation. And this usually does not displease the voting public, which often wants a placebo elected. Whatever the aspirant to office—sharp or dull, honest or cheat, sincere or cunning, man or woman, and now black or white and Catholic or Jewish as well as Protestant—it is money that most often determines the result. The candidates may be labeled liberal or conservative, but they always circle close to that center set by those defending their economic power. In effect, we don't have a two-party system but rather a dual-party system. This also accounts for what is called the stability of American political life.

In general, it may be said that the opposite candidate elected would make small difference.[3] The interests behind the party machines, like pilot fish that act as guides to sharks, strive to find the person who can best be sold to the public, or a very rich individual who can buy the media. Such candidates, to cite from recent presidents, are: a military general who had contempt for politics and never voted; a handsome man with a huge sexual appetite and a super-rich father; a machiavellian liar and crook; and a genial actor with much charm and less wit. And those elected, if not previously wealthy, become millionaires in or after leaving office, through favors given and received. The cynic Ambrose Bierce defined politics as "the conduct of public affairs for private advantage."[4]

The American system has been almost bulletproof for most of our history. Very few questioned the basic premise that the United States was the best of all possible worlds.

There was always what seemed a boundless frontier to seek new fortune. Few indeed thought that the idealistic phrase stamped on the Statue of Liberty, "Give me your tired, your poor, your huddled masses yearning to breathe free . . . ," might also have been stamped, "Give me your cheap labor." Until recently, the African American was *The Invisible Man*, in the clever title of Ralph Ellison's novel. The Native American was corralled in deserts that not even poor white men sought to steal. The immigrant ideal was to become old American in speech, thought, and ethnic osmosis. And since most immigrants were very poor and came from countries where conditions were terrible, the system indeed functioned well.

The first real crack in this facade was the Vietnam War, when millions of young Americans came to realize that many men in high office were fools or liars. This crisis split the country. The second crack was the changing nature of a society starting to be dominated by new technology that rested on employees with great skills acquired only by expensive education. A two-tier society was becoming more and more obvious. The real value of the wages of many employees began to drop, while the wealth of the elite was in sharp ascent, a gap indeed now greater than in all other advanced nations. Drug sales became a major industry for the deprived, with corruption at the top. Combined with this was the rise of extreme factions, some honest and some pushed by fanatics.

New immigrants, often illegal—many crossing a three-thousand-mile Mexican border, which is more a sieve than a border—have also begun to gush into the United States in vast numbers; states such as California and cities such as New York and Houston now have majority nonwhite populations.

The response to rising tension caused by these factors has not been gross repression. That is not the American way. It is to propagate misinformation in order to pander to native prejudice and to the fear of what is different. It is to emphasize that the old ways are the best ways and that if one only accepts the old ways all will turn out for the best. This alchemy calls for more and more money to control the media, for it is so oblivious to many problems that only by magic can it be exorcised. The propaganda drumbeat is to tell people that malcontents and liberals will go away if only the right people are elected.

Candidates above all want to be elected. Illegal immigrants cannot vote, many who are legal rarely do, and the native poor are often cynical or indifferent. Elections, thus, and especially the primaries, are in the hands of those with money. And those with money are in general more concerned with lowering taxes than with the commonweal of a community made up in part of people toward whom they often feel hostility rather than compassion.[5]

How this system works—namely, through the control of the electoral process—may most easily be seen through an analysis of the nomination and election of top candidates for public office. The best example is the election of presidents. Those in office in the second half of the twentieth century are an accurate reflection of the technique.

INFECTIOUS

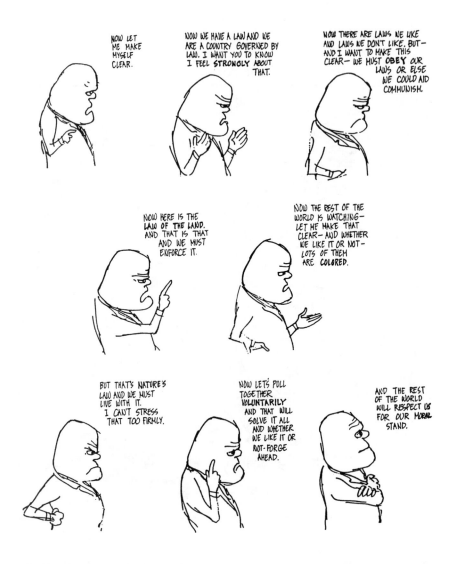

From *Feiffer: Jules Feiffer's America from Eisenhower to Reagan* by Jules Feiffer, edited by Steven Heller, copyright © 1982 by Jules Feiffer. Used by permission of Alfred A. Knopf, a division of Random House, Inc.

# CHAPTER ONE

# DWIGHT DAVID EISENHOWER
## (1953–1961)

> *"To know how to put modest talents to the best use is an art which commands admiration, and often wins a wider reputation than real worth."*
> La Rochefoucauld, *Maxims*, no. 162

> *"Concealment, evasion, factious combinations, the surrender of convictions to party objects, and the systematic pursuit of expediency are things of daily occurrence among men of the highest character, once embarked in the contentions of political life."*
> Robert Lowe, Editorial, *London Times*, February 7, 1852

The second half of the twentieth century began with the two-time election in 1952 and 1956 of President Dwight D. Eisenhower, the American supreme commander and military hero of World War II. After the war and during the growing Communist threat, the country wanted a strong leader, and a victorious general neatly fit the bill. From the hairiest caveman to King David to Alexander the Great to Julius Caesar to Napoleon Bonaparte, the easy choice for most people is to turn to a knight in shining armor.

Americans think themselves a peaceful people, but our wars and our military leaders elected to the supreme office tell a different story. The United States was born in, and nourished by, conflict. Aside from the obvious fact that the country reached its present size through a series of wars swallowing Native American land and lopping off one-third of Mexico, from the Revolution to World War II

Americans engaged in five major foreign wars, as well as the Persian Gulf War and Kosovo. Not included in this figure is a most bloody Civil War, fought for four years, which took some 624,000 lives,[1] as well as the clobbering of its own citizens in such internal actions as Shays's Rebellion, the Whiskey Rebellion, the 1857 Mormon action, the garrisoning of the South after the Civil War, and the use of army regulars in labor troubles and civilian unrest. Nor does this include the numerous direct or covert invasions in Central and South America, China, and Russia. The most obvious example is the creation of an entirely new country by Theodore Roosevelt, who engineered the split of Panama from Colombia in order to build the Panama Canal.

The German military writer Karl von Clausewitz, in his famous book *On War*, defined peace as an interval between wars, but its corollary also has some truth—namely, that civilian rule is often an interval with military leaders spawned by these wars. Nine generals before Eisenhower were elected president.[2] They were George Washington, Andrew Jackson, William Henry Harrison, Zachary Taylor, Franklin Pierce, Ulysses S. Grant, Rutherford B. Hayes, James A. Garfield, and Benjamin Harrison. Four other presidents held lesser rank. Thus, almost 43 percent of all our presidents, up to and including Eisenhower, were high military men.

The usual rationale for these elections is that military men are beyond party and thus more directly concerned with the general welfare. What swept Eisenhower into office can be summarized by a statement made when Ulysses S. Grant ran for office: "General Grant is not a prejudiced partisan nor versed in the crooked ways of politicians. . . . His was not the nomination of a caucus or a convention but the choice of the loyal people."[3] And this was certainly true of Eisenhower, who openly showed contempt for politics and politicians and indeed never voted till 1948, when he was approaching the age of sixty. Democrat or Republican, it was all the same to him; indeed, both parties tried to make him their candidate. He was also the last of the old breed from the previous century, having been born in 1890.

★

What is equally revealing in the Eisenhower sweep is the opposition within both his party and the opposing Democrats. As will be shown over and over, American democracy, better defined as legislative capitalism, in many ways is close to the Venetian Republic, a trading superpower dominated by a hereditary aristocracy for a millennium. Eisenhower's prime contender for the Republican nomination was Robert A. Taft, U.S. Senator from Ohio and conservative leader of the party. Senator Taft was the son of William H. Taft (1857–1930), the twenty-seventh president; President Taft, in turn, was the son of an earlier secretary of war. In the fourth generation, Robert A. Taft's son, Robert A. Taft Jr., was elected a U.S. Senator in 1970. The Taft Ohio seigniory, whose old money comes from Cincinnati real estate and ownership of the Cincinnati *Star-Times*, spans the greater part of the history of our country.

This oligarchic strain in the American system is not restricted to Republicans. The two main Democratic candidates vying to run against Eisenhower in both elections were Adlai E. Stevenson II and W. Averell Harriman. We see here the same story as with Taft.

The first Adlai Ewing Stevenson (1835–1914) was an eternal politician. Illinois state attorney, two-time congressman, U.S. vice president during Grover Cleveland's second term (1892–96), failed presidential candidate in 1896, and William Jennings Bryan's running mate in 1900, he missed by only twenty-three thousand votes becoming governor of Illinois in 1908. In 1912, as a man of seventy-seven, he ran again for the U.S. Senate. A lawyer, he was wealthy from interests in banks, mines, and real estate. In fact, the whole Stevenson-Ewing clan was involved in politics; ten office-holding cousins had influential positions in states ranging from Texas to Virginia.

Adlai E. Stevenson II (1900–1965), who ran without success against Eisenhower in both elections, was a product of Choate and Princeton, with wealthy parents and a still wealthier wife. He mixed in the best society, was heavily tinged with an anti-Semitism muted after entering politics,[4] and, as an eminent gentleman of the upper class, was hardly the man his idealistic backers thought. Slaughtered in the races by Eisenhower in 1948, he was appointed by President Kennedy as American ambassador to the United Nations in 1961. Stevenson supported until his death the American involvement in Vietnam.

The line continues with Adlai E. Stevenson III (1930–). A graduate of Milton Academy, Harvard University, and Harvard Law School, he was groomed by the Chicago Democratic machine for his name. Illinois state treasurer in 1966, U.S. Senator for the decade of the 1970s, two-time candidate for Illinois governor in 1982 and 1986, he now runs a merchant banking company, gaining in cash what he lost in politics: a war chest that will without doubt push forward the future political careers of Adlai E. Stevenson IV and Adlai E. Stevenson V.

The Democratic contender anxious to surpass Stevenson and take on Eisenhower was W. Averell Harriman, the son of Edward H. Harriman (1848–1909), head of the Union Pacific Railroad and one of the richest Americans in all history. Heir to such wealth and a great party contributor, the son was appointed by Franklin D. Roosevelt as U.S. ambassador both to England and the Soviet Union, then as secretary of commerce. He was finally elected governor of New York in 1954.

Harriman's much younger wife, Pamela, a colorful lady in many senses and a leading Democratic fund-raiser after her husband's death, was appointed ambassador to France in 1993 by President Clinton. The Harriman oligarchy, however, now seems muted for two reasons. The first is that W. Averell Harriman had daughters but no sons. The second, of equal importance, is that Pamela Harriman, with the estate trustees, ran through $65 million left by her husband, reducing the trust funds to $3 million—and without big money all family political wheels grind to a stop.

In the case of Eisenhower, the well-known journalist Arthur Krock, a close friend of Joseph P. Kennedy who later was an important cog in the balloon blowup of John F. Kennedy, described him as follows: "His manner is genial . . . his smile is attractively pensive, his frequent grin is infectious, his laughter ready and hearty. He fairly radiates goodness, simple faith, and the honest, industrious background of his heritage." In other words, just one of us ordinary good guys. The truth, however, is that Eisenhower was one of the master politicians of the American twentieth century. His post–World War II career was one of continued disavowal of any interest in the presidency, while with astute cunning he marshalled the political and financial resources to make the run. When chief of staff (1945–48) after the war he said he absolutely disdained, contrary to those who knew his great ambition, the thought of the highest office. On September 28, 1946, for example, he stated: "There is no possibility of my ever being connected with any political office." On July 4, 1947, he reiterated: "I do say flatly, completely, and with all the force I've got, I haven't a political ambition in the world. I want nothing to do with politics." As late as January 23, 1948, Eisenhower paraded the same line: "I am not available for and could not accept nomination to high political office. . . . I could not accept nomination even under the remote circumstances that it were tendered me."[5] In this same period, however, he wrote to an old army buddy: "So-called drafts . . . have been carefully nurtured, with the full even though undercover support of the 'victim.' "[6]

In the middle period of these disarming public statements, Thomas J. Watson, the founder of IBM, convinced Eisenhower, who hated New York City and knew nothing of educational problems, to become president of Columbia University. To make life easier for him, friends in the U.S. Treasury Department arranged a unique deal whereby his memoirs would hardly be taxed so that he received almost a half-million dollars net.[7]

After the freak election of Harry S. Truman over Thomas Dewey in 1948, there was a change. Now Eisenhower, who was actually hired by Columbia University as a fund-raiser and left a mediocre record in his official duties, became deeply involved in social activities in very rich circles. "Eisenhower's relationships with wealthy men grew steadily from 1946 onward, to the point that his friends were almost exclusively millionaires."[8] They were, with one exception, all

Republicans. The inner group consisted of Bill Robinson, vice president of the New York *Herald Tribune*, the semiofficial newspaper of the eastern Republican Party, as well as Ike's closest friend and political manager; Clifford Roberts, an investment broker who handled Eisenhower's money; Robert Woodruff, chairman of the board of Coca-Cola; and W. Alton Jones, president of Cities Service Company. Not a part of the inner circle but passionately devoted to Eisenhower's advancement was the aforementioned Thomas J. Watson.

Still seeming to protest, Eisenhower was drafted as the Republican candidate for the 1952 election, the "gang," as they called themselves, "putting their time, money, energy, experience, and contacts into the cause."[9] The great sums spent by those men and their corporate friends on his candidacy helped Dwight D. Eisenhower become elected our forty-third president, routing Adlai E. Stevenson II.

Eisenhower's cabinet reflected these interests. John Foster Dulles, his secretary of state, was another example of the oligarchic strain in America. More than four generations of his family had served the Department of State. Among the most prominent was his grandfather, John Foster, secretary of state under Benjamin Harrison. His uncle by marriage, Robert Lansing, was secretary of state under Woodrow Wilson. As senior partner in the top law firm of Sullivan & Cromwell, Dulles had the reputation of being the world's highest-paid lawyer.

The ferocious initiator of the Cold War and "brinksmanship," as well as a religious man, Dulles apparently found no problem with Luke 16:13 as well as Matt. 6:24, namely, "Ye cannot serve God and mammon." His son, the Rev. Avery Dulles, must have been so disturbed by this hypocrisy that he converted to Catholicism, became a Jesuit theologian, and, at age eighty-two, was elevated as the first American to the College of Cardinals.

Appointed to run the Pentagon was Charles E. Wilson, president of General Motors, who was allegedly the highest-paid executive in American industry. George M. Humphrey, president of M. A. Hanna & Company, an enormous Cleveland conglomerate centered

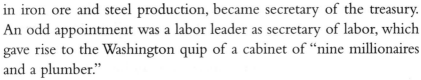

in iron ore and steel production, became secretary of the treasury. An odd appointment was a labor leader as secretary of labor, which gave rise to the Washington quip of a cabinet of "nine millionaires and a plumber."

Under Eisenhower there were eight years of peace, which, though minimal, is actually quite a positive statement when one reflects on American history. Eisenhower must also be given credit as the creator of our modern interstate highway system, which he only succeeded in pushing through Congress as critical for national security because troops could be more quickly moved in case of a national emergency.

However, underneath the surface of peace and prosperity many dirty bubbles boiled. One can mention a few examples. The CIA organized the 1954 military uprising against the democratically elected leftist government of Guatemala. This established a ruthless military dictatorship that protected the American companies with wide commercial interests that feared the loss of their money. Some thirty-five years later, in 1996, with between 150,000 and 200,000 people killed and a somewhat defanged CIA, the military government mediated an agreement with rebel forces to create an uneasy peace. As described by the *New York Times* on September 20, 1996, "The conflict in Guatemala can be traced to the coup in 1954 that the CIA, acting ostensibly to protect the interests of American corporations, sponsored to overthrow an elected left-leaning government and bring the military to power." The CIA took orders from Eisenhower, an American; the corpses were Guatemalan.

The CIA likewise toppled Mohammed Mosaddeq, the popular premier of Iran, in fear of heavy taxation or possible attempts to expropriate oil produced by that country and controlled by American corporations. A general arrested for Nazi sympathies in World War II was installed instead. The CIA action was orchestrated by Kermit Roosevelt, another example of how the same families continue to hold an important role in American politics. This action directly led to the violent ferment that resulted in the coming to

power of the present anti–American regime; with that in view one can perhaps see why the leaders of Iran today call the United States "the Great Satan."

The stage was set for the American entry into Vietnam in this period, the United States financing three-quarters of the French war effort there.[10] After the French left, the CIA gave military aid to the Diem regime in violation of the 1954 Geneva accord. John F. Kennedy picked up the ball from Eisenhower, Lyndon Johnson carried it, and Nixon fell on top of it. We lost our first war in history to a bunch of patriotic fanatics in the jungle who imitated the tactics of the . . . American Revolution.

These were among the foreign issues of the eight-year peace of President Eisenhower. Some of the domestic issues may be touched on.

The regime was shaken by several scandals above which hovered the president, the teflon before Ronald Reagan. Sherman Adams, Eisenhower's chief of staff, accepted gifts from a New England industrialist in return for attempting to influence various federal agencies. Initially supported by Eisenhower, he was finally fired. Harold E. Talbott, secretary of the air force, was ousted for using the official position to advance his own business affairs. In another case, it was proved that IRS agents were receiving large sums for not prosecuting tax delinquents.

The curious aspect is that President Eisenhower accepted personal gifts throughout his presidency. He took some $40,000 worth of equipment and animals for his Gettysburg farm despite the "suggestion" by the New York City Bar Association that presidents should set an example by passing along gifts to charities or museums. The syndicated columnist Drew Pearson estimated the total worth of gifts during his two terms at about $300,000. When questioned, Eisenhower replied, "The conflict-of-interest law does not apply to me." This is an interesting piece of logic, namely, that a presidential underling is influenced by gifts but the president is not. As long ago as the seventeenth century when Francis Bacon, lord chancellor of Britain, defended himself against taking money by stating it did not influence his opinion, the argument was rejected and he was dismissed. Eisenhower's response was an earlier variant of Nixon's reply to David Frost in a televised interview after his resignation: "When the president does it, that means it is not illegal."[11]

Eisenhower is given much credit for sending troops to quell the racial disturbances at Little Rock, Arkansas, in 1957. This is true: What is not mentioned is that he was brought to that decision kicking like a mule. He opposed any action until the Supreme Court, in an epoch-making decision, outlawed segregation in the public schools. Eisenhower strongly disagreed: "I am convinced that the Supreme Court decision set back progress in the South at least fifteen years. . . . The fellow who tells us that you can do these things by force is just plain nuts."[12] Even after sending the troops, he still disapproved: "The obligations of my office required me to order the use of force within a state to carry out the decision of a federal court," but then he added, "Our personal opinions about the Court decision have no bearing on the matter of enforcement."[13] As an old army man, he followed orders with which he disagreed. As an aside, one should also point out that Adlai E. Stevenson II, the hero of the liberals, was of the same mind as the president on this issue. It must be admitted that this reaction was better, however, than the answer of President Jackson who, when hearing the Supreme Court had estopped the state of Georgia from expelling the Cherokees—one of the most disgusting episodes in U.S. history—replied that since the Supreme Court judges had made the decision, let *them* enforce it.

Though the evidence indicates that he despised Senator Joseph McCarthy, particularly in McCarthy's attacks against the patriotism of his bosom friend, Gen. George C. Marshall, Eisenhower tolerated the demagogue almost to the end. This angered even his closest colleagues in the army, who in several cases were denounced as Communist sympathizers. It was Eisenhower's view that McCarthy would destroy himself—which did indeed happen, but not before many good people were maligned and undoubted patriots were denounced as Russian agents.

Toward the end there is some evidence that the president was not in full command of his mind. Some of his statements were odd; some were actually extremely dangerous. For the former, one may quote an exchange at a press conference on August 24, 1960, before the Nixon-Kennedy contest. A reporter asked regarding the extent of Nixon's participation as vice president in decision making while Eisenhower was president:

> Question: "We understand that the power of decision is entirely yours, Mr. President. I just wondered if you would give us an example of a major idea of his [Nixon's] that you had adopted in that role, as the decider and final—"
>
> Eisenhower: "If you give me a week, I might think of one. I don't remember."[14]

Far more serious and indeed foreboding was Eisenhower's view of nuclear war. He actually anticipated Barry Goldwater by approving a recommendation by the Joint Chiefs of Staff that called for employing atomic weapons wherever advantageous against military targets in China.[15] Some of his last statements were chilling. On March 16, 1955, with tension rising between the United States and China over the Formosa Strait, he said, "In any combat where these things can be used on strictly military targets and have strictly military purposes I see no reason why they [atomic weapons] shouldn't be used exactly as you would use a bullet or anything else."[16] By this time even the common man in the street knew that atomic bombs would have incredibly broad destructive effects and could not be limited to "strictly military targets." When Johnson escalated the war in Vietnam, Eisenhower likewise called those opposing it "kooks" and "hippies."

The relation between Eisenhower and his vice president, Richard M. Nixon, varies according to different memoirs, ranging from cool to indifferent to warm. Certainly Nixon snuggled up to a man so popular in the hope of future blessings. Long after Nixon's involvement in the Jerry Voorhis smear campaign (to be discussed later), Eisenhower stated: "The feature that especially appealed to me was the reputation that Congressman Nixon had achieved for fairness in the investigation process. . . . He did not persecute or defame. This I greatly admired."[17] If this was an ultimate judgment, the marriage of Eisenhower's grandson David to Nixon's daughter Julie was quite symbolic.

The final irony of Eisenhower's regime is that, in his televised farewell address to the nation at the end of his second term, he warned, in a statement that has been quoted innumerable times as to his wisdom, that "[w]e must guard against the acquisition of unwarranted influences, whether sought or unsought, by the military-industrial complex." Yet during his two terms, he quadrupled military spending. A master of speaking out of both sides of his mouth, Eisenhower, with his million-dollar smile, was the idol of the American people. Word was brought to him at the hospital when he was dying that Nixon was elected president; as was fitting in every sense, the new president gave the glowing eulogy.

A poll of American historians, published a year after he left office, assigned Eisenhower to the class of presidents well below average, with Chester A. Arthur and Franklin Pierce.[18]

Reprinted with permission from *Drawn & Quartered*, Stephen Hess and Sandy Northrop, editors. Elliott & Clark Publishing Company.

Courtesy the National Library of Wales.

# CHAPTER TWO

★

# JOHN FITZGERALD KENNEDY
## (1961–1963)

★

*"Jack in office is a great man."*
Thomas Fuller (1608–1661), *Gnomologia*

In a technical sense John F. Kennedy was elected president in 1960. But his real election took place years before by an electorate of one. The elector was Joseph P. Kennedy, his father, a colossus in his time for good and bad. The prince of "Camelot" was a very handsome young man with an orgiastic sex drive, hidden from the voters, that made the Bill Clinton scandals of later years seem like those of a vestal virgin. If it had not been for Daddy Joe, young Kennedy would have been merely another playboy whose antics enlivened the tabloids. This charming icon, whose shreds of Camelot are still bandied about, was summed up in the able words of seasoned writer and expert politician Rexford G. Tugwell:

> He had no program. There was nothing he wanted to do if he should be elected—that is to say, he had no cause. He was a Democrat because he belonged to the party by birth and by association, but also because Democrats had a better chance of election. But he had no notion of serving the party any more than he had of serving the people of his district. It was simply a way to office. . . .[1]

The *paterfamilias* of the Kennedy brood was paralyzed by a stroke in December 1961 at age seventy-three but lived until 1969, long enough to see the family triumphs and disasters in a pattern of hubris that a classical Greek tragedian could have written. Joe Kennedy's fortune in the 1960s was around $300 million, with some estimates much higher, and he was among the twenty wealthiest men in the United States. Kennedy was in a direct line of very clever and very ambitious men in American history who, from our country's founding—early examples being Benjamin Franklin and Patrick Henry and a later one being Lyndon B. Johnson—clearly saw the connection between politics and money and acted accordingly.

Joseph P. Kennedy came from a political background. His father, Patrick J. Kennedy, was a Massachusetts Democratic state representative at twenty-eight and a state senator at thirty-two. Joe married Rose Fitzgerald, the daughter of "Honey Fitz," Boston's two-term Democratic mayor. Sharp at making money, he was even sharper to see the wind veer toward the Democrats in the Great Depression, and became one of the few rich men to support Roosevelt, contributing $25,000 to his first campaign, lending $50,000 more, and raising $100,000 among his friends[2]—great sums at that time, especially when almost all rich men violently opposed Roosevelt.

Joe's first reward, engineered through his friend Jimmy Roosevelt, son of the president,[3] was his appointment as U.S. agent for Haig & Haig, Ltd.; John Dewar Sons, Ltd.; and Gordon's Dry Gin Co., Ltd., which meant control of most scotch and gin sales in America under the impending repeal of Prohibition. After the repeal, a grateful Kennedy used to send a truckload of scotch to President Roosevelt at Christmas. Then, in 1934, Joe got his more direct reward: appointment to the Securities and Exchange Commission and, through Roosevelt's pressure, election as chairman. He stayed only a year and a half in this office before resigning, anxious to get back to making big money, but with massive new high contacts.

When Joe offered financial support to Roosevelt for his successful second-term bid (he also wrote an influential book titled *I'm for Roosevelt* [4]), he received a great prize, appointment as ambassador to the Court of St. James in 1937, the first Irish-Catholic ambassador to England. This became his one failure, for he advised Roosevelt that Hitler would win the coming war and that the United States should not back a loser—as he had advised Roosevelt, with more success, not to aid the Loyalist government fighting Franco. Publicity over this political advice forced Kennedy to resign. Joe Kennedy's cold, logical mind had added the evidence together and gave no weight to human spirit; it might be said that these world-shaking events were viewed by him merely as business deals, where profits and losses were the sole consideration. President Roosevelt never called on Kennedy again after his resignation. Disappointed in his political ambitions, Kennedy gave up politics and returned with great success to making a still larger fortune.

With a magnificent sense of timing, Joe Kennedy plunged into real estate after World War II, just as the country entered a boom period. His first arena was New York City, where it has been said that his ruthless raising of rents was a big factor in the city's passage of rent-control legislation. But Kennedy's greatest coup was the purchase of the Chicago Merchandise Mart. Construction began in the summer of 1928 by Marshall Field II, the famous retailer, and was finished in January 1931, just in time to feel the full brunt of the Great Depression. Costing about $30 million, it was the world's largest building until the Pentagon was constructed in the 1940s: It had ninety-three acres of floor space and close to 4 million square feet, with forty thousand persons using the elevators daily.

A key here also was politics. Marshall Field, desperate for tenants, had rented a huge amount of space to government agencies on short-term leases that were about to expire. Kennedy's Washington friends tipped him off that this space would not be renewed in a market that had begun to turn around, with space renting at higher figures.[5] In 1945, Kennedy purchased the Chicago Merchandise Mart for a little less than $13 million and then negotiated a mortgage for $12.5 million. Including commissions and legal expenses his cash investment was about $1 million. The government offices moved out and he re-rented the space for more money. Four years later, he remortgaged for $17 million, pocketing the difference. By 1963, the annual rent roll was greater than the original purchase price, and by 1984 the Mart was worth over $250 million. Taking advantage of the upward sweep in real estate of the late 1990s, the Kennedy family sold the Merchandise Mart in early 1998, as part of a package that included some lesser properties, for $625 million. This deal alone guarantees, one may add, a major Kennedy family presence in politics in the twenty-first century.

At about the time his son John entered the political arena, Joe Kennedy, feeling that the whiskey business did not show a good image, sold his English liquor franchise for $8 million, the original investment having been $100,000; trade sources estimated his annual income from the scotch and gin sales had been around $250,000.

After the demise of his own political ambitions, Joe Kennedy's aim was to use his huge fortune to propel his children into those high posts that he had not be able to reach. This became an obsession. In JFK's first try for the U.S. House in 1946, his father ran the campaign through a cousin, Joe Kane. A great sum of money was spent and JFK won. Asked why they had spent so heavily, Kane said, "It takes three things to win. The first is money and the second is money and the third is money."[6]

The use of money and contacts to push JFK ahead of the opposition had its origins years before. Bankrolling and string pulling, Joseph Kennedy had orchestrated his son's career from the start. When JFK went to Harvard his undergraduate thesis was so poorly written that his father hired a ghostwriter to make it publishable.[7] Then he arranged for his friend Henry Luce, a top publisher, to write the foreword. The famous journalist Arthur Krock, also a pal, reviewed the book in the *New York Times*. When it was published in 1940, *Why England Slept* was featured by Henry Luce on the cover of *Time*, one of his many magazines. Papa Kennedy bought more than thirty thousand copies of his son's book, putting them in a storehouse, which catapulted the book to the best seller list.[8] The renowned English economist Harold J. Laski, under whom JFK had studied as a young man at the London School of Economics, wrote to Joe Kennedy, whom he knew as ambassador to England, "I don't honestly think any publisher would have looked at that book of Jack's if he had not been your son, and if you had not been Ambassador."[9] JFK's second book, *Profiles in Courage*, reportedly was the output of a committee of scholars that included Kennedy speechwriter Theodore Sorensen.[10] It won the 1957 Pulitzer Prize.

Following the same tactics, JFK's political career was enhanced by a war record made mythical by manipulation. Though his PT-boat was rammed by a Japanese destroyer in an action which at worst was negligence and at best inexperience, Joseph Kennedy made sure that, with great publicity, his son was decorated by a high-ranking naval officer.[11]

In 1952 JFK ran for the U.S. Senate against the Republican incumbent Henry Cabot Lodge Jr., a scion of the Old Guard.[12] This was part of the general American movement away from the traditional oligarchic power to the new plutocracy, the vast sums made by newer groups taking over from the old money. It was in this campaign that the twenty-seven-year-old Robert F. Kennedy, JFK's younger brother—fresh out of law school—first surfaced as campaign manager, fronting for his father. Joe Kennedy hired 286 persons to coordinate the campaign. Nine hundred thousand tabloids were distributed showing Lieutenant Kennedy rescuing his shipmates in the PT-boat collision. The various Kennedy family members gave thirty-three formal receptions attended by an estimated 75,000 persons. Joe spent at least a half-million dollars, mainly on billboards, giveaways, and television political commercials.[13] He gave an additional half-million dollars as a loan to the hard-pressed editor of the *Boston Post*, John Fox, who then endorsed JFK.[14]

Lodge, confident of victory and working out of state for Eisenhower's presidential campaign, belatedly recognized the threat and hurried back to Massachusetts just two months before the election.

But it was too late. John F. Kennedy won a thumping victory, though Eisenhower took the state.

The Kennedy drive for the White House began in earnest in 1958, shortly after JFK's reelection to the U.S. Senate and two years before the national election. Joe Kennedy deluged the opinion shapers with money. With a keen nose for the value of early publicity, he flattered, cajoled, and aided editors and publishers. Feature articles began to appear about the handsome young war hero and senator in major magazines such as *McCall's, Redbook*, and the *Saturday Evening Post*. JFK's Washington office received more than a hundred speaking invitations a week. Joe's oft-quoted remark "We're going to sell Jack like soap flakes"[15] not only expressed the truth but was the first sign of a new trend in American politics: the purchase of office—any office—as though it were a rare painting or jewel for sale at a high-class auction house.

The first step in the new technique was to buy primaries. Actually, Senator Estes Kefauver of Tennessee in 1956 became the godfather of this revolutionary shift from boss control of the presidential elections to the ascendency of the state primary.[16] This change permits very rich men with no political experience, and often with far more money than sense, to reach for power by both the purchase of delegates and a direct appeal to a limited group through expensive media advertising. The very small number of people who vote in the primaries means that the right pressure on a small fulcrum can create the illusion of a landslide appeal.

First in Michigan, and then more decisively in West Virginia, the Kennedy money steamroller pressed forward. According to the research of Richard Whalen,[17] Joe Kennedy committed at least $1.5 million to his son's preconvention campaign, a figure lower than some other estimates. His main competitor, Hubert Humphrey, entered West Virginia with $17,000. "I don't have any daddy who can pay the bills for me," Humphrey said bitterly. Perhaps the most witty remark was that of a leading Republican, who said that Kennedy's victory as the Democratic candidate "proves the Amer-

★

ican dream that any boy can hope to grow up to run for President, especially if his father has four hundred million dollars."[18] Fatefully, in order to unite the South behind him, Kennedy chose Lyndon B. Johnson as his running mate.

With Kennedy sewn up as the 1960 Democratic presidential candidate, the fight began. Richard Nixon, who had served as vice president under Eisenhower, was the Republican candidate. He was a favorite of Joe Kennedy and received campaign contributions from him. But that was no longer relevant, for Joe's view of what was best for America was one led by a Kennedy dynasty. The choice of Nixon was indeed a godsend for JFK, because the liberal wing of the Democratic party, which distrusted the Kennedys, hated Nixon more than any other political figure. The nomination of Nixon thus brought together the rival segments of the Democrats.

Bobby Kennedy, who resembled his father ("He's a great kid. He hates the same way I do," remarked the old man[19]) was appointed campaign manager. Edward (Ted) Kennedy, Joe's youngest son, was sent to San Francisco to supervise the campaign from the Rockies to the Pacific Coast. Jack, whose liberalism had nowhere been evident in his previous political career, now wrapped himself in the smile of Franklin D. Roosevelt and called for a rebirth of the New Deal. Joe assured his alarmed conservative friends "that the platform promises were just that—promises."[20] But that was not what the public heard. They were charmed by the young candidate: his youth, his looks, his animal magnetism, even his bland generalities. And Joe—alerted to the fact that his presence would alienate many voters, especially New York Jews[21] who decided that state's large electoral vote—went into the wings, staying mainly with rich California friends. This gave rise to the couplet:

> Jack and Bob will run the show,
> While Ted's in charge of hiding Joe.

No one knows how much money the election cost Joe Kennedy. His bankroll was less decisive than before because the rich conserva-

★

tives poured forth great sums to neutralize the Kennedy fortune in an attempt to elect Nixon. The final result was razor-thin. Kennedy did not receive a majority of the votes when the small vote for minority candidates is included. Of the more than 68 million votes cast, Kennedy won by less than 120,000 votes, 49.7% to 49.6%. Only 24,000 more votes for Nixon, properly distributed in five states, would have changed the outcome. Surely, however, one may conclude that the vision of the "young hero" created by Papa Kennedy (and housebroken academics) brought in far more votes than the tissue-paper difference.

The Nixon supporters had nothing to fear. The top Kennedy cabinet appointments were: Douglas Dillon, heir to the founder of the top Wall Street firm Dillon Reed and Company, as secretary of the treasury; Robert S. McNamara, president of the Ford Motor Company, as secretary of defense; and Dean Rusk, president of the Ford Foundation, as secretary of state. Joe Kennedy was quite right in soothing his alarmed conservative friends.

The rest is history, leading to Dallas.

Joe Kennedy tried, and almost succeeded, in creating an American tribal dynasty equal if not superior to the Adams, Lee, and Bush families. Only fate—those of a meditative cast might say hubris—destroyed this ambition. Joe's first choice had been Joe Jr., his oldest and favorite son, who was killed in World War II. He then settled on Jack. "I got Jack into politics, I was the one," Kennedy told a reporter. "He didn't want to. He felt he didn't have the ability. But I told him he had to."[22]

Then it was Bobby's turn. As noted, he was made campaign manager for JFK's U.S. Senate and presidential races. Appointed attorney general by President Kennedy, though he had never in his life tried a case in court, Bobby had already set plans to emulate his brother before the assassination in Dallas. Joe Kennedy allegedly said at the time he had spent $3 million to elect JFK a U.S. Senator, and the seat belonged in the family. Whether true or false, in 1964 Bobby took on New York's Republican senator Kenneth B. Keating. The

Democrats for Kennedy, an organization fronting for Papa Joe, spent over $2.5 million, a record at that time. All the Kennedy clan members, not only Bobby's father, poured money into the campaign. Almost the entire huge sum was spent on television ads in the last five weeks before election. And Bobby won.

In the 1968 presidential primary, Bobby campaigned hard and took California and South Dakota the same day. Only Hubert Humphrey then remained as a formidable Democratic opponent. The night of Bobby's victory statement in California, he was shot dead after a press conference. The final irony of the twisted brilliant destiny of Joe Kennedy, who with Henry Ford and Father Coughlin was a leading American anti-Semite, was the death of his beloved son Bobby by the hand of an Arab fanatic because of his pro-Israel views.[23]

After Jack and Bobby came Ted, Joe's youngest son. Joe made that decision, too. "You boys have what you want and everybody worked to help you get it. Now it's Teddy's turn. I'm going to see that he gets what he wants."[24] Ted Kennedy, only three years out of law school, was pitted in the 1962 Massachusetts Democratic primary for the U.S. Senate against Edward J. McCormack Jr., the state's attorney general, whose uncle was Speaker of the House in Washington. The Republican opponent was George Cabot Lodge, son of former Senator Henry Cabot Lodge II. Young Teddy, aided by the family money spigot, first drowned his fellow Irish American and then trounced the old-line Yankee WASP.

As the *New York Times* commented sarcastically in an editorial dated March 17, 1962, the race had the flavor of one in which the entrance requirement was a listing in the American equivalent of *Burke's Peerage*. The editorial concluded that it would be helpful for candidates to "present some solid evidence of talent before they make the sacrifice of starting at the top."

Never having held a job, Senator Ted waited seventeen months before speaking on the Senate floor for the first time. Fate intervened in his hopes as well. If it hadn't been for the 1969 Chappaquiddick scandal, when Ted walked away from a car accident in which a female

★

companion was drowned, he certainly would have tried to match his brothers in a bid for the presidency. Indeed, in 1980, he did, but the odor of that scandal could never be overcome.[25]

The Kennedy nepotism applied also to the distaff side of the family. Joe's daughter Eunice married R. Sargent Shriver, who had worked for his future father-in-law as a manager at the Chicago Merchandise Mart. As part of the inner political network, President Johnson later appointed Shriver ambassador to France. Shriver then ran for vice president with George A. McGovern in 1976 after having tried for the presidential nomination. But with the *paterfamilias* paralyzed and useless, the family went separate ways, disunited in bankrolling Kennedy candidates, and the old magic was less potent.

Some of the next generation have picked up the torch. Four Kennedys ran for public office in 1994. In Massachusetts, the home nest, Senator Ted Kennedy was reelected, as was Bobby's son, Joseph P. Kennedy II. After six terms in congress young Joe retired in 1998, probably realizing how short life is after the death of his cousin Michael in a skiing accident. Ted's son Patrick Kennedy, at the age of twenty-seven, gained a House seat in Rhode Island, next door to Massachusetts, and is the youngest U.S. Representative. And Kathleen Kennedy Townsend, Bobby's oldest child, became lieutenant governor of Maryland. Another of Bobby's children, Kerry, married Andrew Cuomo, son of former New York governor Mario Cuomo; President Clinton, in a sweet payoff, appointed young Cuomo secretary of housing and urban development at the age of thirty-nine. It is becoming as difficult to follow the sequence of Kennedys as the genealogic tree of European monarchs.

All this, of course, is propelled by streams of money. In his 1996 campaign for reelection, Congressman Joseph P. Kennedy II spent $1,550,916. "The fifteen other candidates for the seat together spent only $2.3 million, an average of about $150,000. Joe clearly bought the election."[26] But there's plenty more. President Kennedy left an estate worth $10 million. Jacqueline Kennedy, who was as adroit via the marriage bed as was her father-in-law in finance (even keener

than Pamela Harriman), left an estate close to $73 million according
to a preliminary audit of the IRS—which of course does not take
into account lifetime distributions. And, as mentioned, the Chicago
Merchandise Mart in early 1998, with some other properties, was
sold for the huge sum of $625 million.

The old oligarchy does not surrender to the new plutocracy
without a fight. The double name Cabot Lodge constantly shows up
in the Massachusetts annals against the rising Kennedys. In his successful fight to become a U.S. Senator from Massachusetts in 1952,
John F. Kennedy, as noted, challenged the incumbent Henry Cabot
Lodge II, a senator since 1936. This Lodge was the grandson of
Henry Cabot Lodge (1850–1924), who had been a Republican U.S.
Representative from 1887 to 1893 before moving up to the Senate,
where he served until his death. As chairman of the Foreign Affairs
Committee, he was a leading conservative noted for managing the
defeat of the U.S. entry into the League of Nations after World War
I. John Davis Lodge, brother of Henry Cabot Lodge II, was a
Republican representative for Connecticut from 1946 to 1950 and
then governor of Connecticut from 1950 to 1954. George Cabot
Lodge, son of Henry Cabot Lodge II, ran for the U.S. Senate in
1962 but, as noted, was beaten by Ted Kennedy, whose long reign in
Massachusetts has at last smashed the century-long dominance of
the Cabot Lodge patricians. George Cabot Lodge won Republican
primaries but lost his bid to become the 1964 Republican presidential candidate to Senator Barry Goldwater. He was appointed ambassador to Vietnam by the victorious President Johnson, an appointment that effectively destroyed any future political hopes he still may
have had.

When Richard M. Nixon, vice president under Eisenhower, ran
unsuccessfully as the Republican candidate for president in 1960,
Henry Cabot Lodge II, then U.S. Ambassador to the United
Nations, popped up again as his running mate. Jack Kennedy had
beaten Adlai Stevenson in the Democratic primaries for this election—the same Stevenson defeated by Eisenhower in the preceding

two presidential elections. And in 1994, Massachusetts Senator Ted Kennedy was gravely threatened by Republican Mitt Romney, a multimillionaire venture capitalist who was the son of George W. Romney, former head of one of America's top automobile companies, former governor of Michigan, presidential candidate in 1968, and Nixon's secretary of housing and urban development.

The political races were thus rather like a game of musical chairs, with the same players changing seats every four or six years and now and then allowing a new player—either with enormous wealth or the ability to tap such wealth—into the game.

An ultimate question is: How effective was the short presidency of John F. Kennedy? Certainly, though we can never know how he would have evolved, the little evidence we have suggests that he will never join the small core of great presidents. Two events stand out in a dubious, if not negative, sense. They were our growing involvement in the Vietnam War, and the slovenly mess of the Bay of Pigs invasion and its consequence, the Cuban missile crisis.[27]

As to the former, President Lyndon Johnson's massive involvement overshadows the link between President Eisenhower's initial backing with great financial aid to the French, as well as some small troop commitments, and Kennedy's subsequent hesitant but larger involvement. Eisenhower dispatched a total of some eight hundred men to Vietnam as military advisors to the native army, while the figures vary between sixteen and twenty-five thousand troops thrown into that maelstrom by Kennedy. A force less than a thousand can be drawn out of a conflict without too much grief, which was what Eisenhower did after landing American troops to take sides in the Lebanon civil war. But when a much larger army is sent, "saving face"—always a great presidential worry, especially with Congress yapping at one's heels—becomes more difficult. This indeed was the reason that Johnson, who evidently did not believe the previous Vietnam policy made sense, was compelled to intervene massively. And Kennedy was equally at fault.

It is a curious aspect of American thinking on foreign policy

★

issues that we fail to connect, or hold persons accountable for, the consequences of their actions. Just as it is rare indeed for Eisenhower to be blamed for his CIA coup in Iran, which led to the present anti-American regime, or his CIA coup in Guatemala, which led to the deaths of more than 150,000 citizens of that country, the Cuban missile crisis directly flowed from the CIA fiasco called the Bay of Pigs. President Kennedy was praised for "standing up to the Russians," but in reality his endorsement of the 1961 Cuban invasion led directly to the decision by Moscow to send nuclear missiles to Cuba; and, though concealed, his compromise—namely to take out our missiles facing Russia from Turkey while the Soviets removed theirs from Cuba—was in fact a tactical victory for the Russians. Krushchev complained in April 1961 to Ambassador Thompson: "The USA . . . believes that it has the right to put military bases along the borders of the USSR. . . . The Americans had surrounded our country with military bases and threatened us with nuclear weapons," and then later added, ". . . and now they would learn just what it feels like to have enemy missiles pointed at you."[28]

President Kennedy, knowing well the judgment of history if he unleashed nuclear warfare, proposed the compromise. It is to his credit. But he was so ashamed of seeming to be weak that the deal was kept secret for years to protect his image. Presenting this commonsense compromise as a victory, he projected himself as the man who "faced down" the Soviets and drew a line in the sand. Indeed, he even had the impertinence to suggest that his old opponent in the Democratic primaries, Adlai E. Stevenson II, then U.S. Ambassador to the United Nations, had been "soft" during the crisis, favoring a missile trade—the exact thing that Kennedy had secretly done.

In conclusion, we may state that at least Kennedy, like Eisenhower, kept us out of a full-fledged war. This was courageous in those hysterical times when, only shortly before, a psychopathic drunkard like Senator Joseph McCarthy had been the idol of a good many Americans. In his personal morals, John F. Kennedy was a society lecher. In his intelligence, he was above average among presidents. But at bottom he was politically a mediocre image with good looks, a beautiful wife, and natural charm and style, all swollen large by Papa's money and top-grade writers and speech makers.

Reprinted with permission from *Drawn & Quartered*, Stephen Hess and Sandy Northrop, editors. Elliott & Clark Publishing Company.

**"I haven't really lost touch with you—the people—have I?"**

Reprinted from *LBJ Lampooned: Cartoon Crtiticism of Lyndon B. Johnson*, ed. Sig Rosenblum and Charles Antin (New York: Cobble Hill Press, 1968).

# CHAPTER THREE

★

# LYNDON BAINES JOHNSON
# (1963–1969)

★

*"If you do not know how to lie, cheat and steal, turn your attention to politics and learn."*

Josh Billings (H.W. Shaw)

*"To be a chemist you must study chemistry; to be a lawyer or a physician you must study law or medicine, but to be a politician you need only to study your own interests."*

Max O'Rell (pseudonym of Paul Blouet)

Lyndon B. Johnson as a person was a discord of vulgar traits, a bawdy loud-mouth, liar, conniver, show-off, as sex-obsessed as Jack Kennedy but with less style, and a peddler of federal benefits to others and even more to himself. As a warmonger Johnson dumped more than a half-million soldiers into the jaws of a full-scale, though undeclared, war in Vietnam, with some fifty-eight thousand dead young Americans as a result.

At the same time LBJ (as he came to known), probably even more adroit as a wheeler-dealer than FDR, was responsible for the greatest social legislation of the twentieth century: the Civil Rights Act of 1964, the Voting Rights Act of 1965, Medicare and Medicaid, and the Elementary and Secondary Education Act of 1965, which gave federal aid to poor children. He also created the National Endowments for the Arts and Humanities and the John F. Kennedy Center for the Performing Arts. To add to the accolades,

Johnson added 1.3 million acres to the National Wildlife Refuge System.

How does one judge the paradoxes of such a man? Many books have been written, none fully satisfactory. The best approach is simply to state the facts.

The crass vulgarity of LBJ has been often recorded. Johnson liked to sit on the toilet while conducting official business and insisted others come close while he discharged and wiped. He preferred nude male swimming parties and badgered everyone to strip, openly mocking those not willing. His crudeness with women is well noted. His actions were those of a grown-up spoiled infant.

LBJ's lies were prolific. Apparently he lied all the time not because he was a habitual liar in the ordinary sense, but rather because speech was intended to advance his ends, not to communicate thought.[1] A few examples will suffice. To prove his Texan heritage for political purposes, he stated in campaigns that his great-grandfather died at the Alamo, while the simple truth was that his great-grandparents arrived in Texas years after that battle. More devious, to use a polite word, was the invention of his war experience. He had been an observer on a plane in action in the Pacific for thirteen minutes. Five months later, he told a reporter that he was in combat for two and one-half months; this tale grew, and by late 1944 he had not only flown many missions over enemy territory but had been hospitalized in the Fiji Islands. He later added that the men who flew with him gave him the name "Raider" Johnson in admiration.

Like Joe Kennedy did for his son Jack, through political contacts Johnson arranged to receive the Silver Star, which he wore proudly while campaigning though he only served on that one plane as an observer. No one else on that aircraft got a medal—not the pilot who flew the plane, not the corporal who shot down an attacking Japanese Zero—no one, that is, except that thirteen-minute observer of the action.[2]

His lying extended to overt actions. Johnson manipulated situations out of context or through distortion. In one case this even

★

resembled Stalin's wiping out Trotsky and other revolutionary
leaders from group revolutionary photographs pictures taken with
Lenin, in order to seem to be the sole anointed successor of Lenin.
When Johnson first won his seat in Congress in 1937, riding on
Roosevelt's coattails, the president's yacht docked in Galveston at the
end of a fishing trip and both Johnson and the Texas governor had
their picture taken with the president. Johnson later had the picture
altered to make it appear that he was alone with Roosevelt.[3]

A strange quality of Johnson was his use of humor. Apparently,
it was routine for elections to be "stolen" in Texas, and Johnson was
an expert in the matter. The evidence was quite clear that he had
ballot boxes stuffed to defeat Coke Stevenson in the Democratic primary fight—which, in Texas, meant the election—for U.S. Senate in
1948. After the election Johnson delighted in telling this story, not
only to his inner circle but at parties and even to reporters. Lyndon
told it with great gusto, including a Mexican accent:

> A small Mexican American boy named Manuel was sitting on a
> curb in a little town near the Mexican border crying, and a friend
> came up and asked him what was the trouble.
>
> "My father was in town last Saturday, and he did not come to
> see me," Manuel replied.
>
> "But, Manuel, your father has been dead for ten years."
>
> Manuel sobbed louder. "Sí, he has been dead for ten years. But
> he came to town last Saturday to vote for Lyndon Johnson, and he
> did not come to see me."[4]

Johnson's habitual lying and self-deception was an important
factor in the Vietnam tragedy. It could have been foreseen by his previous intervention in the Dominican civil war. In April 1965 the
ruling military junta in the Dominican Republic was attacked by the
opposition, with danger to the lives and property of U.S. citizens.
LBJ reacted as the caricature of a Texan: "It's just like the Alamo.
Hell, it's like if you were down at that gate, and you were surrounded
and you damn well needed somebody."

That "somebody" turned out to be twenty-one thousand U.S. Marines supporting a military dictatorship. Johnson then quoted his favorite schoolroom patriotic stanza: "I have seen the glory of art and architecture. I have seen the sun rise on Mont Blanc. But the most beautiful vision that these eyes ever beheld was the flag of my country in a foreign land." As usual, Johnson lied without concern for the facts. "Some fifteen hundred innocent people were murdered and shot, and their heads cut off, and six Latin American embassies were violated," he stated. The final investigation revealed that no embassy had been fired upon, no one had been beheaded, and no American civilian was hurt. The "Communist and Castroist" opposition leaders list at the U.S. Embassy in Santo Domingo was a story concocted to justify the invasion.[5]

Such reasoning led directly to Vietnam. Alberto L. Camargo, the former president of Colombia and a consistent friend of the United States, said at the time, "A new and openly imperialistic policy in the style of Theodore Roosevelt had been adopted by the White House and that . . . one could only expect—in Asia, in Africa and wherever—new acts of force."[6]

It is not necessary to review the facts regarding our disaster in Vietnam. One point should be emphasized, however. Lyndon Johnson is often given credit for opposing the use of nuclear weapons, unlike his Republican opponent Barry Goldwater (who later admitted he was wrong). This is true, but for reasons that had nothing to do with compassion. By 1952 Johnson, like Eisenhower, was advocating the use of nuclear weapons. Senator Henry Cabot Lodge of Massachusetts, a key Republican and a member of the foreign relations committee, advocated dropping atomic bombs and firing atomic artillery shells in Korea. Johnson went further: "We are tired of fighting your [Russia's] stooges; we will no longer waste our substance battling your slaves. . . . We will strike back not at your satellites—but you. We will strike back with all the dreaded might that is within our control, and it will be a crushing blow." To clarify any ambiguity, two weeks later he added, "We are already in a war—

a major war. The war in Korea is a war of Soviet Russia." And then, shortly thereafter, in February 1952, Johnson stated, "If *any*where in the world—by *any* means, *open or concealed*—communism trespasses upon the soil of the free world, *we shall unleash all the power at our command upon the vitals of the Soviet Union.*"[7]

It should be pointed out that as a result of the Korean War sane opinion was dropped by many in favor of the apocalypse. Because of lies from the top and initial media control, the great majority of the American public—and the military—strongly supported Johnson's actions in the Dominican Republic and the early years of Vietnam. As time passed, with the disclosures of napalm and saturation bombing, the slaughter of innocent Vietnamese civilians and, most of all, the avalanche of body bags coming home to patriotic street marches turning sour, Johnson—who always had a good ear for the man in the street—felt hobbled in making that one last ultimate decision, to start a nuclear war.[8]

In retrospect, the bad taste left by Lyndon Johnson is not so much the Vietnam War. To blame him exclusively is to forget the previous actions of Eisenhower and Kennedy, the unanimous support of the highest civilian and military leaders, and even the bulk of the American people whipped into patriotic frenzy by lies.

There are other serious grounds. Johnson tried to implement his social programs at the same time he poured billions of dollars into the military: his so-called guns-and-butter program. The national debt, the sum of all the annual budget deficits, went up to the almost incomprehensible figure of $5.5 trillion. Before the Vietnam War it was about 30 percent of our gross domestic product; because of Johnson's spendthrift policy, which was later magnified by Reagan's vast military buildup, as of 1997 the national debt stood at the awesome figure of 70 percent of GDP.

Perhaps more serious was the attempt by Johnson to breach the constitutional division of the three branches of government, the executive, the legislative, and the judicial—that tripod upon which the freedom of the American people and the Bill of Rights rests.

Johnson, who knew the legislative branch intimately, tended to treat our lawmakers as a master does a pet dog, instructing it through pet food (grants and favors) to stand on its legs and bark on command. Every strong president does this to some extent but never more sinuously cultivated and trained as in his case. Even more obvious was his approach to the judicial branch. In Johnson's relations with Abe Fortas, his personal lawyer whom he appointed to the Supreme Court and then tried to make chief justice, he regarded Fortas as a patrol post to check the Court's actions and influence its decisions. It was as though the president did not understand, or pay attention to, the constitutional wall created to avoid tyranny. If the aim was worthy, so reasoned Johnson, any means to achieve it was worthy. Here he exposed a fatal flaw. In the name of progress (as FDR equally reasoned when he tried to pack the Supreme Court with more sympathetic members) one invites that all-too-familiar road to despotism so well lighted by history. In this sense the actions of Huey Long, the Louisiana demagogue who spouted social justice shortly before this time, were not so different than the actions of Lyndon Johnson. One may add that Abe Fortas later was forced to resign from the Supreme Court for taking money intended to influence his judicial opinion. Often the measure of the servant is the nature of the master.

Besides these grave defects was Johnson's deliberate misuse of political power to create an enormous personal fortune through monopoly control of an important part of the Texas airwaves, which expanded from one radio station to a radio and television empire and was then parlayed into banking, land holdings, and cattle. President Johnson came to the highest office of our land in 1963 with a background of fraud and payoffs, using his wife as a shield, that had created a fortune totaling between $10 and $20 million according to various estimates. He was one of the richest men ever to enter the White House.[9] The free $375,000 office space, the franking privilege, a military helicopter, and the constant protection of the Secret Service that he received on retirement were peanuts compared to

the great deception he pulled on the American people, one remarkably similar to the practices of the dictators of emerging nations as
well as the present sacking of the resources of Russia by individuals
nominally elected to guide that state. This story requires detailed
analysis because it clearly shows the way Johnson used his political
career to fill his pocketbook.[10]

   LBJ, of rural Texas background, came from a family that already
showed a hunger for political power. His grandfather held elected
office and his father, Sam, served six terms in the Texas legislature.
Lyndon's mother had pretenses to fallen gentility and was a great
influence on the tall, good-looking, bright, and verbal boy. It was a
period of general national hardship as the young man grew up and
he attached himself with fanatical loyalty both to the person and the
image of the Depression-elected Franklin D. Roosevelt. The Texas
Democratic Party machine saw potential in this gangling youth of
twenty-eight and he was chosen in 1937 to run for U.S. Congress
in an election that was probably honest—for to be a Democrat in
Texas at that time was automatic election.

   LBJ had a sure instinct when it came to the sources of power.
He immediately struck up a close friendship with Clifford Durr, a
commissioner of the Federal Communications Commission (FCC),
the organ of government that controled licenses for radio (and later
television). The famed Sam Rayburn, Speaker of the House and also
from Texas, was petted and flattered. Johnson fawned in such an unc-
tuous way on President Roosevelt that his letters make a person with
some sense of dignity wince. He moved up in the system, from five
terms in the U.S. House of Representatives to U.S. Senate in 1948
to Democratic majority whip in 1951 and then to majority leader
in 1955.

   In 1943 Lady Bird Johnson bought radio station KTBC-TV in
Austin, Texas, for $17,500. The station sold cheaply because it was
losing money due to its inability to get federal approval to affiliate
with a network and operate at night. Under the new owner, the
FCC almost immediately granted the station unlimited broadcasting

hours as well as the right to quadruple its transmitting power. KTBC then became a cash cow; in less than twenty years that $17,500 investment grew to close to $4 million, according to the station's 1962 FCC filing, with an actual estimated value of around $17 million. As stated in an analysis made shortly thereafter: "Unlike most businesses, a broadcasting enterprise can exist and expand only with government approval. . . . The practical effect of a long series of FCC rulings has been to create the Johnson local TV broadcasting monopoly, expand its sphere, and defend it against incursion."[11]

Behind this, of course, was LBJ. Making sure to control FCC decisions, when elected a U.S. Senator in 1948 he immediately attached himself to the Commerce Committee, the senatorial overseer of the FCC. In 1952, for example, when Johnson was Senate whip, the FCC, which had awarded the Austin area just one high-frequency channel (KTBC, of course), gave five competitive channels to the Dallas–Fort Worth area and three to Corpus Christi, a city with a smaller population than Austin. In fact, Austin was the largest city in the entire United States to have only one TV station. Not unrelated, Johnson's income each year from 1948 to 1964 was more than $1 million.

LBJ's pious explanation to these events was the claim that it was his wife's station, not his, and her business acumen—with which he had nothing to do—created the profits that solely belonged to her. It can be pointed out in answer to this fairy tale that under Texas community property laws, any of a wife's income becomes the joint property of her husband.

The Johnson deceit was no dark secret. When he ran in 1946 for a fifth term in Congress, an Austin resident named Hardy Hollers opposed him. Hollers, who charged that Johnson enriched himself in office, asked a question: "Will Lyndon Johnson explain how the charter for KTBC, owned by Mrs. Johnson, was obtained?" He then concluded with a devastating remark: "If the United States Attorney was on the job, Lyndon Johnson would be in the federal penitentiary instead of in Congress."[12]

But the shrewd congressman held the trump card, for he had sprinkled federal money liberally in his congressional district with large rural electrification projects, installations such as the big Bergstrom Air Force Base, and dams on the Lower Colorado River: Indeed, Johnson boasted that the Pedernales River Electric Cooperative was the biggest co-op in the world. These benefits, and the resultant Texans on the federal payroll, were what the voters cared about. Johnson was voted back into office by more than a two-thirds majority.

The KTBC-TV purchase was the rivulet that turned into a river of payoffs. Actually, Johnson got his political start as a protegé of Richard Kleberg of the fabulous King Ranch family, and his advisers all represented the cattle owners, the oil companies, the big public utilities, and the building contractors. Foremost among these was the construction firm of Brown & Root. Herman and George Brown (Root had died earlier) poured large sums into LBJ's political campaigns and in return won fat federal contracts that made them very rich men.

Admiral John J. Manning, retired chief of the navy's Bureau of Yards and Docks, publicly said that Johnson's friends "get the first look at what we're going to do." For Brown & Root's first big contract, to build the Mansfield Dam on the Colorado River near Austin, the firm made the low bid of $6 million to get the job; before they finished, $25 million was authorized. In 1937 LBJ discussed with President Roosevelt putting a naval base in Texas. Naval Committee Chairman Carl Vinson said Johnson "played a dominant role in setting up the naval base in Corpus Christi"; and Brown & Root, with a partner, got the $78-million contract to build the base, with extra millions in the base's expansion.[14] In this same period Brown & Root received the contract to string the almost two thousand miles of electric lines for the Pedernales River Electric Cooperative.[15] In a letter dated November 5, 1941, Johnson wrote to George Brown, "I will talk to Admiral Moreel as you suggest and do all I can." Moreel was then chief of the navy's Bureau of Yards and Docks. The letter does not refer to a specific project, but less than eight months later Brown & Root received a $58-million contract to build an ammunition depot in Oklahoma, and a letter on record indicates that Johnson's wife found out by checking with Admiral Moreel.[16]

By 1954 a public relations man for Brown & Root said the relatively obscure firm had done a billion dollars worth of work for the army and navy. "It was indeed, a partnership, the campaign contributions, the congressional look-out, the contracts, the appropriations, the telegrams, the investment advice, the gifts and the hunts and the free airplane rides—it was an alliance of mutual reinforcement between a politician and a corporation. . . . In its dimensions and its implications for the structure of society their arrangement was a new phenomenon on its way to becoming the new pattern for American society."[17]

It should be mentioned that the Brown brothers were noted as the most effective large antiunion firm in the United States and hired only nonunion help. To this LBJ, the great liberal and union defender, raised no objection. The relationship between George Brown and LBJ was so close that it was on Brown's Virginia estate that Johnson suffered his first heart attack in 1955.

President Johnson organized a new group called the President's Club. This club, "bearing the imprimatur of Lyndon Johnson, has no rules, keeps no minutes . . . and transacts no business that anyone talks about."[18] For $1,000 minimum dues (1966 money) more than twenty-five hundred rich Americans of both parties joined the club. This entitled them to a "direct relationship" with government officials, invitations to the White House, and consultation on federal appointments. In 1966 the President's Club raised more money for the Democrats than all contributions to the party's national committee.

LBJ, in response to an inquiry as to the club's function, told reporters that club donations did not influence the awarding of government contracts. Yet there followed a series of amazing coincidences, of which several can be noted.

★

- On May 10, 1966, the House voted to kill a $20-million appropriation for Project Mohole, a controversial attempt to drill through the earth's crust. On May 13, George Brown contributed $23,000 to the President's Club. On May 18, President Johnson sent a request to Congress that the Mohole funds be restored. Brown & Root got the contract, though its bid was almost double the lowest offer. Chairman Brown said it was "ridiculous" to suggest any connection between the events.
- An employee of Anheuser-Busch, Inc., the nation's largest brewery, alerted the Republicans that company officers and their wives contributed $10,000 to the President's Club less than a month before the Justice Department dropped an antitrust suit against the company. The brewery stated that any possible connection between the events was "preposterous."
- An Atlanta architect was awarded a design contract for a Veterans' Administration hospital; the architect then gave $10,000 to the club. The architect denied any connection between the contract and his gift.

Early in his career, Lyndon Johnson had started to buy land outside Austin, and by 1966 he owned fourteen thousand acres whose worth he calculated only at book value. With a quick sense of humor, Dean Burch, chairman of the Republican National Committee, then quipped that New York City's real estate should be listed as worth $24, the amount paid to the Indians by the Dutch settlers.[19]

Johnson always had an inner logic to his investments. The rapid rise in value of his land purchases was due to the fact that LBJ then funneled taxpayers' money into the construction of highways and bridges nearby. An airport was also built conveniently close to his land, financed in part by federal funds. The Texas Board of Water Engineers, for example, gave Johnson a permit to dam the Pedernales River in order to provide water to irrigate his land. All parties, of course, denied that any favoritism was involved. The report of these schemes

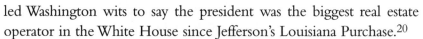

led Washington wits to say the president was the biggest real estate operator in the White House since Jefferson's Louisiana Purchase.[20]

LBJ seemed to have magic powers that would have made future president Ronald Reagan's teflon skin seem like a thin coating by comparison. Three buddies and business associates in President Johnson's last ninety days in office formed a nonprofit corporation and then received twenty-six and one-half acres of government-owned choice real estate in the center of Austin to build a nursing home and apartment building. The land, being used as a fish hatchery by the Interior Department, was declared surplus without any screening of other federal agencies as to its possible use or competitive bidding. Although valued by earlier appraisal as worth more than $2 million, its value was arbitrarily reduced to $642,000. Furthermore, Johnson's three buddies received large cash grants from the Department of Health, Education, and Welfare (HEW) as well as loans totaling $8.5 million from the Federal Housing Administration in order to proceed.[21]

Senator John J. Williams, a Republican from Delaware, somehow heard of this sweetheart deal. He investigated and reported "White House pressure was on, and no attention was paid to any of the adverse reports."[22]

As a result of Senator Williams's exposé, the HEW Department declared the nursing home did not have the proper income tax status to receive the surplus land. But Johnson displayed his usual cunning. A reshuffling of the three Texans put in command Frank C. Erwin Jr., chairman of the University of Texas Board of Regents. With such an illustrious Texan as head, in less than two months the building corporation was granted a tax exemption by the IRS that qualified it to receive the surplus land.

These are examples of the rapacious face of LBJ. Turn Janus to the other side and we have the greatest figure in social legislation of the twentieth century. It is almost an unbelievable paradox.

That Lyndon Johnson was sincere in his passion to better the lot of the common man, almost all commentators agree. From a poor background, coming to consciousness in the Depression years in

Texas where Mexicans were viewed as trash—there were fewer blacks in the high grazing lands of the Austin region, which is more than five hundred feet above sea level—one of the first jobs the young man had was to teach these maligned Latinos. This sympathy extended to blacks, and Johnson himself considered the passage of the Voting Rights Act of 1965 his greatest achievement. Related to this was his appointment of Thurgood Marshall, a black man and an outstanding liberal, to the Supreme Court.

Yet here again we see the contradictions in LBJ's character. As a congressman for eleven years he voted against every civil rights bill, not only against ending the poll tax and segregation in the armed forces but also against lynching. He attacked President Truman's civil rights program and up to 1957, both in the House and Senate (twenty years in all), was consistently against all such legislation. Indeed, in speeches several years after the death of President Roosevelt, LBJ stressed his repudiation of various aspects of the New Deal and placed himself in the conservative ranks of southern senators.[23] If President Kennedy had not been killed, Johnson probably would have gone down in history as just another weathercock produced by the accidents of politics, veering with the winds from liberals and then the winds from conservatives as personal ambition dictated.

What happened that night in Dallas on November 22, 1963, when John F. Kennedy was assassinated and Lyndon B. Johnson, hastily sworn in as president, moved in a sense from the vice president political morgue to the high throne of president? We will never know. Did LBJ sense the time was again ripe for a bold program of social change? Was he always a concealed liberal on the issue of civil rights but voted against all such programs because he felt his Texas constituency would then reject him? Did his immense ego twit him that he would only be remembered if he created laws attached to his name that would never be forgotten? Again, we will never know.

In science the difference between what is considered true and what is considered a hypothesis rests on overwhelming factual evidence. And the evidence suggests that, putting aside psychological

motives (which in an ultimate sense are irrelevant when stacked against the facts), Lyndon B. Johnson will be forever regarded as the stuff of a great president who tragically pushed us deeper into a ill-conceived war and thus lost his chance to go down in history as the heroic figure he dreamed himself to be.

Perhaps the best single-sentence summary of LBJ was made by Joseph A. Califano Jr., who was Johnson's closest domestic adviser at the White House: "He gave new meaning to the word Machiavellian, as he gave new hope to the disadvantaged."[24]

★　★　★

MILHOUS I
Lord of San Clemente
Duke of Key Biscayne
Captain of Watergate

Reprinted with permission. Edward Sorel.

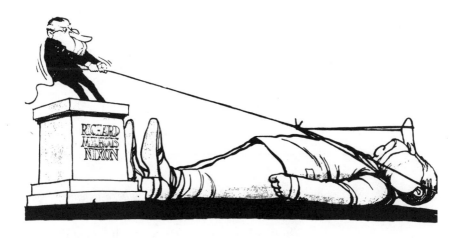

**OLIPHANT**                                    by Pat Oliphant

'I NEED A NICE POLITE PARROT WHO'LL SIT ON MY SHOULDER AND SPEAK WHEN HE'S
SPOKEN TO!'

# CHAPTER FOUR

★

# RICHARD MILHOUS NIXON
## (1969–1974)

★

*"Whenever a man has cast a longing eye on office, a rottenness begins in his conduct."*
Thomas Jefferson, Letter to Tench Coxe, 1820

*"Men who are engaged in public life must necessarily aim at reducing opposition to a minimum, and one of the most obvious means to that end is by misrepresenting, discrediting or ruining their opponents."*
Frederick Scott Oliver, *Politics and Politicians*

Richard M. Nixon stood out from the start. At Whittier College, a Quaker institution in a suburb of Los Angeles, which he entered in 1930, the young man was elected freshman class president with 90 percent of the vote, student body vice president in his sophomore year by 75 percent of the vote, and by the same great margin student body president in his junior year. Finishing second in his class in scholarship, Nixon won the college's highest service award. The very bright and popular graduate then received a full-time scholarship to Duke University Law School.

Though Richard Nixon became noted as an actor in campus plays at Whittier College, his specialty was debating. Through all four years at college his team was tops, winning twenty-four of twenty-seven debates among the small schools of Southern California. In 1933 he won the coveted *Reader's Digest* speaking contest among conference colleges. "He was a merciless opponent," one teacher commented.[1] In the acorn is the future tree.

At Duke Law School, Nixon's great memory was a high asset. Dogged as ever, he was remembered by fellow students as studying every day and night the library was open. In his first year he achieved an A average and was third in a class that included thirty-two members of Phi Beta Kappa. His grades dropped a bit in the second year but he was still sixth; and in his last year, when he also was an editor of the *Duke Bar Association Journal*, he again rose to third. In a popular article he argued with force for granting free legal service to the poor, a position he would, thirty-five years later, just as passionately reject. Nixon was also remembered as being an ardent liberal on race relations, in fact seeming to the southern students as one of their harshest critics.[2] Indeed, as late as the latter part of the 1930s Richard Nixon opposed General Franco's revolt in Spain, a position very much at odds with California conservatives who usually painted loyalists (anyone who opposed Franco) as Communists. He also openly despised Hitler.

After graduation from Duke, where the shining young man had received profuse character references from the dean, he took and passed the California bar examination with ease in a year in which more than half the applicants failed. Joining a law firm in his home town of Whittier, Nixon in two years was invited to become a full partner. In the next decade he became Whittier assistant city attorney, headed the alumni of both Whittier College and his class at Duke University, served on the Whittier Chamber of Commerce, and taught Quaker Sunday school classes. Falling in love with Pat Ryan, he paid no attention to her poverty-stricken background and different religion at a time when he could easily have married upward in his own circles.

When the Japanese struck Pearl Harbor and war broke out, Richard Nixon applied for a job, and was accepted, in the Office of Price Administration (OPA): "I would stay working with the government rather than compromising our Quaker principles," he wrote home.[3] But by spring of 1942 he felt impelled to join the armed forces, requesting a position in naval procurement rather than direct action. While on active duty he studied the Bible daily and was popular wherever he served.

The reason for this rather detailed report on the young Nixon is to wonder why, given this background, he struck what might be called a Faustian bargain with the demon of power. Nixon was extremely bright, clean-cut, good-looking, religious, hardworking, sober, and righteous without being a prig. He was the model of the Horatio Alger ideal American. But his tacking toward another path was soon apparent. The change can be followed quite clearly.

To understand Nixon's somersault one must touch on the California political scene shortly before and after World War II. By tradition smugly Republican, and even more so in Southern California, the state was hit by waves of Okies (refugees from the Oklahoma dust storms), Mexicans, and idealistic Americans like Jerry Voorhis, son of a devoutly Episcopal and Republican home from the Midwest who, galvanized by the social gospel, had become a left-wing (though anti-Communist) Democrat. In this churning scene the fear of the might of the postwar Soviets fused with the resentment of high taxes and the federal bureaucracy to create a flaming hatred by old, rich Californians who identified the New Deal with pro-Communism. Backed by the major newspaper and radio web, this powerful elite appealed to all the frustrations of the electorate. Jerry Voorhis, Congressmen from California's twelfth district, was vulnerable but there seemed to be no vigorous Republican opponent to unseat him. The only prospective candidate to fill the ticket died suddenly of a heart attack. It was then—such is fate—that the Republicans turned to the hometown Richard Nixon, with his sterling credentials.

Their choice in this cocoon of his political career considered himself, though Republican, a liberal. At his audition before the committee deciding the primary candidate, Nixon stated, "I will be prepared to put on an aggressive and vigorous campaign on a platform of practical liberalism." His mentor in spirit was the young Harold

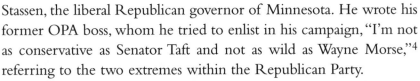

Stassen, the liberal Republican governor of Minnesota. He wrote his former OPA boss, whom he tried to enlist in his campaign, "I'm not as conservative as Senator Taft and not as wild as Wayne Morse,"[4] referring to the two extremes within the Republican Party.

It was at this time that a public relations expert named Murray Chotiner came on board. Chotiner was a brilliant rattlesnake who matched violent anti-Communism with cynicism and a philosophy of winning no matter what, which fitted Nixon's submerged side. Chotiner electrified the rather listless Nixon campaign by claiming that Jerry Voorhis was the front for the Political Action Committee (PAC) of the Congress of Industrial Organizations (CIO), the body of big-labor leftists: an ironic charge because the CIO had endorsed every other major Democrat in the California elections except Voorhis, who had publicly expressed contempt for Communist influence in labor unions. But this meant nothing to Chotiner, and Nixon studied, admired, and came to imitate the tactics of Chotiner.[5]

Now major newspapers began ferocious attacks, particularly on the bogus PAC issue, against Voorhis. Most important to Nixon was the strident support of the *Los Angeles Times*, with its virulent anti–New Deal policy, which led to campaign money from large banks and insurance companies. By May, Voorhis was almost completely frozen out of paid advertising that Nixon money had preempted. Fifty thousand postcards were sent to voters urging a vote for Nixon. The change from "practical liberalism" to a different figure began to take shape. Nixon ended the primary campaign with a new oratory: "On Tuesday the people . . . will vote for me as a supporter of free enterprise, individual initiative, and a sound progressive program . . . or for the continuance of the totalitarian ideologies of the New Deal administration." On election day he repeated this theme, namely that voters could choose Nixon or Voorhis, "who had supported by his votes the foreign ideologies of the New Deal administration."[6]

The strength Nixon showed in the election primary proved to Republicans that Voorhis could be beaten. The money really began to pour in. Oil companies especially hated Voorhis, who had blocked their efforts to take over the tidelands offshore oil, and were large contributors. Others were the Bank of America and the California utility companies. The main source was a large diversion of extra funds from the Republican National Committee, engineered by former president Herbert Hoover, a fellow Quaker whose wife served with Nixon on the board of Whittier College.[7]

Fresh from a vacation taken after the primary, Nixon came out fighting. At a kickoff dinner he charged that Voorhis was allied with "the left-wing group which has taken over the Democratic Party in California." He then said in Whittier, "I welcome the opposition of the PAC, with its communist principles."[8] Other examples may be quoted: "Today the American people are faced with the choice between . . . the radical PAC and its adherents, who could deprive the people of liberty. . . ." When the CIO opened a campaign office to aid local candidates—excluding Voorhis, whom they never endorsed—Nixon repeated in speech after speech, "The communist-dominated PAC has opened campaign offices right here in our district. This organization has endorsed my opponent, Jerry Voorhis. They will flood the district with paid workers to spread their doctrines . . . to seek the defeat of those who stand for the preservation of the American way of life."

The harder Voorhis worked to disavow these lies the more damning the Nixon ads grew. In speeches Nixon perfected the technique he would use throughout his career. The OPA, where he had worked—and from which short months before he had asked his former boss to manage his campaign—was "shot through with extreme left-wingers . . . boring from within . . . to bring about the socialization of America's basic institutions." Communists were infiltrating everywhere "to gradually give the American people a communist form of government."[9]

Nixon won by a landslide, 57 percent to 43 percent.[10] The lesson he had learned from Murray Chotiner, the Big Lie, now became his technique to rise to power. And that also became his sole objective: to win. We have precise evidence he knew exactly what he was doing because years later in a recorded conversation Nixon was introduced to Stanley Long, a former Voorhis aide, who chided him on the Red smears. Nixon responded, "Of course, I knew Jerry Voorhis wasn't a communist. You know I know better than that. But it's a good political campaign fire to use." Long then asked the usual question of the relation of means to end. Nixon answered, "I had to win. That's the thing you don't understand. The important thing is to win."[11] The transformation was complete. From Nixon to men like Joseph McCarthy was only the next step. And Watergate was not an aberration; it was simply the end of a continuous unfolding.

The rest is well-known history. It is not necessary to review the Whittaker Chambers–Alger Hiss case, the smashing of Congresswoman Helen Gahagan Douglas, the clawing upward to become vice president under Eisenhower, and, finally, Nixon's presidency. Every opponent—whether the charges were half true or false—was a leftist, pinko, or communist.[12] Every opponent was suspect or working for a foreign power. "True Americans" had only one basic choice and that was to vote for Richard Nixon. And, with certain interesting exceptions, Nixon devoted himself to smashing or weakening unions, destroying federal legislation aimed at helping the poor and helpless, and pushing measures to increase the power of the rich. This, of course, was payoff for the great sums he received to finance his election campaigns.

The result was that this strange and brilliant man came to be more hated or more loved—except for Joseph McCarthy—than any other political figure in twentieth-century American history. Hated, we may add, even by people who shared his basic philosophy. Republican Governor Earl Warren of California, later elevated to the Supreme Court, openly despised him. His fellow California senator, conservative Republican William Knowland, when requested to introduce Nixon's name as vice-presidential nominee to Eisenhower, asked bitterly, "I have to nominate that dirty son of a bitch?" And Nixon gave back in kind. He described aging Eisenhower, to whom he owed his presidency, as "that senile old bastard."[13] His various comments about others as recorded on the Watergate tapes are too filthy to print in respectable journals.

One of Nixon's main goals when he became president was to control the Internal Revenue Service in order to blackmail or destroy his enemies. Following the summer of 1969, a persistent attempt was organized to make the IRS Nixon's political arm. Specific enemies were pinpointed by White House memos or through John Dean (White House counsel), and files were maintained on such individuals as Jimmy Breslin, Tony Randall, Elizabeth Taylor, Julie Andrews, and organizations such as the Urban League, the National Council of Churches, the American Jewish Committee, and the National Organization of Women. About 225 audits were ordered under intense pressure from Nixon. An interesting aspect of this vile approach was the stubborn resistance on the part of first IRS Commissioner Randolph W. Thrower, and then his successor Johnnie McK. Walters. One of the heart-warming aspects in the study of American history is to stumble on such decent men who, often anonymously, are responsible for the continued success of the American system. When Walters balked in 1972 after Dean asked him to investigate the main contributors to the McGovern campaign, warning it would be disastrous for the IRS, Nixon was thrown into a rage: "After the election . . . the whole goddamn bunch go out . . . and if he [Secretary of the Treasury George Schultz] doesn't do it he is out. . . . I look forward to the time that we have the agents in the Department of Justice and the IRS under our control after November 7."[14] The mentality was underscored by Egil Krogh Jr., the assistant to presidential aide John D. Ehrlichman, who blatantly stated, "Anyone who opposes us, we'll destroy. As a matter of fact, anyone who doesn't support us, we'll destroy."[15]

On June 17, 1972, at the Watergate office building in Washington a group of men were arrested trying to break into the offices of the Democratic National Committee.[16] Their credentials showed they worked for the Committee to Re-Elect President Nixon, the purpose of the robbery being to steal documents involving Democratic

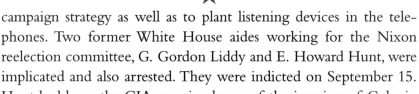

campaign strategy as well as to plant listening devices in the tele-phones. Two former White House aides working for the Nixon reelection committee, G. Gordon Liddy and E. Howard Hunt, were implicated and also arrested. They were indicted on September 15. Hunt had been the CIA man in charge of the invasion of Cuba in 1961. No one at that time connected the Nixon reelection com-mittee or the White House to their break-in.

An October Gallup poll showed that most Americans hadn't heard of the botched burglary. In November, Nixon was resound-ingly reelected.

On February 7, 1973, amid recurring rumors and innuendo about corrupt financing and dirty tricks done by the Nixon reelec-tion committee, the Senate established a Select Committee to inves-tigate. On March 3 one of the men convicted in the case, a former CIA agent, admitted that he and the other defendants had been pres-sured to keep silent. He eventually implicated John Mitchell, attorney general and chairman of the Committee to Re-Elect Pres-ident Nixon, as the "overall boss."

Pressure started to mount. On April 20 L. Patrick Gray, acting director of the FBI, resigned after admitting that on the advice of Nixon aides he destroyed Watergate evidence. Ten days later Nixon's chief of staff, H. R. Haldeman; domestic affairs assistant, John Erlichman; and presidential counsel, John Dean III, all resigned. In a televised speech, Nixon denied any knowledge of Watergate. In this same period it came out that Watergate conspirators Hunt and Liddy had also burglarized another office to seek records involving a Nixon critic. Then, on June 25, John Dean testified before the Senate committee that not only was Nixon involved but he had authorized payment of "hush money" to the men caught in the Watergate break-in. It was eventually established that $400,000 was given on Erlichman's orders.

On July 16 White House aide Alexander Butterfield told the Senate Select Committee that the president secretly recorded all Oval Office conversations.[17] The committee asked for the tapes but was refused. On October 20 Nixon ordered Attorney General Elliot Richardson to fire the Watergate Special Prosecutor Archibald Cox, who had asked for the secret tapes. His assistant, William D. Ruckelhaus, backed Richardson and both resigned. Solicitor General Robert Bork, third man in the Justice Department, did as told and fired Cox. (This was a major reason Bork, when nominated by Ronald Reagan for the Supreme Court, was rejected by the Senate.) The dual resignation of Richardson and Ruckelhaus and the firing of Cox led the House to consider impeachment of the president. On October 20 Nixon reluctantly turned over all but two of the tapes.

On November 21 an eighteen-minute gap was discovered in one of the tapes, which Nixon claimed was due to an accident. Expert analysis proved this was almost impossible; later it was established that the erasure was deliberate. In this same month the officials of five big corporations pleaded guilty to the charges of making illegal contributions to the Nixon campaign. It was also uncovered that Commerce Secretary Maurice Stans had taken a secret payment of $250,000 from a fugitive financier, Robert Vesco, to squelch a Securities and Exchange Commission investigation of Vesco's criminal acts.

The plot was unraveling slowly, but surely. On March 1, 1974, seven former White House staff members, including Halderman, Ehrlichman, and former Attorney General John Mitchell, were indicted for conspiring to obstruct the Watergate investigation. On May 16 Richard Kleindienst, who followed Mitchell as attorney general, pleaded guilty to a charge of lying before a Senate committee, becoming the first attorney general ever convicted of a crime. On July 27 the House Judiciary Committee approved two articles of impeachment against Nixon: obstructing justice and violating his oath of office.[18] And on August 8 Nixon conceded at last to "a serious omission" to his earlier statements—namely that six days after the Watergate burglary he had ordered a halt to the FBI investigation. His last congressional support began to fade.[19] Key Republican congressmen told him there were enough votes for impeachment; on August 9, 1974, Nixon announced his resignation,

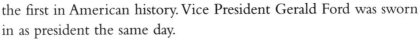

the first in American history. Vice President Gerald Ford was sworn in as president the same day.

On September 8 President Ford granted Nixon "full, free, and absolute pardon . . . for all offenses against the United States which he . . . has committed or may have committed or taken part in while president."This pardon guaranteed Nixon's large annual federal pension and free offices, secretaries, and secret service protection.

To summarize Watergate in one sentence: President Nixon was party and partisan to an overt burglary, lied to cover up his involvement, destroyed material evidence of the burglary, and attempted to use federal agencies to silence political opponents.

Though less known than Watergate, the history of Nixon's personal investments is equally revealing because it shows the same mindset at work in the private field as in the public. The best example is his purchase of an estate in Southern California.

In 1969 Nixon paid a $100,000 down payment on a $1.4 million, twenty-six acre oceanfront property in San Clemente, with a lavish fourteen-room Spanish-style house. Despite a mortgage, he was short of cash and borrowed $625,000 from two rich bosom friends who were also neighbors at his other residence in a private compound at Key Biscayne, Florida. In 1970 the two men, Robert A. Abplanalp and Charles G. ("Bebe") Rebozo, set up an investment company, which bought the property—except 5.9 waterfront acres and the house—for $1,249,000. Thus, Nixon acquired the best land and the house for $151,000—the difference between the original $1,400,000 purchase price and the sale price of $1,249,000. The house was then separately mortgaged and Nixon had very little money, or none at all, in this acquisition.

A later investigation showed that the Abplanalp-Rebozo purchase was encumbered by a mortgage, probably a refinancing, of $1 million, which meant that the purchasers personally invested less than $250,000. Most curious in this transaction is that the San Clemente property records indicated that the $1 million mortgage covered the entire original property, including the 5.9 waterfront

acres and the house, a situation hard to believe. The mortgage company either did not know or ignored (as a title search would indicate if the sale to Nixon had been recorded) that the acres and house
had been removed by a private deed. This oversight would have been
impossible in a normal sale and deed.[20]

Payoffs, of course, were involved in the form of special favors.
Two can be illustrated. In 1971 it was disclosed that the federal government paid Rebozo more than the appraised value for land it
bought from him for the Biscayne National Monument. Mr.
Rebozo also had special relations with the Small Business Administration (SBA) in Florida. The regional administrator of the SBA in
that state guaranteed the rents on a shopping center, amounting to
close to $1 million, that Rebozo was developing.

The story of San Clemente does not stop with its purchase.
Nixon ordered the General Services Administration to make
improvements for what he later described as "security reasons."
These included a high masonry wall around the entire twenty-six
acres (though Nixon officially only owned 5.9 acres), and such items
as a new electric system and new windows for the house, walkways
to the beach, gazebos, new furniture and silver service, a beach
cabana, and golf carts.[21] When questioned, the White House said the
improvements amounted to some $40,000. City building permits
and subsequent government record searches indicated the sum was
$703,000. When asked about the discrepancy, the White House
refused to comment. Nor did it respond to questions as to why
"security reasons" extended to improving property owned by
Nixon's friends.

The pressure of these investigations grew to the point that Nixon
finally accepted a congressional committee, which then reviewed his
finances. This probe showed that during his four years as president,
Nixon had more than tripled his net worth, becoming a millionaire,
largely through tax evasion. He had not paid any taxes in California,
though he was a registered voter there, nor did he pay any capital gains
tax on the sale of his New York City apartment. He took tax deduc-

tions for operating costs at San Clemente and Key Biscayne even though the government paid for the facilities. Nixon gave his vice-presidential papers to the National Archives, taking an $80,000 deduction, but did not sign a deed of gift, explaining later that the deed had been lost. For the gift to the same archives of his presidential papers, he took a deduction of more than $2 million. The gift was illegally backdated to fall within a deadline, but this was uncovered.

The final result of this investigation was a determination by the IRS that Nixon, who had paid less than $79,000 taxes on an income of some $1.2 million between 1969 and 1972, owed $467,000. Under great pressure, he settled.

After his resignation and pardon by President Ford, Nixon sold the television rights for interviews to TV personality David Frost for $600,000. Then he published his story, RN: the Memoirs of Richard Nixon, for which he was paid an advance of $2.5 million. Thereafter he published several other books "that became his economic salvation,"[22] as though $3.1 million was merely a starting point. He ended his life many times a millionaire.

One can never draw a final conclusion on the Nixon years, regardless of his personal offenses, without reviewing his foreign policy, so intertwined with the Vietnam War. It took a great deal of what is called "Realpolitik"—accepting reality—to awaken President Nixon to the changes taking place in the world. After he did, however, dragged as he was to the altar, his contribution was enormous.

In late 1968, when Nixon was elected president, he pledged the withdrawal of American soldiers from Vietnam. Indeed he did greatly reduce the troops, with fewer than 150,000 left by early 1972. His approach was "Vietnamization," i.e., American money and air power supporting the native South Vietnamese. It did not work. In the spring of 1970 Nixon arranged an invasion of Cambodia backed by a huge bombardment. This, too, did not work. Then Nixon supported the South Vietnamese in an invasion of Laos. That failed also. The North Vietnamese continued to gain strength.

From 1964 to 1972 the United States, the most powerful nation in the world, dropped 7 million tons of bombs on Vietnam, more than twice the total tonnage employed in Europe and Asia during World War II. Also, poison spray called Agent Orange leveled plant life. Yet the peasant army of this small country, about the size of Massachusetts, defeated our effort.

Why? It was nationalism, the same force that motivated the small farmer army of Colonial America to defeat the Redcoats and hired Hessians of a powerful Great Britain. U. S. leaders screamed communism and indeed the revolt was under the Communists. But it was nationalism, the will to die for their country's freedom from foreigners, that made those heroic soldiers fight, not the abstruse dialectics of Karl Marx. This our brightest people, including men of the caliber of William Fulbright and Adlai Stevenson, did not grasp.

But students who would be sent to die could understand. After four college students were killed at Ohio's Kent State University in 1970, the first general strike of its kind in the nation's history was called when students at four hundred colleges and universities united to protest. As the war went on desertions mounted, mainly to Canada: the estimates range from fifty thousand upward. In Vietnam, servicemen started to roll fragmentation bombs under the tents of officers who were ordering them into combat: The Pentagon reported 209 such incidents in 1970 alone. By Christmas 1972 came the first defiance of B-52 pilots who refused to fly missions. Altogether, about seven hundred thousand military personnel received less than honorable discharges. By 1973 the United States was in effect forced to throw in the towel, although the final South Vietnamese collapse took almost two more years. And two months after the end of the war only 20 percent of Americans polled thought the collapse of the Saigon government was a threat to U.S. security— which indeed it never had been, except in the fevered heads of American leaders.

Nixon at first opposed violently and then, degree by degree, accepted reality. The passions created over Watergate often obscure the fact that President Nixon, besides ending the Vietnam War, was

★

responsible for our first serious efforts to achieve detente with China and the Soviet Union. One might retort that only a right-wing president could navigate these devious channels but, whether so or not, it was Nixon who did it. What was called the Nixon Doctrine, despite the frightful aberrations of the invasions and bombings in Cambodia and Laos,[23] was at bottom more than gradual withdrawal but, finally, an American acceptance of political pluralism, changing the conflict from a "strategic contest between the proxies of two great powers—the U.S. and China—into a dirty little war that could . . . be lost or settled in a way that would not gravely damage American interests or increase threats."[24]

This was the basic building block that led to our further achievements in settling relations with China and Russia and reducing the supreme threat of nuclear war. The Nixon Doctrine was the first recognition of a new world reality.

Nixon's twisted personality included many contradictions. As mentioned earlier, he held some views that are usually associated with very liberal persons. Despite many of his mean-minded admirers, he was not a racist. Perhaps due to his Quaker background, his voting record on civil rights before becoming president was better than most of his opponents and far superior to that of Lyndon Johnson. Jews were close to him and among his most trusted admirers, the best examples being Murray Chotiner, his éminence grise throughout, and national security advisor and secretary of state Henry Kissinger at the end. He seemed to prefer refugee Cubans in those few intervals when he could relax, Bebe Rabozo being his primary companion. His record on Native American rights is perhaps the most extraordinary of any twentieth-century president. Nowhere—except in occasional epithets when maddened under extreme pressure—did he categorize with contempt different people as a whole.

Even in politics he adopted some positions opposite to those usually ascribed to him. Nixon proposed universal health coverage. He supported wage and price controls, as well as automatic cost-of-living adjustments in Social Security. The Clean Air Act of 1970, which he endorsed, was at that time the greatest effort to control air pollution. His environmental record was excellent, including federal regulation of oil spill cleanup and pesticides dumped into the ocean as well as control of noise pollution.[25]

It is usual liberal policy to increase executive power in order to aid those at the bottom of the economic chain. Curiously, this coincided with Nixon's view, but for another reason. As president, he continually strove to redirect power from Congress and the federal bureaucracy to the presidency and his inner circle. In an important sense, Nixon's effort to redistribute this power to himself and then to the states and cities meant in fact increasing executive authority by siphoning off that formerly belonging to the legislative branch. Ronald Reagan, then governor of California, was the most prominent Republican opposing these measures, based on his opposition to almost all centralized government. After attacking the 1972 Fiscal Assistance Act, a gesture in that direction, Reagan as president ended the program in 1987. Ironically, a full circle was thus made between the two most right-wing presidents.[26]

To what extent was Nixon unique among presidents? In his defense, he insisted that he had done nothing different from others but was a victim of liberals and the Eastern Establishment. Probably the final opinion circles around the question of degree. Without doubt Lincoln's suspension of habeas corpus (the basic foundation of American liberties) during the Civil War and Franklin D. Roosevelt's internment of Japanese Americans and the Aleut tribe in Alaska during World War II (racist acts, since he didn't do the same with German Americans) were in some senses worse than Watergate. Yet Lincoln and Roosevelt are American idols while Nixon is generally vilified. The justification for these two cases was the U.S. involvement in crucial wars; but Nixon during the undeclared Vietnam conflict was also trying to win that war and considered Daniel Ellsberg's publishing of the Pentagon Papers and other similar acts as treason.

The Watergate tapings have an ambiguous side as well. They were not unique. Eisenhower, Kennedy, and Johnson all taped conversations. The Kennedy tapes, for example, reveal that when he called the Justice Department's Nicholas Katzenbach on July 25, 1963, the topic was James M. Landis and the IRS. Landis, the Kennedy family lawyer, was in trouble with the IRS. These, as other Kennedy tapes, are blotched or segmented. However, Nixon not only attempted to use the IRS to break his political enemies but spoke openly of them with loathing and crude epithets on his tapes.

Considering his enormous popularity at the time—in the 1972 election, after Watergate but before the final hue and cry, Nixon won almost 62 percent of the vote, took forty-nine states and received 520 of the 538 electoral votes, a smashing victory—if Nixon had admitted his role from the start and apologized to the American people, Watergate would probably have ended up as a minor footnote in history. But Nixon denied his role to the end until the evidence was overwhelming. It was cynicism that brought him not only to believe he was above the law, but to be contemptuous of it as well.

A big factor was that Watergate, a burglary, was a blue-collar crime. Presidents, senators, and congressmen—as well as governors, mayors, and other state and city officials—constantly commit white-collar crimes and get away with them, sometimes with a slap on the wrist or a fine. Many, if not most, public officials are on the payrolls of large pressure groups in one way or another and vote according to the sources of their funding. Sometimes it is done legally; many times, in the shadows. But burglary is different: As the American humorist Finley Peter Dunne (1867–1936), writing at the turn of the century under the name of Martin Dooley, said, "Steal a purse, go to jail; steal a railroad, become a U.S. Senator." Nixon committed an offense against conventional values by organizing a blue-collar crime.

It was not his only one. In 1971 he tried to organize raids on the office of the *Los Angeles Times*, an opposition newspaper, as well as calling for an IRS audit of its publisher.[27] He told H. R. Haldeman, his chief of staff, "I want this whole goddamn bunch gone after." Two weeks after the Watergate burglary, the tapes show that Nixon proposed sending thieves to make a "shambles" of Republican Party

★

headquarters and then to blame it on the Democrats. As for Watergate, when Nixon learned that G. Gordon Liddy, with some Cubans, would take the blame for the break-in, talking of their silence Haldeman said, "It's very expensive." Nixon answered, "They have to be paid. That's all there is to that." When John Dean decided to tell the truth, Nixon said in a fury, "I think we can destroy him—we must destroy him."[28]

In a way, one can understand Nixon's cynicism because he learned early on that almost everyone can be bought in politics, indeed almost everywhere, when there is big money and the stakes are high. He was also convinced, with some reason, that John F. Kennedy had bought, with his father's money, the election in 1960. But, as pointed out before, there are still persons of integrity who cannot be bought.

All the living Presidents respectfully attended the funeral of this master of under-the-table monies and dirty tricks, this expert equally in lies and foreign diplomacy. Always the politician, President Clinton delivered the eulogy, as he would later for Barry Goldwater. While Nixon was still alive, Yorba Linda, the small town where he was born, made the Nixon family farmhouse a museum while across the street a $25 million archives and library was built. In a final postmortem triumph, the U.S. Justice Department agreed after a twenty-year legal battle to pay $18 million to the Nixon estate in compensation for the presidential papers and tape recordings seized after his resignation in 1974.

★    ★    ★

*Post Script.* In July 2000 the United States and Vietnam completed a sweeping trade agreement that would allow unfettered commerce between the two nations. U.S. companies expressed satisfaction because they could then use Vietnam's low-wage workers to produce in bulk for the American market.

Hanoi also said that it planned to open its first stock market.

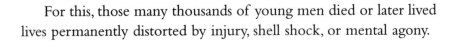

For this, those many thousands of young men died or later lived lives permanently distorted by injury, shell shock, or mental agony.

**OLIPHANT**                                                    by Pat Oliphant

# WHO LOST VIET NAM?

"NOT I," SAID IKE. "I JUST SENT MONEY."

"NOT I" SAID JACK. "I JUST SENT ADVISORS.

"NOT I," SAID LYNDON. "I JUST FOLLOWED JACK."

"NOT I," SAID DICK. I JUST HONORED JACK AND LYNDON'S COMMITMENTS."

"NOT I," SAID JERRY "WHAT WAS THE QUESTION?"

"YOU LOST VIETNAM," SAID HENRY, "BECAUSE YOU DIDN'T TRUST YOUR LEADERS."

# CHAPTER FIVE

★

# GERALD RUDOLPH FORD
## (1974–1977)

★

*"Some people are like popular songs that you only sing for a short time."*

La Rochefoucauld, *Maxims*, no. 211

*"If one were to draw up a list of full-time American politicians whose mental reach encompassed anything more than an encyclopedia of misinformation and outworn maxims, one would surely come close to naming 90 percent of them."*

Ferdinand Lundberg

John Tyler, James K. Polk, Millard Fillmore, Franklin Pierce, James Buchanan, Rutherford B. Hayes, James A. Garfield, Chester A. Arthur.

Who? What?

These men were all presidents of the United States. So was Gerald R. Ford.

People often ascend in politics by strange paths, but rarely by miracles. Ford arrived by way of three miracles. In January 1965 the Republicans elected Ford as Speaker of the House of Representatives—not because of any superior talent or leadership qualities, but simply due to the fact that various candidates had clashed so harshly for the position that they settled on a well-liked person who was without enemies. Then, in December 1973, when Nixon's first vice president, Spiro T. Agnew, resigned, Ford was nominated by Nixon

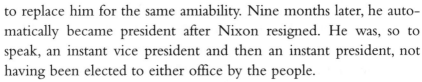

to replace him for the same amiability. Nine months later, he automatically became president after Nixon resigned. He was, so to speak, an instant vice president and then an instant president, not having been elected to either office by the people.

Who, indeed, *was* Gerald R. Ford? "I am a moderate in domestic affairs, an internationalist in foreign affairs and a conservative in fiscal policy,"[1] he once explained. In the climate of the time, this was like coming out for mother's love and apple pie, so ambiguous it gave the former Speaker leeway on any issue. In practice, he was a right-wing Republican.

Ford acted both as a loyal soldier and drill sergeant in this cause. He admired greatly and supported the extreme positions of Barry Goldwater, including the use of nuclear bombs in Vietnam: "I'm 100 percent behind Barry Goldwater," he declared.[2] He constantly pushed for the expansion of the war into the north of Vietnam, being "by instinct a Cold Warrior of the Eisenhower-Dulles school."[3] His congressional career was marked with two high spots, both in error.

Early in 1968 the Senate passed by a bipartisan majority and sent to the House a bill forbidding discrimination in the sale or rental of housing; indeed this bill was the handiwork of the conservative Senate Republican leader Everett M. Dirksen. Ford tried to kill the bill, allying himself with South Carolina's Republican Senator Strom Thurmond, the notorious apologist for southern racists. His own Republican House colleagues revolted, "an anti-leadership revolt without precedent in Ford's tenure as Republican floor chief."[4] Thereupon Ford issued a statement "reassessing" his stand—finally yielding. It has been claimed that this very unpopular action made Nixon decide to choose Agnew for vice president in 1968, bypassing his good friend.

The second stain on Ford's political life (in a certain way resembling Ken Starr's later vendetta against Clinton) was his obsessive attempt to impeach the popular Supreme Court Justice William O. Douglas, calling him senile, attacking his writing in what was called a pornographic magazine, and claiming he took money from a man with business connections to organized crime. Neither the Justice Department nor the CIA, both of which investigated the charges, could find any grounds for impeachment. Ford later admitted, "It was a mistake."[5]

There is little one can write about Ford's career as president. He was a Tyler, Polk, Fillmore, Pierce, Buchanan, Hayes, Garfield, Arthur. A folk expression states that a happy nation has no history, and Ford's tenure was a time of healing from the catastrophe of Watergate. Ford retained in his cabinet Nixon appointees viewed with great suspicion. But it was a safe group; as the well-known columnist Stewart Alsop wrote, it would give off "a Grand Rapids smell [Ford's hometown] . . . a nice comfortable smell."[6] Others were less charitable. Seventeen months into his presidency three national columnists—George Will, Tom Braden and Joseph Kraft—wrote variously that Ford was "a caretaker," "a joke," and "a man who brought his decline and his troubles upon himself with his own stupidities." Reporters were quoting "martini speeches."[7] And one severe critic stated that "Gerald Ford really is Archie Bunker, slightly modified, and that he was depending for a future election upon the nation's Bunkers in their numerous variations."[8]

Like the other hypocrites who pretended to dislike supreme power—as noted, the best example was Eisenhower—Gerald Ford claimed during his instant presidency that he had no interest in seeking election after his interim term. He testified before the Senate Rules Committee on November 23, 1973:

> Mr. Ford: ". . . I first should reiterate a comment I made many times since October 12 [when he was nominated for the vice presidency]—that I had no intention of seeking any public office in 1967."
>
> Senator Allen: ". . . You have . . . said that you do not intend to run for President or Vice President in 1976. . . . Do you think you might be subject to a draft?"
>
> Mr. Ford: "Well, the answer is still 'no.' I have no intention to run, and I can foresee no circumstances when I would change my mind. I have no intention of seeking public office in 1976."[9]

★

When 1975 arrived, Ford did not run but rather galloped. He desperately fought off Ronald Reagan's aggressive drive, stomping up and down the country for delegates. Jettisoning Nelson A. Rockefeller, whom he had chosen in his interim term as vice president, he picked Senator Robert Dole to ingratiate himself with the diehard Republicans. But all to no avail. He lost to Jimmy Carter.

Time has lent perspective on the figure of Gerald Ford. Unlike Nixon, he was a rather decent though undistinguished president who mirrored some of the better qualities of the American people, being kind, loyal, and blessed with a good sense of humor. Two anecdotes can illustrate this. When running for election in 1976, in a debate with Carter, Ford insisted (let us graciously assume through inattention) that Poland was not under the domination of the Soviet Union. After losing the election, he told reporters that he was considering becoming a professor at the University of Michigan. He then paused, and added: "I'm not going to teach Eastern European history, however."[10]

The second example he also told whimsically: After a speech in Omaha in this same 1976 campaign, an old lady came up to him and said, "I hear you spoke here tonight." Ford answered modestly, "Oh, it was nothing." The old lady nodded. "Yes, that's what I heard."

A final summary is probably correct. "Gerald R. Ford was an ordinary man called to serve America in extraordinary circumstances. In his plain ways and plain speaking, in his forthrightness and genial ways, in his trust in others and their trust in him, Ford was Everyman become President."[11] Oddly, he resembled Eisenhower without shoulder stripes. What ultimately lost him the 1976 election, more than decent mediocrity, was the taint of the quick Nixon pardon. Campaign polls consistently showed that 6 percent of the voters would not vote for him because of that decision, and he lost by 2 percent. In fact, Jimmy Carter won 49.9 percent of the vote, Ford 47.9 percent, with the electoral vote being one of the closest in sixty years.

Gerald Ford has mellowed through the years, perhaps softened by the suffering of his wife, who has had chronic alcohol problems. In the summer of 1998, having just turned eighty-five, he gave an interview in which he said that the hard-right, family-value extreme emphasis of certain Republicans was the road to political disaster. He stated that the welcome mat must be put out for those Republicans who support abortion rights, gay rights, and federal funding of the arts, summarizing, "If Republicans are going to win, they're going to have to have a broad enough umbrella."[12]

Gerald Ford, whose net worth in late 1973 was $256,378, is now a multimillionaire, as are all the living former presidents. After leaving office, he hired an agent from the William Morris Agency who negotiated a TV deal, with Ford earning large sums for his appearances on NBC. Ford and his wife then agreed to write their memoirs, with a $1-million advance for the two books.

Ford joined the boards of several prominent corporations, the most valuable being as an "adviser" (one of three, including Henry Kissinger) to American Express. The *Los Angeles Times* calculated that he received $541,300 alone in 1986 as a corporate director and consultant. As a very old man he sits on the boards of American Express, the National Association of Securities Dealers, and the Chase Bank of Texas; and as an emeritus director of Citigroup he is paid $125,000 a year. His government pensions amount to about $250,000 a year.[13] Being a top politician is a good business indeed.

President Ford was associated with two men who represented, at least in some senses, the worst and best of America. The vice president Richard Nixon chose instead of Ford was Spiro T. Agnew, a vulgar crook and indeed a funhouse mirror image of Nixon.

Agnew was a tart-tongued hatchet man worshiped by the far right for his cocky and abusive style. Strange in a man whose birth name was Anagnostopoulos, he derided immigrants and spoke of "Polacks" and a "fat Jap," to cite two examples. In another famous case, he derided black civil leaders at a time of urban riots. Critics of the Vietnam War were "pusillanimous pussyfooters," "an effete corps of impudent snobs," "ideological eunuchs," "hopeless, hysterical hypochondriacs of history," and "vicars of vacillation"—some of these remarks being crafted by Patrick J. Buchanan, a colonel in Nixon's army. In fact, Buchanan praised Agnew as "the voice of the silent majority."[14] In his heyday, Agnew—and unfortunately this tells much about an important segment of America—was rated the third most popular figure in the country, behind President Nixon and the Rev. Billy Graham.

Spiro Agnew was a Republican hack who rose in the political sewers of Baltimore, first as a party appointee on a local zoning board, then as Baltimore County Executive, and finally as governor of Maryland.

A month after Nixon's reelection a grand jury in Baltimore started looking into charges about Agnew's public service there. For eight months Agnew pleaded innocence against mounting evidence of corruption. Outraged, he bellowed to an audience, "I will not resign if indicted!"

Forty pages of charges were issued. In the final accounting it was proved that Agnew solicited $147,500 in bribes during ten years as Baltimore county executive and governor, accepting money even while vice president. Forced to reimburse the state of Maryland $268,482 in bribes and interest, he kept insisting these were political contributions but finally pleaded nolo contendere to tax evasion, which the judge pointedly reminded him was the "full equivalent" of a guilty plea.

However, the judge—as usually happens in cases of top politicians—ordered three years of unsupervised probation and a fine of $10,000. Agnew's cohorts—as also usually happens—were treated more harshly. One served four months in jail; the other six months. If the three had stolen a woman's pocketbook they might have been dealt with more harshly.

Twenty-one years after being disgraced Spiro Agnew attended the unveiling of his marble bust in the Capitol. Three hundred loyal friends, including top political figures, attended the event. He had made a fortune after his downfall; using influential contacts was his

★

specialty, Agnew proudly said. In one such well-known business transaction he served as the agent in a complex $181-million deal by former Nixon aides to sell information to Saddam Hussein of Iraq, recommended for his role to the supplier by Nixon himself and the Romanian dictator Nicolae Ceausescu.[15]

On news of his death, Bob Dole, then the Republican candidate for president, said, "Spiro Agnew earned the support of his countrymen because he was never afraid to speak out and stand up for America." Former President George Bush intoned, "He was a friend." One must conclude that justice is not only blind, deaf, and dumb, but takes a court recess when judging politicians.[16]

When interim President Gerald Ford chose Nelson A. Rockefeller as vice president he reached out to a world of values far different than those of the sleazy Spiro Agnew. This was another face of America, for Rockefeller was a deputy of the monied class and the aristocrats who flow through different regimes regardless of their political color: the Tafts, the Cabot Lodges, the Stevensons, the Harrimans, the Roosevelts, the Bushes, and the more recent Kennedys. In sum, this was the Eastern Establishment so scorned and yet at heart envied by Nixon.[17]

Nelson A. Rockefeller was a grandson of John D. Rockefeller, probably the richest man in American history.[18] Though the Rockefeller billions have been dispersed among a huge brood of children, grandchildren, great-grandchildren, and now great-great-grandchildren, there are still many Rockefeller multimillionaires because the family—unlike some other super-rich nineteenth-century families—has had the good fortune in each generation to produce prudent and hard-working members.

Nelson A. Rockefeller (the "A" is for Aldrich, his mother's maiden name★) was the most politically active of this tribe, which is an older and more refined species than the Kennedys. After several

---

★Money marrying money: Abby Aldrich was the daughter of the wealthy Senator Nelson Aldrich of Rhode Island, a leading Republican responsible for the Gold Standard Act of 1900.

early important offices he was elected Republican governor of New York in the 1958 elections, defeating Averell Harriman in the usual political round of musical chairs.[19] Rockefeller was four times governor, from 1959 to 1973, when he resigned to take office as vice president under Ford. Before, he had been a leading contestant in three Republican primary fights for president during the 1960s, but because his moderate views offended right-wing Republicans he was passed over for Barry Goldwater and then Richard Nixon.[20] In effect, Nelson Rockefeller was too civilized for the aggressive, new-money Republican rich.

Nelson's brother David chose money over politics and—the family owning a large stock position—became chairman of the Chase Manhattan Bank. But there were others who followed Nelson's route. Winthrop Rockefeller was elected Republican governor of Arkansas and served two terms, from 1967 to 1970. His son Winthrop Jr. was elected lieutenant governor of that state after his father's death in 1973. And still another Rockefeller, John Davison IV (called Jay), was governor of West Virginia and then elected U.S. Senator from that state in 1997. The wheel of fortune is reputed to be errant, but with a name like Rockefeller it has an uncanny ability to know where to stop.

Gerald Ford tried to appease the Republican right wing by dropping Nelson A. Rockefeller for Robert Dole as his vice-presidential partner in the bid for reelection, but the dismal showing of Dole when running later against Bill Clinton—and the closeness of Ford's loss to Jimmy Carter—indicates that he might have been reelected with Rockefeller as a running mate of such known integrity.

Reprinted with permission. Creator's Syndicate, PAULSZEP@peoplepc.com.

Jimmy's admission

Reprinted with the permission of the *Augusta Chronicle*.

# CHAPTER SIX

★

# JAMES EARL CARTER JR.
# (1977–1981)

★

*"The word virtue is as useful to self-interest as the vices."*
La Rochefoucauld, *Maxims*, no. 187

*"It is in the ability to deceive oneself that one shows the greatest talent."*

Anatole France

James ("Jimmy") Carter came from a Georgia political family. His father, Earl Carter, served on the Sumter County school board and was a director of the local Rural Electrification Association (REA). He hated FDR and supported Herman T. Talmadge, the violent Georgia segregationist. In 1952 Earl Carter was elected to the state legislature, dying shortly after of cancer. Jimmy Carter's uncle Alton, Earl's older brother, was mayor of Plains, the Carter hometown, several times in this same period. Thus, Jimmy Carter had been familiar with politics since childhood.

The Carter family, involved in peanut growing and processing, was upper-middle-class (Jimmy's father was the wealthiest man in the area) and lived the style of that class in the small towns and suburbs of America. Young Carter went to elementary school in Plains and then to Georgia Southwestern, a junior college in Americus. Neither at elementary school nor at junior college did he make any unusual impression, though he was considered smart and likeable.

After applying to, and being rejected by, Annapolis, Carter attended Georgia Tech, where he entered the Navy ROTC. In the top 10 percent of his class, he was finally accepted at Annapolis in June 1943. His career there was similar to those before, showing affability and intelligence but nothing extraordinary. "No one seemed to consider Jimmy Carter as the man most likely to succeed. He was capable, but not marked for greatness."[1] His classmates later were amazed when he became governor of Georgia, and even more astounded when he was elected president.

In August 1946 Carter began a naval career that extended over seven years, during which time he applied for a Rhodes Scholarship, but was rejected. Moving from desk officer to training officer, he then went on submarine duty as an electronics officer, a result of his training as an engineer.

It was at this point that there occurred a change that marked his whole life. Carter applied for the atomic submarine division headed by the mythical Admiral Hyman Rickover, a rigid disciplinarian responsible for the great superiority of the U.S. nuclear submarine fleet. Accepted by Rickover after a personal interview, he stated that the rear admiral—who exerted constant personal pressure on his subordinate officers to attain their highest potential—was (after his parents) the most profound influence on his life.

In October 1953 Carter applied for release from the navy. After World War II naval promotion was slow, and his father had died leaving a messy estate. His resignation accepted, Carter, as executor of his father's will, returned to Plains and to the family peanut business.

Jimmy Carter was a joiner: Besides his attachment to the Plains Baptist Church, where he taught Sunday school, he was a scoutmaster for the Boy Scouts, an active member of the Lions Club, a member of the local chamber of commerce, a participant in several agricultural groups, and a lieutenant in the U.S. Naval Reserve. All these activities directly related to his business interests as well as his political hopes, which now began to dominate his life. He immediately entered politics.

Carter's ability to straddle issues was an outstanding trait. In the 1950s and 1960s, despite the great turmoil over the attempt of blacks to gain civil rights, he avoided a public position. "Carter was essentially uninvolved. . . . Had Carter been pulled into these conflicts, it would have created serious problems for his political future."[2] By 1961 he was chairman of the Sumter County Board of Education in a period when the board was forced to integrate. He evaded the issue by concentrating on multicounty development planning. Two years later, elected a state senator, he followed the same technique, urging more efficient government, a balanced budget, and the economic development of southwest Georgia, bypassing the highly charged issues of school integration and equalization of services between white and black schools in the rural districts. As a result, in 1965 he was selected as one of the eleven most influential legislators of Georgia.[3]

Later, it was a carefully nourished myth that Carter had been a liberal on the matter of the color issue. The opposite is true. In 1964, as a Georgia senator, he voted for a state constitutional amendment aimed at preventing school integration. He was in the die-hard minority even for Georgia because the measure failed to carry. The next day the racists attempted a second time and failed, Carter again voting with them. Carter also voted for a constitutional amendment to prevent enactment of fair employment laws by Georgia counties; here, again, he was allied with the worst elements of the state. At that period and for some time he was quite frank as to his views. When running for the Democratic nomination in the later gubernatorial campaign, he defined himself "as a local Georgia conservative Democrat. . . . I'm basically a redneck."[4]

In fact, Jimmy Carter's ties to Georgia's governor Lester Maddox, an outspoken racist, were very close. Running to succeed Maddox, prohibited from immediate reelection by Georgia law, Carter said that he was "very proud to be part of a party that is great enough to have men like Governor Maddox heading it up in Georgia," and later added that Maddox was "the very essence of

what the Democratic Party stands for."[5] His position was obvious to
the racists. At that election Carter met with Roy Harris, the leader
of Georgia's White Citizens Council, and Harris then announced
that he would vote for Carter.[6] Reg Murphy, first political editor
and later editor of the *Atlanta Constitution*, knowing Carter would
trim his sails when governor, his eye set on the national scene,
declared: "Jimmy Carter was one of the three or four phoniest men
I ever met,"[7] a statement endorsed by Julian Bond, a leader in the
black community and also a Georgia state senator at the time, who
later changed his tune on being elevated by Carter. A good example
might be Carter's refusal to speak up—despite his known reli-
giosity—when his friend, supporter, and pastor, Bruce Edwards, was
forced to resign from the Plains Baptist Church because he favored
the admission of blacks. It should also be added that Carter's support
of the Vietnam War was one of the most prolonged and persistent of
any major political figure, continuing as late as 1974. Yet, seeking the
presidency two years later, he attacked the war as immoral. The redneck racism of the earlier period compared to the later liberal
rhetoric, like the pro-war enthusiasm up to 1974 and the antiwar
condemnation in 1976, were similar in purpose: to advance himself
politically.

This hypocritical thread is a consistent theme throughout his
political career. In 1970 Carter ran for governor of Georgia. His
great talent here, as well, was to speak opposite things from two sides
of his mouth. This, of course, is attempted by every hack politician
but is not usually associated with the religious fervor of someone
like Carter.[8] His political positions were similar to the Republican
candidate he defeated. He attracted hardcore conservatives by his
refusal to endorse Andrew Young, a black Democrat then running
for U.S. Congress. As mentioned, he gained the support of Roy
Harris. In an unguarded but remarkable statement he compared
government officials to "the icing on a cake or the froth on a glass
of beer"[9]—the cake and beer in this phase of his political career
being the money received from top officers of Coca-Cola, a vice

president of Southern Bell Telephone Conpany, Delta Airlines, and the owner of the Atlantic Newspaper Company. The largest corporate contributor was Rabhan Associates of Savannah, a business empire that ran nursing homes and day-care centers; later Ervin David Rabhan, under investigation by several federal agencies for questionable business dealings, skipped the country and vanished.[10]

The other side of Carter's mouth was equally facile. It was defined by his pollster Bill Hamilton as "stylist populism." Though rejecting Andrew Young's candidacy, he suggested that Democrats should vote a straight-line ticket. He emphasized Christian morality, preaching justice and equality, not so obliquely alluding to his born-again conversion in strongly Baptist Georgia. Supporters linked him with John F. Kennedy as a young-looking man with a slim wife and four handsome children. As one reporter wrote of his fancy gubernatorial inauguration, it was "Camelot—all over again."[11] That evening there were four inaugural dances with thirty thousand invited guests.

Similar indeed to Kennedy in many respects, although a less sophisticated version, one of his first acts as governor was to put his family on the government payroll. His oldest son, Jack, twenty-four, did liason work with the Georgia General Assembly; he then interned in the Fulton County District Attorney's office. Chip, twenty-one, worked in the governor's office, as did his third son, Jeff, who was only eighteen and a recent graduate from high school.

As governor, Carter was friendly and sympathetic with George Wallace, the notorious racist who was then governor of Alabama. In May 1971, he hailed Wallace and wrote that they both "are in agreement on most issues."[12] He opposed George McGovern in 1972 in his bid for the presidency, finding him too "dovish" on Vietnam. After McGovern got the Democratic nomination, in his usual fence trimming he sought the vice-presidential nod without success.[13]

Events indicate he had already set his hopes on the presidency. In November 1972 his close friend Hamilton Jordan wrote Carter a memo in the form of a blueprint, which included: "He was to expand his contacts in Washington and cultivate the 'fat cats' and the 'Eastern Establishment' press"; he should work out policies to deal with George Wallace, Senator Henry Jackson, and Ted Kennedy; and he must "cultivate his Kennedy smile."[14] The following month Carter told his inner circle he had decided to run for president. And in December 1974, one month before his term as Georgia's governor ended, he declared his candidacy.

Carter's basic tactic was the same, though now on a national level, namely, to appeal to liberals and northerners as a moderate southern alternative to Wallace while retaining Wallace's populist appeal in the South. The polling tricks at the primaries first used by Estes Kefauver and perfected by Joe Kennedy for JFK were adopted by Carter with great success. A minor event in Iowa was first. In late October 1975 the state Democratic Party held a fund-raising dinner to which the presidential aspirants were invited. The Carter people shrewdly guessed that a poll would be taken among the dinner guests and drummed out his supporters. Of 4,000 persons attending only 1,000 voted in the poll and Carter came in first with 250 votes, or about 6 percent of the total attending. Yet the vote was ballyhooed as a "solid lead." This was followed by a presidential straw vote at Florida's Democratic state convention, where Carter was better known, and he won with 697 of 1,035 votes. No other major candidate attended this event, but the tiny votes in Iowa and Florida were blown up to seem a national upsweep, and major newspapers and columnists began to pay attention.

The initial commitment in Iowa—Carter had been working the state for a year—paid off in the primary. The other candidates had been spending their time in the larger states and only came to Iowa at the last minute. Ten percent of the eligible Democrats voted: 37 percent for uncommitted candidates, almost 28 percent for Carter, the rest distributed among other candidates. Carter was announced the victor. The *New York Times* now proclaimed Carter a major contender.

The follow-up in New Hampshire, a conservative state, was enhanced by the fact that Carter was considered to the right of his

Democratic opponents. Ninety volunteer Georgians, called the Peanut Brigade, flew up and knocked on doors in Manchester and Nashua, where most Democrats lived. On primary day Carter got 30 percent of the votes. The more liberal candidates took over two-thirds of the total but their votes were split among five persons. Now Carter was a major contender in fact.

In Florida, where Carter had spent much time, he won with 24 percent of the vote, the rest split among other candidates. This led to his picking up almost without opposition the primary vote of the other southern states. And then when Carter, who had courted the machine boss Mayor Richard Daley of Chicago, won in Illinois with 48 percent, he became the Democratic forerunner. At this point, Wallace dropped out, swinging his votes to Carter; Henry Jackson ran out of money; Jerry Brown entered too late; and Hubert Humphrey, who had hoped to be drafted, didn't campaign. Previously, Ted Kennedy had decided not to run. Lady Luck changed her name to Carter.[15]

Much of the so-called spontaneity of this campaign was backed by large sums of money. Phil Walden of Capricorn Records, the largest independent recording label in the United States, got performers under contract with him to give benefit concerts—about $400,000 was raised this way. Smart money looking for future favors started to follow what might be a winner, and after he won key primaries Carter contributors poured $2.25 million into the campaign. Carter's bank friends in Georgia (of which more will be said later) lent him $1,275,000. California friends raised $1.5 million. A Wall Street Committee for Carter, headed by top partners and executives of Lehman Brothers, Paine Webber, Jackson and Curtis, and Dean Witter and Company, raised great sums; as one partner stated, "Carter's positions on some economic issues are closer to traditional Republican positions than are those of other Democrats."[16]

The final note was the benediction given by Martin Luther King Sr. at the Democratic Convention: "Surely the Lord sent Jimmy Carter to come on out and bring America back where she belongs."[17]

In sum, Jimmy Carter won the Democratic nomination because the other candidates made terrible mistakes or didn't try hard; it was not so much that he won but that they lost. Carter never received a majority of the state primary votes. He was not even the favorite of Democratic voters in the national polls.

In the final, squeaky presidential victory over Gerald Ford, it was the black vote, a key in major urban centers, that made the ultimate difference, Carter getting over 90 percent.

As might have been foreseen by those following closely Carter's rhetoric and later his performance, as president he was no different than a conservative Republican—basically his was a Gerald Ford second term. Six weeks after Carter took office, nine hundred survivors of the Roosevelt age gathered in Washington to celebrate the anniversary of FDR's first inaugural, including all the living members of the "Brain Trust," the intellectuals surrounding FDR. Jimmy Carter, six blocks away, didn't bother to show up. He turned down a memorial park in FDR's honor which, ironically, Ronald Reagan later sponsored. Carter tried to trim Social Security benefits and cut back on urban, health, and welfare programs. As he himself declared: "My main political problem was with the so-called liberal wing of the Democratic Party. . . . This was the biggest political problem when I was in office."[18] He was often called Jimmy Hoover, and indeed George Meany, head of the AFL-CIO, told reporters in 1978 that Carter was the most conservative president he'd seen in his lifetime.

Jimmy Carter had great affection for and stuck closely throughout his career to what was described as the "Georgia Mafia." Foremost was Bert Lance, a banker Carter met in 1966 who became his personal banker. When Carter was elected Georgia's governor he named Lance his commissioner of transportation. Following Lance's failed attempt to run for governor of Georgia in 1974, President Carter in 1976 appointed him U.S. Director of the Office of Management and Budget, the prestigious post that established all the budgets for government agencies.

Bert Lance was a small-town extrovert whose tie to Carter was also

★

based on their shared religious passion. His ultimate values may be stated by a remark he often repeated, "The only thing I know about are people and money, and that's all there is anywhere."[19] A shrewd man in the worldly sense, Lance defended Carter as a great campaigner: "He was a moderate to the moderates, a conservative to the conservatives, and a liberal to the liberals. He was all things to all voters."[20] Carter's inner clique, consisting of Hamilton Jordon, Charles Kirbo, Jody Powell, and Bert Lance, were all WASPs from small Georgia towns. This more than anything gives an inner view of Carter's psychology.

Bert Lance was president and had a controlling share in the stock of the National Bank of Calhoun and two other smaller Georgia banks when he met Carter, and was reputed to be worth some $3 million. Their mutually lucrative relationship was enhanced by loans Carter received. The Carter family business corporation borrowed $4.9 million in the period before his campaign in the presidential primaries. One million dollars was secured from the National Bank of Georgia, in which Lance also held a controlling stock interest and of which he had become president. It was later learned that the loan was above the amount spent by the Carter corporation, raising questions whether the money went into his campaign. In this same period Lance loaned the bank's plane for Carter's use without payment, for which the bank was fined. In the midst of the presidential campaign, the National Bank of Georgia increased the line of credit for the Carter Warehouse to $9 million; and after Carter received the Democratic nomination Lance, as president of the bank, reduced the interest rate on these loans.

Charges about Lance surfaced in the first year of Carter's administration. Lance had used the same bank stock as collateral for different loans. He had borrowed $3.4 million from the First National Bank of Chicago and the Manufacturers Hanover Trust Company of New York to buy the National Bank of Georgia stock; this money was lent a month after the National Bank of Georgia deposited funds in non-interest-bearing accounts at both lending banks.

The investigations grew. The Lance family had overdrafts of

★

more than $400,000 from the National Bank of Calhoun despite a federal law that prohibits banking executives from borrowing more than $5,000 from their own banks, except in certain circumstances not relevant in this case; further testimony showed that a bank examiner as early as 1971 had told him his overdrafts violated the law. The final total showed fifty-four loans amounting to $12.3 million that Lance, his relatives, and associates had received from twenty-three different banks. It was disclosed that Lance did not file financial reports with the banks of which he was an officer, as required by statute or regulation. It also revealed that the regional director of the comptroller's office had rescinded a disciplinary order involving the National Bank of Calhoun.[21]

Despite this evidence, Carter completely backed Bert Lance. Attorney General Griffin B. Bell, also a Georgian and a stockholder in the National Bank of Georgia, named a special prosecutor who was part of the Carter inner circle, a situation critics compared to Watergate tactics, still fresh in all minds. The IRS and two separate Senate committees launched independent investigations. When all the facts came in, the pressure was overwhelming. On September 21, 1977, President Carter read a letter from Bert Lance announcing his resignation, and characterized this action as "a courageous and also a patriotic gesture."[22]

Sleeping dogs sometimes wake up, even in politics. In 1978 Justice Department investigators contacted Billy Lee Campbell, who had been convicted of embezzling more than $300,000 from the National Bank of Calhoun. Campbell reported that Bert Lance was his silent partner in Campbell Farms, which had received the embezzled funds, and that Lance had encouraged him to take the money so they could split the profits. Because he was a silent partner, no papers had been signed.[23]

Investigation was then made of the tax returns of all the parties involved and it was discovered that President Carter had taken tax credits in 1975 and 1976: a tax credit of $695,000 in 1975 for a peanut sheller appraised at $300,000 in Sumter County records, and an investment credit of $367,000 in 1976 for equipment valued by the county at $50,000 for tax purposes. Billy Carter, the buffoon brother of the president and a member of the Sumter County tax assessment board, said there was nothing wrong with the differences.[24]

Neither Bert Lance nor any other of the persons involved was indicted. But it is a travesty of common sense and ordinary justice to refer to these people—from the top down—as having great dignity. Jimmy Carter might be called the American *Tartufe.*[25]

In 1979 two-thirds of members of Congress—including both Democrats and Republicans—rated Carter's presidential performance below average. Three years into his term inflation had risen to 16 percent, doubling in the period, and interest rates were rising close to 20 percent.[26] The American people were fed up. Lady Luck deserted Carter: Now his Republican opponent was no party hack, but the charismatic Ronald Reagan. Clever at being elected but a vacillator in office, Carter went down to defeat, the first time that an elected incumbent president had lost since Herbert Hoover in 1932. The huge difference in vote was 51 percent to 41 percent.

Probably Jimmy Carter, like Michael Dukakis in his presidential bid years later against George Bush, was defeated not so much for abandoning a reformist social vision as by his lack of an avowed high purpose. The American people look for inspiration in their leaders; they seek an activist in troubled times, not a leader who passively reacts to events. The New Deal, the Great Society, the Fair Deal, even Reagan's later Morning in America Again, no matter how histrionic, were symbols of hope. Trained as an engineer, Carter was a technician, indeed competent as one, but his kind of competence involved fixing an electric circuit or a plumbing leak, not running a country. Nor do Americans want a Sunday school teacher lecturing on what's wrong with them. The indefinable word "vision" was lacking in Jimmy Carter, and even those things he did right seemed to be unimportant compared to that lack.

As one reviews Jimmy Carter in historical perspective, two things are apparent. The first is that his so-called high moral ground was to a

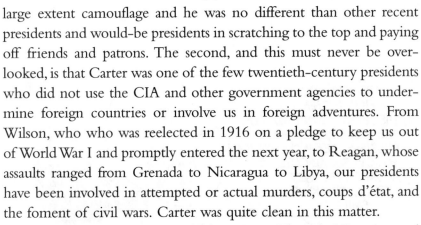

large extent camouflage and he was no different than other recent presidents and would-be presidents in scratching to the top and paying off friends and patrons. The second, and this must never be overlooked, is that Carter was one of the few twentieth-century presidents who did not use the CIA and other government agencies to undermine foreign countries or involve us in foreign adventures. From Wilson, who who was reelected in 1916 on a pledge to keep us out of World War I and promptly entered the next year, to Reagan, whose assaults ranged from Grenada to Nicaragua to Libya, our presidents have been involved in attempted or actual murders, coups d'état, and the foment of civil wars. Carter was quite clean in this matter.

There are other commendable actions. Though Nixon started the process, it was Carter who established full diplomatic relations with China. He agreed to turn over the Panama Canal to the Panamanians against a large part of public opinion. His Camp David accords brought peace between Egypt and Israel. He accelerated the move to SALT II, eliminating bombers as well as cruise and mobile missiles, and cut $3 billion in defense money to show our sincerity in striking a nuclear deal with Moscow. Perhaps in the eyes of history these may be seen with greater favor than his domestic fumblings; Carter may thus be viewed, certainly in foreign policy, as a superior president.[27]

Jimmy Carter is now a multimillionaire. The family peanut business, which had lost money during his absence as president, was sold for $640,000 after he left the White House. Emory University hired him as a professor, paying him in excess of $100,000 a year. A family partnership owns about twenty-five hundred acres of timber and farmland in Georgia. But Carter's specialty has been grinding out books appealing to those of his religious bent; over the last eighteen years he has written fourteen books, often hitting the bestseller lists, with advances of up to $400,000.[28]

GREAT DEBATE #1

"OTHER THAN YOUR FRIENDSHIP WITH THE PRESIDENT, MR. BONZO, WHAT QUALIFIES YOU FOR THIS CABINET POSITION?"

# CHAPTER SEVEN

★

# RONALD WILSON REAGAN
## (1981–1989)

★

*"When I was a boy I was told that anyone could become President. I'm beginning to believe it."*

Clarence Darrow

*"The more ridiculous a belief system, the higher probability of its success."*

Wayne A. Bartz, *Human Behavior* magazine, 1975

The early days of Ronald Reagan show a similar pattern to those of Richard Nixon. Born in Tampico, a small town in Illinois, he attended the Disciples of Christ College in nearby Eureka, where his girlfriend was the daughter of a town minister. He was the school's best swimmer, played on the football team—his favorite sport all through life—was active on the student newspaper, and a member of both the debating team and dramatic club. Elected president of the booster club three years in a row and president of the student council, Reagan became seriously interested in acting and played a leading role when the Eureka Players reached the finals in competition at Northwestern University's annual play contest. The real difference with Nixon, though Reagan possessed a good memory in his youth, was his mediocre scholastic marks.

Molded by this atmosphere, Ronald Reagan remained throughout his life an exuberant and optimistic small-town boy from the Midwest, boosting its values, doubting the worth of other values, certain that the truths he had learned in youth were the only authentic American ones.

After graduating in 1932, Reagan drifted into radio broad-casting, where his ability to ad lib and his glib enthusiasm led to a quick rise in sports announcing. When in Southern California with the Chicago Cubs at spring training, he was introduced to a Holly-wood agent. Strikingly handsome and with great charm, he was offered a movie contract at Warner Brothers Studios.

Acting in movies, Reagan, though never a featured star, was believable and a hard worker. His career flourished. By 1948 he was earning over $150,000 a year, a very large sum at the time. During World War II, Reagan played roles in morale-boosting pictures for the air force. Later, when questioned about his wartime activity while running for office, he replied he had served in the war as an adjutant of an air force base, not mentioning that the base was Hollywood.

A member of the Screen Actors Guild, Reagan soon became one of the union's leaders, and then its president. In the period during and after the war he was considered a left-leaning Democrat. He supported both Franklin D. Roosevelt and Harry Truman, and campaigned for the very liberal candidate Hubert Humphrey in the 1940s.[1] He backed Helen Gahagan Douglas against Nixon in 1950 for California's U.S. Senate. The organizations he joined were all on the leftist side: Americans for Democratic Action (ADA), where he was a member of the national board; the American Veterans Com-mittee, set up to oppose the policies of the American Legion; and the United World Federalists, which advocated world government. His intense involvement in these causes, as well as the presidency of the Actors Guild, left him with little time at home, and his marriage to actress Jane Wyman soon broke up.

At thirty-nine, his movie career slipping, Reagan found himself without an anchor. In 1951 he met Nancy Davis, stepdaughter of Dr. Loyal Davis, a wealthy, conservative Chicago neurosurgeon, and they soon married. It is said that this marriage pushed his political change of heart, for the new Mrs. Reagan strongly shared her father's views.

In 1954 General Electric Corporation, looking for a man to host its new half-hour television series, came to Hollywood. Reagan was recommended, hired, and became an instant success. Eight years with GE was the final goad to his extreme political shift, buttressed as well by heavy taxes on his high salary. In 1952 Reagan, though still considering himself a Democrat (he adored FDR all his life as an individual and war leader), supported Dwight D. Eisenhower for president, as he did again in 1956. By the late 1950s he questioned every social program of the New Deal, opposed medical care for the aged and all aspects of Medicare, disapproved of Social Security, and was especially vehement against the progressive income tax, which, he claimed, was "spawned by Karl Marx and declared by him to be the prime essential of a socialist state."[2]

GE dropped the television show in 1962, but Reagan's eight years at a high salary and an investment in valuable Malibu Hills ranch land had made him wealthy. He returned as president of the Screen Actors Guild and then was hired as host for a new weekly television program. At the same time Reagan plunged into politics, only changing his registration to Republican in 1962. In 1964 he was appointed California cochairman of Citizens for Goldwater. Considered the best orator of that state's Republican Party, now a die-hard rightist, his position was so extreme that the party leadership, while proposing him for governor, demanded and received his pledge to mute his Goldwater views to hold moderate Republicans in line.

Opposing Reagan in the campaign for California was Governor Pat Brown, who was running for reelection. Brown, considered a moderate liberal, was met by the mass defection of strong elements of the Democratic Party for various reasons. Brown supported President Johnson's increasing involvement in Vietnam, which alienated the antiwar group that was strong in California; this was also true for the California Democratic Council, which could muster forty thousand political volunteers. Calling out the National Guard after Los

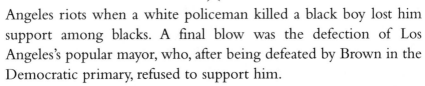

Angeles riots when a white policeman killed a black boy lost him
support among blacks. A final blow was the defection of Los
Angeles's popular mayor, who, after being defeated by Brown in the
Democratic primary, refused to support him.

Reagan, on the other hand, focused on generalities, in which his
television style had smoothed to a fine round crystal: morality, old-
fashioned integrity, less bureaucracy, and cutting taxes. He was the first
political figure to perfect the use of television spot announcements.

The result was a landslide. Reagan won the governorship in
1967 by a margin of almost a million votes. This crushing victory
over a man who had been considered a popular liberal governor
automatically pushed him to the front for those national conservatives disoriented by the loss of Nixon and the sweeping defeat of
Barry Goldwater.

As California governor, Reagan acts were consistent with his
views, though he was often compelled to compromise by Democratic opposition in the state legislature supported by moderate
Republicans. He opposed abortion, cut back on welfare, and refused
to increase state aid to urban-slum public schools or to award money
for job training. On the very important issue of land conservation,
especially for the remaining redwood forests, he always sided with
the lumber companies. "In his speeches the poor became the enemy,
trying to take away the hard-earned savings of the middle class. . . .
His mandate from the voters had been to reverse a trend, and his goal
was to convince the rest of the nation he had done so."[3] In foreign
policy Reagan remained true to Barry Goldwater, being consistently
a hawk on Vietnam. He publicly held to the view that Nixon was
victim to a "lynch mob," and stuck with him to the end.

What seemed like Ronald Reagan's startling rise to power
reflected a new mood in the American people, the reversal of a trend
initiated by Franklin D. Roosevelt as a result of the Great Depression. Now uppermost was the view of the enlarged middle class to
reduce taxes and government spending on the poor. Reagan's ascent
was due to the fact that he was the first charismatic politician to

embrace with conviction that a problem-solving government was out of style. It also revealed for the first time since the 1930s that voters who believed in social justice through such government action were now a national minority. Law and order and traditional morality had become more important than social activism. In sum, the middle class, always a larger voting group than the poor, felt that government should protect their wealth rather than tax them to extend social equality. For those people Reagan's simple but well-formed answers in a magnetic voice and a likeable style gave them a formidable leader.

The rest is history. Twice put up by the Republican Party's most conservative wing for the 1972 and 1976 elections and twice thwarted by more moderate forces as the party's nominee for president, in a third attempt the tide flowed with Reagan and he easily defeated Jimmy Carter's attempt to be reelected. Relevant, however, is that the Republicans raised $108 million from individual contributions in the 1980 campaign while the Democrats garnered only $19 million.[4]

In his 1980 acceptance address before the Republican national convention in Detroit, Ronald Reagan concluded: "I propose to you, my friends, and through you, that government of all kinds, big and little, be made solvent and that the example be set by the president of the United States and his Cabinet." And then this darling of the conservatives began a program of tremendous deficit financing that only has begun to be reversed by larger government tax receipts due to the prosperity of the 1990s.

In his first thousand days in office Ronald Reagan increased the U.S. national debt by half; and in eight years the debt rose to $2.8 trillion, almost three times that which the Reagan administration had inherited. Since debt service rises in proportion, this also tripled. And the trade deficit quadrupled.

The main reason was that defense spending rose greatly while taxes were sharply lowered. "Supply-side" economics, the new magic wand, might have worked if the decrease in taxes had been

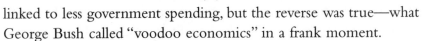

linked to less government spending, but the reverse was true—what George Bush called "voodoo economics" in a frank moment.

The Economic Recovery Tax Act of 1981 slashed social spending by about $30 billion while increasing military spending by almost the same amount, the largest single increase in U.S. peacetime history up to that time. With tax income down 25 percent, the federal deficit turned out to be almost $58 billion. In fact, the drop in the corporate tax rate from 33 to 16 percent, plus larger depreciation schedules, led to many corporations paying no taxes and even receiving rebates. And the top personal tax bracket fell from 70 percent to 28 percent over seven years.

The magical theory behind supply-side thinking was that tax revenues would leap upward to close the gap. It did not happen, as Bush and any first-rate economist could foresee. Lower taxes equal less income while more spending is greater outlay. The federal bureaucracy, in its inert mass and vested interests, can seem to survive any onslaught. Health expenditures continued to rise. Congressmen, Republican as well as Democratic, screamed when benefits for their baronies, such as obsolete military bases or federal subsidies for agriculture or industries, were scheduled to be eliminated. Middle-class pressure groups battered their legislators whenever there was a suggestion that Social Security benefits might be reduced or payments no longer adjusted for inflation. Vested interests in the various branches of the military—and the generals and admirals hired by business after retirement for their invaluable contacts—always called for more money. Foreign aid kept client states from collapsing. Washington thus became a giant deficit bank lurching toward bankruptcy.

The results were clear by 1985. The operating expenses of the federal government declined to less than 13 percent of the Gross Domestic Product (GDP) compared to 18 percent in 1965. Of this sum, 6.3 percent went to defense and 3.4 percent to interest on the skyrocketing paper debt, leaving only a little more than 3 percent for all other functions of government. David Stockman, the idealistic conservative who tried to manage early Reagan economics, finally realized where this upside-down system was going. In a postscript to his memoirs he wrote: "With the benefit of hindsight historians will know the immense damage to the nation's balance sheet and living standard that resulted from these eight years of fiscal profligacy. The records will show that within the span of a few short years the United States flung itself into massive hock with the rest of the world."[5]

Overall, income for the bottom tenth of the population fell by almost 11 percent from 1977 to 1987, while that for the top tenth went up over 24 percent; and for the tip-top 1 percent, income rose more than 74 percent. In 1980 there were some four thousand individual tax returns listing income of more than $1 million; by 1987 this rose to almost thirty-five thousand. And by 1989 the richest two-fifths of families had almost 68 percent of the national income, while the poorest two-fifths had little more than 15 percent of the national income. One out of five American children lived in poverty, suffering various problems of malnutrition, a 24 percent increase over 1979. Reagan's explanation for to the radical increase of the homeless was that "a large percentage" of them were "retarded people."[6]

In one nation Ronald Reagan had recreated two different—and, one may add, separate—populations. It was not the Reagan Revolution but the Reagan Counterrevolution, a return to what historians call the Age of the Robber Barons, reminiscent of the period following the Civil War up to President Theodore Roosevelt. Yet such was the Reagan razzle-dazzle that he left office with the highest approval of any president since Franklin D. Roosevelt, the Pied Piper of Hamelin for the lowest class of wage earners but a real piper for the super-rich.

Ronald Reagan's character was a maze of contradictions over which he built a bridge by his charm and sense of humor. His off-the-cuff quips, many being scraps of film dialogue that he memorized, were famous. Like Lincoln and Johnson, he also had a barrel of off-color stories told only to his closest friends. His most notable one-liner was when he said to the doctors preparing for his surgery after an assassination attempt in 1981, "Please tell me you're Repub-

★

licans." Also well-known is his comment about the young protesters gathered against his policies outside the White House: "Their signs said make love not war, but they don't look like they do either." Alan Greenspan, appointed by Reagan as chairman of the Federal Reserve Board, said he was a professional comedian. Clark Gifford, a secretary of defense, went further, calling Reagan "something of an amiable dunce."[7] Lou Cannon, his most noted biographer, stated, "Reagan's sense of humor was a key to his character. He was the resident humorist and gag writer in a White House where nearly everything else was done for him while he engaged in governance by anecdote."[8] Reagan knew little about the law, his national security advisers found him ignorant as to the capabilities of the respective U.S. and Soviet weapons, and his economic aides discovered the same thing in their field. Conservative columnist George Will, though in total agreement with Reagan's values, wondered how anyone so uninformed could become president. In sum, he reigned as a European-style monarch rather than ruled as an American president.

In part, this was due to laziness and advanced age. In his usual disarming way he admitted this in a manner that reminds one of the dry humor of W. C. Fields. He responded to his critics, "It's true that hard work never killed anybody, but I figure why take the chance?" When Reagan wasn't sure of a decision he would say, "I want to sleep on it a while," and then indeed did so, quipping later that he'd been burning the midday oil. Deflecting criticism of his age in front of a mass audience, he cracked, "When Andrew Johnson left the White House, he was seventy-five, and he was still vigorous." Then he paused. "I know that because he told me." The crowd burst out laughing. Even his harshest critics were disarmed by this humor.

Reagan's work schedule fit this same pattern. He came to his White House office after nine and went to his residence by half-past five, earlier if possible. Usually he took off Wednesday afternoons. On Fridays he left early. And he napped two to three hours in the afternoon. Sometimes he napped as well during cabinet meetings; in a famous incident he actually fell asleep during his appearance with

the pope in the papal library in June of 1982. Reagan visited his California ranch 345 days, almost one year's time, while president. And his favorite pastime was watching movies. He went to Camp David on 183 weekends, usually watching two films each time. He also saw movies in the White House family theatre, on television in the family quarters, and in guest quarters while traveling.

One of Reagan's noted qualities was complete self-absorption to the point that, besides his mother and his second wife, people didn't seem to exist to him as real people. He forgot the names of heads of state and even of his own cabinet members. In his second term he sometimes didn't remember old friends. Michael Reagan said that when his father attended his high school graduation he didn't recognize him. His daughter, Patti, admitted that she was unable to communicate with her father. His beloved wife, Nancy, stated in her autobiography that even for her there was a wall around him she could not break through, claiming this was a reaction to his father's alcoholism. Others have felt this wall was to stop anything entering that disturbed his inner picture of an earlier idyllic America.

Nancy Reagan's obsession with astrology was shared to a lesser degree by her husband; they both believed that his presidency had been foretold by a college teacher with psychic powers. Mrs. Reagan was a devotee of Joan Quigley, called "Madame Zorba" privately by the White House staff. She was convinced that Quigley's powers saved her husband from assassination attempts; this usually consisted of establishing favorable or unfavorable days for travel.[9] The changes of schedule caused by the Quigley charts drove Reagan's staff crazy but the president followed his wife on this as well as other matters. An astrologist on a monthly stipend thus determined the schedule of the president of the United States. Donald Regan in his later memoirs claimed that Mrs. Reagan's reliance on Quigley was responsible for Reagan's bad handling of the Iran-contra disclosures.

By some magic mesmerism Ronald Reagan absorbed and integrated wild contradictions into a unified personality. He claimed that he wasn't really divorced because his first wife, Jane Wyman, deserted

him against his wishes. He fought environmentalists, stating a tree was only a tree, but loved to escape to his isolated mountaintop ranch in California where he would ride horseback, alone on trails through the magnificent old forests. Reagan dwelt on his father's Irish heritage but was indifferent to Ireland and an ardent Anglophile. He was consistently pro-Israel and yet visited in tribute a German cemetery containing the graves of Nazi SS officers. Reagan openly adored FDR, having voted for him in 1932, 1936, 1940, and 1944, but then claimed that Roosevelt headed a government that sought to bring fascism to America.[10] And in yet another breath he stated his program was based on similar principles to those of FDR. Reagan supported the Vietnam War to the end, and endorsed nuclear bombing if necessary, but as president avoided any action that could lead to war. He called the Soviet Union the Evil Empire though endorsing concrete steps toward mutual disarmament. Reagan spoke idealistically of universal peace and then through subversion or direct action invaded any nation he perceived as left-drifting, being very careful, however, to pick countries—Grenada, Honduras, and Nicaragua are examples— that could not fight back. Thus, the American invasion of Grenada was a "rescue mission"; the Russian invasion of Afghanistan was a "brutal Soviet occupation."

Sometimes his imagination was so vivid and so hyped by the movies he constantly watched that Reagan would outright lie, as when he said he had served as a Signal Corps photographer filming the horrors of the Nazi death camps, when in fact he fought the war in Hollywood.[11] These contradictions defy belief and require the interpretation of a psychologist rather than a political analyst.

Though little remarked upon, Ronald Reagan's greatest domestic success was to transfer the judicial system to strict conservatives. Because he served two terms in a time of one-term presidents, he was able to appoint more federal judges than any other president since FDR. In total, he reformed into a conservative bloc—the school of "judicial restraint"—slightly more than half of the federal judiciary. Like FDR, but for opposite reasons, he set up an Office of Legal

Policy that collected information on the slant of prospective candidates, studying their published writings and their decisions as lower-
court judges, and interviewing them on their judicial philosophy. The
final triumph was the choice of William Rehnquist, the most conservative member of the Supreme Court, as chief justice. His sole
failure was the attempt to make Robert E. Bork, the man who did
Nixon's dirty work, a Supreme Court justice. Bork had actually tried
to make the use of contraceptives illegal and this, with the Nixon
background, was just too much for Congress to swallow. The result
of his appointments, however, was a reversal of liberal judicial interpretation that is still with us. It was this core of Reagan appointees
that decapitated the popular vote of the United States in November
2000, crowning George W. Bush as the new president.

Ronald Reagan's cabinet appointments conformed to his belief
that top businessmen should run the country. Donald T. Regan, the
head of Wall Street's Merrill Lynch, was appointed secretary of the
treasury and then chief of staff; he put $40 million in a blind trust
to take these posts. Regan had been a Marine officer; the president
seemed to have an affinity for the Marines as well as for fellow Irish
Americans, as had Richard Nixon for German Americans. William
Casey, head of the CIA, had made a fortune as a tax lawyer and previously served as the top man at the Securities and Exchange Commission. Secretary of State George Shultz was president of Bechtel
Group, the giant international construction firm, where Secretary of
Defense Caspar Weinberger was also general counsel. A Connecticut
businessman, Malcolm Baldridge, became secretary of commerce.
John Block, a rich Illinois corn and hog farmer and a protégé of
Senator Bob Dole, was appointed secretary of agriculture. Another
chief of staff in the eight-year reign of Reagan was James A. Baker
III, scion of one of Houston's wealthiest families. The vice president
Reagan chose was George Bush, cofounder of Zapata Oil, a very
successful oil drilling company. And the close friends on whom he
so depended formed a shadow auxiliary group called the "millionaire kitchen cabinet."

These men were clean as Washington appointments go. It was less true for many other appointments. President Reagan had little interest in details and made the naive assumption that all government employees would be honest. He did not seem to understand that appointing certain businessmen tied to a web of contacts might further these contacts for mutual advantage. The result was the most scandal-ridden presidency since Ulysses S. Grant.

In Reagan's first term Edwin Meese III, who served under Chief of Staff James Baker, was for years a funnel for those seeking government favors. Two of the main scandals were when he helped a personal friend obtain a large federal contract for the company that became Wedtech Corporation; he did the same for another friend who secured U.S. backing for an oil pipeline from Iraq to Jordan. The corruption ran so deep that two impeccable Republicans serving under Baker resigned in disgust—one being William Weld, who later became governor of Massachusetts. Ironically, Meese was later appointed attorney general, the nation's top law enforcement official.

Michael Deaver, deputy chief of staff, set himself up in the very lucrative lobbying business after leaving federal employment. Breaking the law concerning such activities, he committed perjury five times when investigated, and was convicted. Lynn Nofziger, another Reagan pal in government, was also indicted and convicted of illegal lobbying.

The list is so long it must be briefly itemized. The Environmental Protection Agency (EPA) under Anne G. Burford was such a miasma of political favorites she was forced to resign, along with a dozen senior aides. Deputy Secretary of Defense Paul Thayer served almost two years in jail for passing insider trading information to friends. Samuel R. Pierce Jr., secretary of housing and urban development (HUD), ran an agency steeped in influence peddling, fraud, embezzlement, and theft.[12] Deborah Gore Dean, Pierce's assistant, was convicted on twelve felony charges based on shifting programs intended for the poor to the financial benefit of friends and associates. One of the beneficiaries was John N. Mitchell, attorney general in the Nixon administration; another was Secretary of the Interior James G. Watt. Mitchell had already died; Watt pleaded guilty to a misdemeanor charge, thus avoiding a trial on eighteen perjury and felony charges. Watt was famous in Washington—and forced to resign—because of his violent racist and religious remarks.[13] Guy Fiske, deputy secretary of commerce, also resigned when confronted with similar felony charges, as did Robert Nimmo, head of the Veterans Administration, and C. McClain Haddow, chief of the Health and Human Services Department.

In more general terms, one can give other examples. The SEC enforcement chief resigned after admitting that he beat his wife several times, leaving her with a broken eardrum, wrenched neck, and multiple bruises. The second top man at the CIA had to quit over questionable stock transactions. So did a White House national security officer, who was forced to repay $427,000 to those defrauded. A third case of this kind, involving a deputy defense secretary, also led to his resignation. The secretary of labor became the first U.S. cabinet member in history to be indicted while in office, though he was later acquitted. He came from a New Jersey construction company, where he had previously been investigated for alleged ties to organized crime. The attorney general had to repay money to the government for private use of federal property, as did the chairman of the National Credit Union. A White House aide very close to Reagan was convicted for being paid by TWA to block a hostile corporate takeover. And all these cases were relatively minor compared to the Iran-contra affair in its flagrant lawbreaking, which, though in a different category, led to the resignation of Secretary of Defense Caspar Weinberger. Put in less polite terms, government employment under Reagan was considered by many a post to sack government. During the eight years of the Reagan presidency more than 225 appointees faced charges of criminal or ethical offenses.

Perhaps even more serious were the cutbacks by the Reagan administration, obsessed by the desire to free business from any regulation, that led to the relaxation of regulatory enforcement. The best example is the abolition of the requirement that savings and loan associations (S & Ls) have at least four hundred stockholders. This danger was increased by a new law passed by a business-dominated Republican Congress that extended the right of S & Ls to make loans not solely to homeowners but to any other kind of business. That allowed individuals such as Charles Keating to bilk the system by reckless lending, sometimes to friends in exchange for favors. The result was a colossal collapse, estimated to be nearly $500 billion, that forced a bailout by American taxpayers. Curiously, this collapse—which could easily have been foreseen by prudent men—was an early curtain call to its repetition on a still larger scale in many Asian countries during the last few years.

Such was the magic of Reagan, the "Teflon President,"[14] that he was never held accountable for appointing scoundrels to high office or endorsing such dangerous legislation. One possibility is that the general public, aware that corruption in Congress was just as common as in that the executive branch, had become cynical about government in general. This very dangerous attitude has led to less than half of all eligible voters bothering to vote even in the most important elections.

Ronald Reagan's personal fortune, though not weighted with the dirty details of Richard Nixon's rise to many millions, is also dotted with some odd happenings.

Reagan earned an upper-class living before his run for governor of California in 1966. His salary, as previously noted, rose to $150,000 a year as a secondary movie star in the 1940s, and was thereafter about the same when he worked eight years as a television master of ceremonies and public relations representative for the General Electric Company. But his net worth skyrocketed only after he was elected governor.

The basis for the Reagan fortune came in the 1950s, when he paid $80,000 for two parcels of land along Mulholland Highway in the Santa Monica Mountains, north of Los Angeles.[15] One was 236 acres; the other, 54 acres. This land abutted 2,500 acres owned by 20th Century Fox, which used the steep, barren land as a setting for movies.

Impressed by Reagan's passionate television support for Barry Goldwater in his 1964 unsuccessful presidential campaign, a group of very rich Californians persuaded him to give up his acting career, in exchange for which they would manage his finances.[16] In December 1966, less than a month after he was elected California governor, Ronald Reagan sold the plot of 236 acres to 20th Century Fox for $1,930,000. Reagan had paid about $276 an acre; the sale price was $8,178 an acre.

The purported aim of the purchase was for Fox to move its studios to this land, a rather laughable idea since 60 percent of the 236 acres had a slope exceeding thirty-one degrees and was classified as "very steep to precipitous." In a 1968 tax hearing it was concluded that the sale was "not a fair market sale." When the president of Fox's real estate department was questioned, she said tartly, "Why should we want to air those dirty linens? It would just dirty Fox's name. Maybe management decided they owed Reagan a favor. Who knows? Who cares?"[17] Adding to this less-than-opaque mystery, when a Fox executive was asked at the tax hearing how his company learned of the availability of the land bought, he was told by the company's lawyer not to answer.

Fox, of course, never moved its studios to this acreage. In 1974, while Reagan was still California governor, the 236 acres were sold to the California State Parks and Recreation Board at a price of $1,800 an acre. Thus, about eight years later, in a period when land values had greatly risen in California, Fox got rid of the land at about a fifth of the price it paid Reagan; but at least the company was off the hook due to a California state agency under Governor Reagan.

The second plot of 54 acres, which Reagan purchased at the same time, also has a curious history. This land was even less usable; 80 percent was classified as "very steep to precipitous," topped by a 1,515-foot rock pinnacle. At the same 1968 tax hearing, the land was appraised at a fair market value of $556 an acre, with a total value of $30,000. In June 1968 Reagan bartered this land as part of a deal for 771 acres of the Kaiser Aluminum Company Rancho California development in Riverside County east of Los Angeles. A trust acting for Reagan bought the 771 acres for $346,950;[18] Reagan paid almost $182,000 in cash while the remainder, valued at $165,000, was the 54 acres thrown in to close the deal. Thus, the land valued at a fair market price of $30,000 was sold for $165,000.

The picture becomes even more convoluted at this point. Kaiser Aluminum had a clause whereby Reagan would take back the land at the sale price of $165,000 if the company decided not to hold the property. It exercised this right. Then a firm called Fifty-seventh Madison bought the 54 acres for exactly $165,000. Documents showed that this New York City commercial real estate outfit was controlled by Jules C. Stein, cofounder and a director of MCA, Inc., the Los Angeles entertainment company. When repeated inquiries were made by investigative reporters as to why a New York City company owning office buildings would buy very steep and barren land in the Santa Monica Mountains, Stein refused to take the telephone calls. We may presume he had his reasons. It may be added that Stein was, at the time of the trade-for-land deal with Kaiser and the Kaiser sale to Fifty-seventh Madison, a trustee of the Reagan trust involved in these deals. Like the earlier sale, these 54 acres were also bought by California for a park, in this case netting a small profit for the company.[19]

In 1974 the Reagans bought the Rancho del Cielo ("Sky Ranch" in Spanish) for $527,000, with a down payment of $90,000. The property of 688 acres sits atop the Santa Ynez Mountains, more than twenty-two hundred feet above sea level, where the Pacific Ocean can be seen on clear days. Some thirty miles northwest of Santa Barbara, the property has a Spanish-style adobe house next to a small man-made lake put in by Reagan.

The former owner had used the land as a working cattle ranch. Under California law such use qualifies under "agricultural preserve" zoning and has an extremely low tax base. Reagan preserved this special tax status by grazing a mere twenty-two head of cattle. The assessment under this special law was only $20,423 and the annual tax bill was $862. If the ranch had been assessed at fair market value—and by 1980 local real estate sources valued it at between $1 and $2 million—Reagan would have paid annual property taxes of $42,000 even at the lowest valued figure. This enormous discrepancy works to the advantage of very rich landowners like Reagan, who see no contradiction between attacking government interference in the workings of the free market and taking advantage of a state gimmick aiding those in high tax brackets. To compound this void between Reagan theory and practice, the Reagans were able to take a deduction of $9,105 against their taxes because of a loss on the ranching operation.[20]

In this same category, despite his tirades against government, in 1980 Reagan accepted $7.3 million to finance his primary campaign and another $29.4 million to finance his election campaign, a gift of a total of almost $37 million from Uncle Sam—which is to say, the American taxpayer. He did not complain about this subsidy given to qualified candidates.

The Reagan administration touched its low-water mark in the Iran-contra affair, ranking among the greatest stupidities of twentieth-century American foreign policy. It started out as a rather simple idea in 1985. Robert C. ("Bud") McFarlane, a retired Marine colonel—who later pleaded guilty to a misdemeanor charge of lying to Congress—was the national security advisor who organized a method to release Americans kidnapped in Lebanon. Faced with the opposition of Caspar W. Weinberger at the Pentagon, who refused to deal with Iran's radical leaders, McFarlane endorsed a roundabout method in which Israel would sell missiles to Iran, which controlled the Lebanese kidnappers, with the United States replenishing the stock, whereupon Iran would release the embassy captives. The Iranians, fighting a war with Iraq, agreed. Reagan gave the go-ahead, "although we would have to waive for Israel our policy prohibiting any transfer of American-made weapons to Iran."[21]

The Israelis, on being informed that Reagan was supportive, delivered the missiles. But Iran reneged after receiving them. It was

★

at this point that Lt. Col. Oliver ("Ollie") North became involved. North, a Marine and a National Security Council (NSC) staff aide, was our government liaison in charge of supporting the Nicaraguan contras fighting their Marxist government. The Iranians, working with North and middlemen, now stated that for additional missiles they would honor the original agreement.

The next step was a comedy of errors. North arranged for this second shipment to be made through Portugal, keeping Adm. John Poindexter, McFarlane's deputy, alerted to events. This was done because the Iranians objected to deliveries on Israeli airplanes marked with the Star of David. The Portuguese, however, refused to ship the missiles, so they had to be sent back to Israel.

North then arranged the missile shipment to Iran on a charter operated by St. Lucia Airways, a CIA-controlled airline. The HAWK missiles, however, were found to be an older model, useless for shooting down Iraqi bombers (even the newer HAWK missiles were designed to hit lesser aircraft, a fact nobody seemed to know). The Iranians, feeling cheated, called off the deal. The sole beneficiary, aside from the middlemen who received commissions, was North. He took the money involved and put it into a Swiss bank account to funnel additional aid to the Nicaraguan contras.[22]

This was against an act of Congress which, fearing another Vietnam-like involvement, had voted a limit on the amount of money that could go to the contras. McFarlane, who already had friction with Reagan, became depressed and soon resigned, to be replaced by Poindexter as the new national security advisor.

On the same day Poindexter was elevated to this post, North sent him a note proposing a new and larger arms sale to Iran. This approach at least had the advantage of being clever. Delivery of an improved missile type would be coordinated with a serial release of hostages. The CIA, concerned that Congress had not been briefed, requested specific instructions to be signed by the president. Poindexter brought the papers to Reagan, who signed. When the Iran-contra scandal was revealed a year later, Poindexter tore up this approval because he realized it would cause "significant political embarrassment"[23]—in that the president had thus authorized a trade of arms for hostages.

At this point almost all factions in the top brass united to oppose the newer missile sale. Secretary of State Shultz, Secretary of Defense Weinberger, Chief of Staff Regan, and CIA Deputy McMahon argued against dealing with the terrorists dominating the Iranian government. This collective view was most impressive because almost always there had been friction among these men.

President Reagan, who usually went along with such a united front, "demonstrated an awesome stubborness."[24] He ignored them, feeling his top priority was to get back the hostages by any means. The CIA, again concerned with accountability, requested and received a signed approval from Reagan that authorized covert action, permitted the sale of arms to Iran, and, most important, on the insistence of the legal counsel of the CIA, got authorization to keep the new initiative secret from Congress. North then went ahead. Reagan indeed wrote in his diary, "I agreed to sell TOWs [the newer missile type] to Iran."[25]

Iran was sold fifteen hundred TOWs, along with a quantity of spare parts for the earlier delivery of HAWKs. The additional millions of dollars created by the sale were again deposited by North in the Swiss banks to pay off the middlemen and to send more money to the contras.

The Iranian radicals then released some of the hostages. But as Weinberger and Shultz had warned, the Iranian-supported Hezbollah (the "Party of God") immediately replenished their hostage stock by kidnapping more Americans. There was also evidence that the middlemen, refugees from the Khomeini regime, were deliberately misleading the Americans to make more money.

North then advanced the idea of a secret mission to Teheran to negotiate directly with the Iranians. This harebrained idea was approved by Reagan. Bearing false passports and carrying suicide pills, McFarlane (who was called out of retirement) and North flew to Teheran. A high-level Iranian official blandly informed them that

★

his government merely would consult with Beirut about the hostages and, without any guarantees to that effect, stressed the need for more missiles and spare parts. He also upped the ante, stating that Israel had to withdraw from the Golan Heights and southern Lebanon, and insisted that prisoners held by Kuwait for terrorist bombings, including the U.S. Embassy, be released.

McFarlane pointed out that the terms of the agreement only involved the release of all American hostages. The Iranians retreated a bit, then insisting on the single point of the release of the Kuwait prisoners. North agreed to a further modification, a partial release of the hostages, but McFarlane held firm. The U.S. delegation flew out of Teheran, its cockamamie mission a failure.

During the same period, Libyan terrorists bombed a West Berlin disco, killing two American servicemen. Reagan ordered a retaliation. U.S. planes struck the Libyan cities of Tripoli and Benghazi, dropping more than ninety two-thousand-pound bombs. A target was the barracks of dictator Muammar al-Qaddafi; though he was not there, the bombs killed his adopted two-year-old daughter, wounded two of his sons, and killed 150 Libyans. This act, which may be called reciprocal terrorism and was certainly disproportionate to the death of the two U.S. military personnel, was widely condemned by other countries but greeted with enthusiasm by most Americans. Reagan's popularity soared, reaching shortly thereafter a 68 percent approval rating. And the president, despite the lunacy of the Iran negotiations, never abandoned his hope for a deal. Heady with his great popularity after the bombing of Libya, Reagan approved military plans to rescue the hostages. But the CIA was unable to discover where they were held, so the idea fell through.

Then it was revealed that the middlemen employed to broker the arms deal were overcharging the Iranians by 600 percent on the HAWK parts shipped. The furious Iranians wanted compensation. North responded by asking the CIA to forge a phony price list, which the agency refused to do. But Reagan, seemingly obsessed, agreed to another delivery of five hundred TOW missiles if more hostages were

★

released, and Iran agreed. Following the same pattern as before, in the next short period four more Americans were kidnapped in Beirut. This approach of releasing hostages and immediately kidnapping more seemed obvious to everyone but the president.

North continued to press for more arms delivery to Teheran and conceded point after point to the Iranians in exchange for their promise to release captives, including hints that the United States would not object to freeing the prisoners held by Kuwait, which included those who had bombed the U.S. Embassy there. An accord was signed whereby more missiles were to be delivered in exchange for one hostage; and, incredibly, those Americans newly kidnapped were not mentioned. A single hostage was then released for more military supplies. Negotiations continued.

It was about this time a counterlash beyond the control of the White House began. It came not from the tight-lipped circle around the president, but rather from the other side. Radical students in Iran printed a widely distributed pamphlet describing McFarlane's trip to Teheran. An account of this mission was also published by a Hezbollah newspaper in Lebanon. And in a speech to the Iranian parliament, the visit was openly acknowledged.

The story broke in U.S. newspapers after this news. Congress was in an uproar over the disclosures. Even Republican Senate Majority Leader Bob Dole, a devoted Reaganite, expressed concern that the administration was rewarding terrorists. And Reagan befuddled the situation by claiming that the initiatives had no foundation, and then stating that Weinberger and Shultz had supported the initiatives that he denied existed.

With Congress and the general public asking questions, there was much controversy within the administration as to how to react. The final strategy was to lie. A statement was issued denying that the White House had sought to reward hostage takers by meeting their demands and incredibly concluded, "Our policy of not making concessions to terrorists remains intact."[26]

A two-hour briefing with congressional leaders at the White

House did not satisfy these men. Reagan, who with some justification had a mystical belief in his powers of persuasion on television, spoke to the nation in a speech that was a pack of lies, including, "We did not—repeat, did not—trade weapons or anything else for hostages, nor will we."[27]

For once the public was not suckered by Reagan's magnetism. There were too many inconsistencies. Polls after the speech showed this disbelief. North, very concerned with his role, had what he called a "shredding party," destroying all the documents involved.

The next strategy of the group close to the president was to claim that Reagan was an innocent victim of Poindexter and North, who independently set up policies without clearance. Under pressure Poindexter resigned and North was fired. And Reagan blamed publicity: "This whole thing boils down to great irresponsibility on the part of the press."[28] In other words, a free press was to blame for describing the lies, deceit, and illegal actions of the administration.

Under pressure from Congress the president appointed a board chaired by former Republican Senator John Tower of Texas, called the Tower Commission. When Reagan testified before the Tower Commission his answers were so muddled and contradictory the members were appalled. Poindexter and North hid behind the Fifth Amendment. McFarlane attempted suicide. And shortly thereafter Weinberger resigned as secretary of defense. Respectful of the president, the board concluded, bypassing Reagan's direct role, that the Iran actions ran directly contrary to the administration's own policy on terrorism. Republican Senator William Cohen, a member of a subsequent separate congressional investigation and later appointed secretary of defense by President Clinton, after hearing the president's garbled explanation, summed up the matter correctly: It was a "waste of time" to talk to Reagan because "with Ronald Reagan, no one is there. The sad fact is we don't have a president."[29]

The question, though theoretical, still exists as to how much Reagan understood the implications of what was going on. He had a habit of signing papers without reading them. It is obvious that his primary concern was to free the American hostages. He considered North a hero and patriot in relentlessly pursuing this policy. As to Poindexter, he was an admiral by background who automatically followed orders from his commander in chief. Weinberger and Shultz fought hard against the many stupidities but bowed to the will of the president. And Reagan was never clear or caring about details, fixed as he was on freeing the kidnapped Americans. Long before these events, Reagan had been operated on for intestinal cancer, with a large section removed; in this same period he underwent prostate cancer surgery; and for years he had been very hard of hearing, poor of eyesight, and sleepy most of the time.[30] At seventy-six, he was a classic case of near-senility apart from the distinct possibility of being in the early stages of Alzheimer's disease. Nancy Reagan, who knew her husband better than anyone else, pleaded with him not to run for a second term: She knew what she was doing.

The belief system of Ronald Reagan circled around three basic points: the reduction of taxes, the release of American hostages held by fanatic Muslims, and the elimination of the threat of nuclear war. Reagan felt passionately that lower taxes would release the creative energy of the American people, resulting in greater prosperity for all. This belief, known variously as "supply-side economics," the "trickle-down" theory, "Reaganomics," or, before Reagan's time, "What is good for General Motors is good for America," had disastrous results. Lower taxes and greater military expense turned the United States into a debtor nation, pushing the day of reckoning to future generations, while at the same time it cleaved the nation, making the rich richer and the poor poorer. The disastrous consequences of the second belief, the release of American hostages, have just been analyzed.

However, it is to Reagan's credit that his strong hope for nuclear disarmament led to real progress in this matter despite the violent opposition of some of his most devoted followers, such as Caspar Weinberger and the ultra-right journalists William F. Buckley Jr. and George Will. In effect he followed the initiatives of Richard Nixon

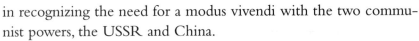

in recognizing the need for a modus vivendi with the two communist powers, the USSR and China.

This shift was only possible because the reformist Soviet leader Mikhail Gorbachev came to power in Reagan's second term. Here was a man with a vision similar to Reagan's. Both leaders sensed that a continued arms race could bankrupt their respective countries. Reagan refused to accept the axiom of some of his top military advisors that nuclear war was inevitable. Instead, he was willing to meet concession with concession. The first and perhaps most important came from the Soviets, who had previously refused to talk until the Americans removed the Pershing and cruise missiles on the borders of their country. Gorbachev declared a moratorium on the deployment of Russian SS-20 missiles, the Soviet equivalent of ours; and followed by actually reducing them. This so encouraged Reagan that he agreed to meet Gorbachev, whom he immediately liked. Though nothing was accomplished at this first meeting, the ice had been broken.

The sticky point was Reagan's obsession with his Strategic Defense Initiative ("Star Wars"), which the Soviets considered a plan to protect the United States while it could strike the Soviet Union with impunity. However, Gorbachev put this problem on hold by offering a trade-off of intermediate and shorter range missiles if those held by the Germans were included. This Reagan accepted, partly because he truly hoped for nuclear disarmament and partly to deflect domestic attention from his lies about the Iran-contra affair.

Although only 4 percent of the world's nuclear arsenals were affected by the 1987 agreement, it was the first U.S-Soviet treaty to provide for the *destruction* of nuclear weapons as well as on-site monitoring. Launched as an idea by Gorbachev, Reagan's agreement rattled hard-line conservatives, many of whom muttered about the president's dotage, which, when he followed their bidding before, had never been a problem. They mounted a stiff campaign against the proposed treaty but Reagan's obvious reputation as an anti-Communist convinced Congress to ratify the treaty. Gorbachev then withdrew Russia's troops from Afghanistan and his popularity soared in the United States. Rather than repeating a favorite theme—the USSR as the Evil Empire—Reagan now referred to the Soviet leader as "my friend," to the disgust of the military establishment. When he traveled to Moscow in May of 1988 and spoke of human freedom as tolerance for diversity and the value of the individual, that was his finest hour. If one believes that nuclear warfare is the single greatest threat to the world, Reagan's rapport with Gorbachev and the resulting thaw in the Cold War atoned in some measure for his other disastrous actions.[31]

The dialogue between Reagan and Gorbachev set the stage for the next step, in the George Bush presidency, when the Soviet leader released the communist grip on Eastern Europe and forced the East Germans to tear down the Berlin Wall. History will probably give the most credit to Gorbachev, under whose initiatives these events occurred; but action must meet with counteraction and it was Reagan, against harsh resistance from the right wing, who made this possible. The two leaders met again briefly in June 1990, when Bush was president. George Shultz complimented the Soviet leader on his accord with the agenda. "Yes," Gorbachev said, "but Reagan was there when times were really tough."[32]

As a postscript, it is claimed that Reagan brought down the Soviet Union by forcing it to spend so much on defense that the system collapsed. This oversimplification of a complex series of events that led to the rise of Gorbachev was a real watermark in twentieth-century world history. Actually, it was Richard Nixon's overtures to China that gave the Soviet Union four thousand miles of troublesome border with its rival Asian neighbor. With Russia's resources stretched to the limit, growing dissent at home, and sharp economic shortages, the Communist giant was not the terror seen by our militarists. Such liars who spoke ominously of nonexistent bomber gaps, then missile gaps, then spacecraft gaps, created a mass American hysteria. The great deficit caused by Reagan's military spending was a factor, but only one factor, bringing about the end of the Cold War.

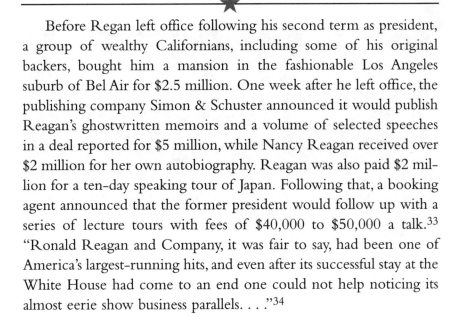

Before Regan left office following his second term as president, a group of wealthy Californians, including some of his original backers, bought him a mansion in the fashionable Los Angeles suburb of Bel Air for $2.5 million. One week after he left office, the publishing company Simon & Schuster announced it would publish Reagan's ghostwritten memoirs and a volume of selected speeches in a deal reported for $5 million, while Nancy Reagan received over $2 million for her own autobiography. Reagan was also paid $2 million for a ten-day speaking tour of Japan. Following that, a booking agent announced that the former president would follow up with a series of lecture tours with fees of $40,000 to $50,000 a talk.[33] "Ronald Reagan and Company, it was fair to say, had been one of America's largest-running hits, and even after its successful stay at the White House had come to an end one could not help noticing its almost eerie show business parallels. . . ."[34]

Reprinted with permission from *Drawn & Quartered*, Stephen Hess and Sandy Northrop, editors. Elliott & Clark Publishing Company.

## OLIPHANT                                                    by Pat Oliphant

Reprinted from *Eyes on the President: George Bush: History in Essays and Cartoons,* ed. Leo E. Heagerty (Occidental, Calif.: Chronos, 1993).

# CHAPTER EIGHT

# GEORGE HERBERT WALKER BUSH
# (1989–1993)

*"An honest politician is one who, when he is bought, will stay bought."*
Simon Cameron (1799–1889),
Republican boss of Pennsylvania and U.S. Senator

*"The less a statesman amounts to, the more he loves the flag."*
Elbert Hubbard

George Herbert Walker Bush came from big money. Samuel Prescott Bush, his grandfather, was president of Buckeye Steel Castings, a company that manufactured railway car equipment. He became the first president of the National Association of Manufacturers as well as a charter member of the U.S. Chamber of Commerce. In 1921 his son Prescott, later U.S. Senator from Connecticut, married Dorothy Walker, daughter of George Herbert Walker, who also came from a line of two generations of wealth. Prescott first worked for his father and then joined the Wall Street investment banking house of W. A. Harriman and Company, whose president, not so coincidentally, was his father-in-law. W. Averell Harriman, scion of one of the richest American families, was chairman of the board; his younger brother, Roland, was Prescott's close friend at Yale University. Prescott soon became vice president of the company, part of the inner nest of the very rich WASP coterie that still casts a long shadow over the United States despite the polished glitter of democracy.

In 1931 W. A. Harriman and Company merged with Brown Brothers, and Prescott became one of the twelve partners of Brown Brothers Harriman. The Banking Act of 1934—trying to correct some of the excesses that led to the Great Depression—forced the separation of commercial banking from investment banking. The firm split into two parts, with Prescott assigned to attract new investment business. While W. Averell Harriman, who had liberal tendencies, went to Washington on the start of his political career as a top national Democrat, Prescott, through the power of the firm, moved to the directorships of such companies as the Columbia Broadcasting System, the Prudential Insurance Company of America, the Simmons Company, Dresser Industries, and the U.S. Guarantee Company. As Herbert S. Parmet, a leading biographer, wrote, "Prescott Bush's way of life resembled the cultural setting one finds in the fiction of John Cleaver."[1]

George Herbert Walker Bush, Prescott's second son, conformed to this pattern and indeed continued to do so all his life. In the aristocratic old-money atmosphere of Greenwich, Connecticut, during the 1920s to 1940s, this meant the Greenwich Country Day School, followed by Choate, Hotchkiss, or Phillips Andover prep schools, and then on to Harvard, Yale, or Princeton. The aim, of course, was to cultivate from the start not only the manners of the ruling class but the youthful associations with which later financial connections intertwined. George, called "Poppy" by friends, followed this welltrodden path. He was a high example of the budding product, captain of the junior and then senior baseball teams at Andover and of the soccer team; his marks, however, were mediocre. The Andover Academy Yearbook student poll in 1942 listed George Bush as third best all-around fellow, third most respected, third most popular, third best athlete, and second with the "most faculty drag [influence]." His name was not listed in the categories of scholastic honors or most likely to succeed.[2]

The bombing of Pearl Harbor and the entry of the U.S. into World War II likely brought the eighteen-year-old into the real world, shedding at least part of his rich but isolated parochial background.

Accepted at Yale, George Bush insisted on enlisting in the naval aviation program. After completing training in June of 1943 he was commissioned a naval pilot, the youngest pilot in naval air service.

Unlike those bluffers Lyndon Johnson and Ronald Reagan, George Bush was a true war hero. As a squadron leader he was assigned to a Pacific Fleet carrier and quickly saw action with strikes by his torpedo plane against Marcus and Wake Islands. The important June 1944 invasion of Saipan began the greatest carrier air battle in history. His plane, struck by antiaircraft fire, was shot down over water with no time to jettison the bombs. After ditching their aircraft, Bush and his two crewmen were saved by a cargo net dropped over the side of a destroyer.

Back in action, Bush helped to prepare for the invasion of Guam a month later with ten successive days of bombing, taking part in thirteen strikes against the enemy. Then came the push against Iwo Jima. Now a lieutenant junior grade, his was one of the planes assigned to destroy seven radio towers, the main Japanese military listening posts, on the island of Chichi Jima. Preparing for the dive to drop bombs through a cloud of tracer fire, the aircraft was hit. Bush continued, unloading the bombs over his target, but his plane was doomed. Bailing out, his parachute snagged on the plane tail and ripped, and he fell quickly.

Supporting fighter planes drove off the Japanese boats sent out to catch his inflated raft and a "lifeguard duty" submarine picked him up. His two crewmen were never seen again. One's parachute did not open on ejection; the other was trapped in the crashing plane.

Bush was awarded the Distinguished Flying Cross. An allegation was later made that he could have landed in the water, saving his two comrades, but the plume of smoke seen by other nearby pilots refutes this accusation. Though eligible for rotation back home, Bush flew eight more missions. Considering his future pandering for power, these were probably his finest hours.

While home on leave Bush married Barbara Pierce, his youthful sweetheart, and then reported again for duty. Due to return to the

Pacific zone, he received news of the Japanese surrender. One month later, because of his extensive combat duty, Bush was discharged. He reentered Yale, where his father and uncle had also gone, and went back to the rich, cloistered life of former years. Only fifteen new members of Skull and Bones, the aristocratic Yale secret society, were chosen each year and George Bush was among them. This was one of the inner breeding grounds to perpetuate America's caste system, forming a network of the super-rich and well connected. Though not intellectual or a young activist—his conservative economic orthodoxy was already ingrained—Bush did make Phi Beta Kappa, "an achievement that perplexed some friends and teachers who remembered him from Andover."[3] Baseball was another matter and at Yale, as at Andover, his teammates chose him as captain during his senior year.

A close associate of his father on the top of the financial pyramid was Neil Mallon, president and general director of Dresser Industries, where the elder Bush was chief adviser and a stockholder. Among the properties of Dresser Industries was the International Derrick & Equipment Company (Ideco), a chain of sixteen equipment stores catering to the needs of the drilling industry and a leading manufacturer of portable rigs.[4] Like his father, Prescott had cushioned into finance through family, so after graduating from Yale, George Bush followed the same pattern, in his case into Texas oil.

Texas in the post–World War II period was like the California Gold Rush a century earlier. The oil industry, through the influence of its Texas politicians, was almost free from the high taxation imposed on other industries. There was a 27.5 percent oil depletion allowance; even more advantageous, the law allowed a 70 percent write-off of development costs for oil wells against the year incurred. This meant a very small tax on oil drilling compared to the almost confiscatory rate of 80 percent then pertaining elsewhere. A successful oil strike therefore was a "gusher" in more than one sense. But this was only open to those with large sums to gamble. And George Bush, through his family, had that.

It was in this same period that George's father entered Connecticut politics. Prescott was endorsed by Joseph McCarthy and campaigned on the slogan of "Korea, communism, confusion, and corruption,"[5] echoing right-wing Republican orthodoxy. He was narrowly defeated—partly because his family was not opposed to birth control[6]—by multimillionaire William Benton, of the famous advertising firm of Benton & Bowles. But Lady Luck, inscrutable as always, intervened. Brien McMahon, the other U.S. Senator from Connecticut, died in the summer of 1952, and Prescott Bush was elected by the bare margin of 51.3 percent, on the coattails of Eisenhower's victory in the same year. Now George Bush's future was even more assured because in addition to the two legs of old WASP family and great money he could include a third leg, high political connection, which assured the tripod on which power stood.

After an appropriate apprenticeship with Dresser Industries, young George was ready to strike out on his own. He had met a very clever oil prospector, John Overby, and the two formed a team shortly thereafter to be joined by two brothers, J. Hugh and William C. Liedtke, sons of the chief counsel for Gulf Oil. Backed by Bush's family money, Overby's nose for oil, and the Liedtke legal contacts and know-how in the oil business, the new firm bought up mineral rights and arranged oil exploration for customers. Senator Prescott Bush did his part in Washington, fighting off the Democratic minority's attempt to federalize offshore oil and use the money to fund support for education.[7]

By the late 1950s strains developed among the partners. Overby objected to the emphasis on venturing offshore and was bought out. Hugh Liedtke resented the dominant control from Bush's uncle Herbert Walker, the funnel for the money from Wall Street. The separation led to a complex stock swap and a split into two companies, with Liedtke holding control of their original Zapata Petroleum Company, while George Bush and his uncle retained the offshore drilling operation, now called Zapata Off-Shore Company. By the age of thirty-five the young man was close to becoming a millionaire and, inflamed by his father's rise in politics, began to cast his eyes on a political career for himself. In 1959 he moved to Houston to anchor this new pursuit.[8]

After World War II, with Texas producing nearly 40 percent of all the oil in the United States, Houston had swelled to become the sixth largest American city. It was also a center for fanatics of the right, for the more money the new millionaires made the worse they hated taxes and the more they saw communists in every Washington bed. Foremost among these extremists was the group called John Birchers. Though on the fringe, Birchers infiltrated the Republican Party in Texas.

Somewhere in this time period a change came over George Bush. Its origin was an enormous hunger for power. It might most easily be described as genteel Nixonism, a decision to rise by whatever means, though in a quieter and more reticent style as befitted Bush's origins. The clash between the Houston Republican Party right-wing regulars and the Bircher fanatics gave Bush an opportunity to be a peacemaker, to declare that one happy family should unite rather than quibble: such a quibble, for example, as the statement of Robert Welch, head of the John Birch Society, that President Eisenhower was "a dedicated conscious agent of the Communist conspiracy."[9]

Republican leaders in Harris County, where Houston is located, had already impressed Bush into party speaking and fund raising. They were drawn to the handsome, tall, and relatively young man with an impeccable war record, an attractive family, and a fine background. They elected him chairman. Bush strove to integrate right-wing radicals into cooperating against their mutual enemy—liberals—to the point that he put a Bircher in charge of a precinct, composing a memo, "We're not going to divide ourselves, calling anyone 'crazies,' or nuts."[10]

The tactic was a success. After a brief period as county chairman, George Bush announced his candidacy for the Republican U.S. senatorial nomination. He won easily against opponents—some, incredible as it might seem, even more right-wing. But he

clearly identified himself as a Goldwater conservative and an opponent of equal rights, arguing against provisions of the civil rights bill
that would guarantee blacks equal access to restaurants, hotels, and
restrooms. Congress, he stated, had passed "the new civil rights act
to protect 14 percent of the people," but he was as much concerned
about "the other 86 percent."[11]

What defeated Bush in his race was not so much his political
positions but rather an event over which he had no control; namely,
the assassination of John F. Kennedy in Texas and the consequent
elevation of Vice President Lyndon Johnson to the presidency.
National revulsion over the killing of a president, with a new president authentically Texan, led to a sweeping victory for Democrats in
which Republican George Bush was drowned.[12] After the election,
Bush confessed to his Episcopalian minister in Houston, "You know,
John, I took some of the far right positions to get elected. I hope I
never do it again. I regret it."[13] He was wrong on both counts. He
did it again. And he was elected because he did it again.

The next congressional election was a different story. By now a
chastened Bush had learned the lesson essential for every rising
politician, namely to talk much but say little. In 1966 the favored
Republican in his congressional district, he became a moderate to
moderates and a conservative to conservatives. "Labels are for cans,"
he said. An observer noted he was "an extremely likeable person"
with a kind of "haziness about exactly where he stood politically."[14]
What helped was that his Democratic opponent was as far to the
right as he was—a common phenomenon in Texas—and the voting
public in the Houston area preferred a Republican in their antipathy
to the remnants of the New Deal. Bush was swept into office. What
really mattered in these elections was Big Oil and gerrymandering
districts to segregate the rising black vote.

During his brief period in Congress George Bush was a well-liked
conservative. He earned a zero voting rate from the AFL–CIO Political Education Committee. His father's connections helped him to get
a seat on the powerful House Ways and Means Committee, where he

was an ardent fighter for the oil interests. He backed President Johnson's war policy in Vietnam to the hilt and, after a tour in that country, said that dissenters were "tragically"out of touch "in the light of what I have seen and heard in South Vietnam."[15] He ran unopposed for reelection in 1968. Most important, Bush had caught the attention of Richard Nixon, who was attracted by his undivided support.

In his fever to rise in politics, Bush attempted to jump to the next level, the U.S. Senate, despite the warnings of his politically savvy father, who told him first to build a reputation. Harris County, with Houston its urban center and the site of its fanatic right-wing millionaires, was not typical of the long-time agrarian Democratic tradition of the entire state. George Bush, with his Yankee speech inflections (which he tried in vain to rid) was still considered by some a carpetbagger from New England. Probably more important, Lloyd Bentsen had knocked out a more liberal opponent, Ralph Yarborough, in the Democratic primary and Bentsen represented the same interests as Bush. They were, wrote a Texan journalist, like "two interchangeable peas in a pod . . . with many friends, business associates, and campaign donors in common." Given a choice, was the conclusion, "Texas'll take the dude with the Democratic label."[16] Campaign money dwindled. Bush was deprived of smearing his opponent as a liberal, as he had hoped in a fight with Yarborough, and, ironically, was even hurt by being considered Nixon's handpicked candidate. As a result, Bush lost heavily, and at forty-six he was out of a job, having sold his oil-drilling stock for $1.1 million while running for Congress. It was a devastating blow.

Nixon, however, never forgot his friends. Although he considered Bush a lightweight—he allegedly blamed Bush for being too much of a gentleman to play sufficiently dirty to win—the Texas Republican Party implored Nixon to reward one of their faithful. Mulling over the situation, Nixon offered Bush the job as head of the U.S. delegation to the United Nations, though Bush's experience for the position was nil.

The appointment was actually a poor ground for advancing his public image because Richard Nixon and Henry Kissinger ran foreign affairs and simply told Bush what to do as a glorified lackey. Bush stayed at the UN, faithfully parroting the official line with as much eloquence and resignation as can be imagined. He was so undercut that when he led the U.S. delegation in attempting to preserve a seat for the island of Taiwan as official "China," he was unaware that Henry Kissinger was meeting with officials in the Chinese capital of Beijing to end China's isolation.

While Nixon was moving to disaster over Watergate, the ever-loyal George Bush defended him to the end. Nixon had switched his job from the UN to head of the Republican National Committee, a major credential being his contacts with big money. He assured the Republican faithful in audiences around the country that "Watergate was the product of the actions of a few misguided, very irresponsible individuals who violated a high trust and who served neither the president nor their country well." Nixon, he emphasized, has "said repeatedly he wasn't involved in the sordid Watergate affairs. I believe him."[17] He emphasized in his contacts with Republican state chairmen that the accusations were baseless; and that Watergate was unrelated to the basic needs of the party.

As more revelations surfaced, his explanations became less and less creditable. Now Bush emphasized that hounding Nixon out of office would not be in the nation's best interest. Even at a late date, with the sky falling in on Nixon, he wrote, "I support the president enthusiastically. . . . I am confident that full disclosure on Watergate will vindicate the president."[18]

When the truth was revealed at last, it is curious that Bush, always considered a man who prided himself on personal integrity, had a very different reaction than Barry Goldwater, who also defended Nixon to the end. Both men took this position because they believed Nixon. Yet when the tapes revealed Nixon's direct knowledge of Watergate and his attempts to conceal involvement, in utter disillusion Goldwater called Nixon the greatest liar he had ever met. Bush, on the other hand, wrote: "All the people he [Nixon]

★

hated—Ivy League, press establishment, Democrats, privileged—all of this ended up biting him and bringing him down."[19]

After Nixon's resignation and the ascension of Ford to the presidency, the ever-faithful Bush was considered a candidate for the vice presidency but was rejected in favor of Nelson Rockefeller.[20] Instead, with his background at the UN, Bush was appointed as U.S. liaison officer to Beijing.

It was another short-term post and, similar to his position at the UN, Bush was simply neglected and outflanked by Henry Kissinger in his dealing with the Chinese leadership. In fact, the State Department didn't even bother to tell Bush about the U.S. surrender of the Vietnamese countryside north of Saigon. Bush learned of the decision at a Beijing party. He was fully aware of his impotence and that he was "playing in Kissinger's sandbox."[21] It was a wasted year for the very ambitious man.

Another wasted year began when Bush was appointed by President Ford to head the CIA, an agency mired in scandal by its surveillance of Americans as well as foreign enemies. An investigative reporter for the *New York Times*, Seymour Hersh, published a series of chilling articles showing the CIA out of control, unaccountable to Congress, going after dissidents and journalists, including wiretapping and mail tampering, with dossiers on at least one hundred thousand American citizens.[22] Bush's job was a delicate fence-walking act, stressing the need for covert actions while deploring spying on U.S. citizens. He quieted the worst critics of his agency by making fifty-one Capitol Hill appearances during his year of service and accepting without protest a three-person congressional oversight board. With Ford's defeat and the election of Jimmy Carter, however, he was asked to resign. The peripatetic Bush, again without a job, went back to Houston.

The Yankee in Texas went about two things with his usual energy: money and politics. Because of his name, various institutions paid him a high stipend. The largest bank holding company in Texas, Interfirst of Dallas, made Bush chairman of its executive committee and a director of a London affiliate at a salary of $75,000 yearly. Other directorships gave him an added $33,000. Old friend and oil magnate Bob Mosbacher put together a partnership, giving Bush a piece for $60,000, from which he received $115,373 in the next decade with an expected continuing annual income of $30,000. The president of Pennzoil gave him another piece of a deal, which returned a profit of almost $500,000. He was brought into a real estate group by an old Connecticut friend who had moved to Dallas. The deal yielded capital gains that totaled $217,278. And Bush traveled widely through the Far East and Middle East representing the oil companies that had provided the money for his political success. Even Texas billionaire Ross Perot cottoned to a man with such rising political momentum, offering him a job to run an oil company in Houston. But sinecures were one thing; a job with no time to move ahead in politics was another, so he turned down Perot.[23]

Always thinking of the national platform, Bush was glad to accept honorary positions that would bring him repute. He headed the American Heart Fund, became a director of Baylor University, a trustee of Trinity University in San Antonio and of Phillips Academy, as well as cochair of Yale's fund-raising in 1978. And he charged fees for speaking.

But his heart was in political advancement. James A. Baker III and Bob Mosbacher put together two money-raising funds, Baker's Fund for Limited Government and Mosbacher's Congressional Leadership Committee, which paid for Bush's precampaign travels. The money flowed in from executives of Pennzoil, McCormick Oil & Gas, Houston Oil & Minerals, Texas Instruments, Exxon, McDonnell-Douglas Aircraft, and even Clairol, which was headed by an old Andover schoolmate. In 1978 Bush traveled on these funds to forty-two states, reviving and adding to his friends from the time when he was head of the National Republican Committee. Some of these trips aided their businesses as well. For example, Bush took his old partner Hugh Liedtke to China with him; this led to Liedtke's contract there for oil drilling.[24]

In May 1979 Bush announced his presidential candicacy. However, he had against him an insurmountable obstacle, namely, Ronald
Reagan. The handwriting indeed was on the wall early, because a
survey released at the end of the year showed that among the
Republican Party faithful he trailed Reagan by a 13 to 57 margin.
Except for an initial setback in the Iowa primaries, where Reagan
hardly bothered to campaign, the charismatic man from California
swept the primaries. Bush's former support for gun-control legislation and his ambiguous attitude toward birth control, both hastily
abandoned years before, worked against him with the Republican
hard core, who accused Bush of being two-faced. Also diluting his
monied contacts was the huge sums pouring in for Reagan. And
thus the good soldier dropped out, holding back tears, and
announced that he would stop his campaign and support Reagan to
the hilt against Carter.

"Always a bridesmaid, never a bride" seemed to be Bush's fate.
Other than a brief period as congressman, he had never won an
election, but rather spent his whole political career in appointed
offices. The only true advantage of his aborted 1979 presidential race
was that he met Lee Atwater, an unscrupulous but brilliant young
man from South Carolina who would be the éminence grise of his
later presidential campaign.

Originally Ronald Reagan did not want Bush as his running
mate, since his views were considered too moderate for the clique
around the Californian. But by process of elimination he was reluctantly accepted, a Yankee by origin with roots in New England and
a lifestyle from Texas being a boost to the Western background of
Reagan in balancing the ticket. And thus, in the movement to the
right among the American people, with the colorless Carter as the
Democratic opponent, the Reagan–Bush ticket won.

Ever faithful, ever obedient, ever compromising, Bush rose in
Reagan's appreciation during his two terms. Bush's promise, dictated
as a condition to his vice-presidential candidacy, was an absolute and
flat condemnation of abortion. He then denied using the term

"voodoo economics" to describe the Reagan program, although it was well documented.[25] Probably he loathed many of the vulgar, newly rich millionaires who formed the "kitchen cabinet" of the president, but he kept his mouth shut. "Not only would he never be seen or heard disagreeing with Ronald Reagan on any matter, but he also would never publicly offer any substantative opinion of his own."[26] His most fawning acts concerned support of corrupt regimes. As Reagan's representative in Manila for dictator Ferdinand Marco's presidential inauguration, he said, "We love your adherence to democratic principles and to the democratic process."[27] Perhaps most humiliating was his position as liaison to Manuel Noriega, the disgusting drug purveyor of Panama who was a fair-haired favorite of Washington until he got too big for his britches. Noriega, among his other activities, served as an agent who enabled the narcotics trade to market cocaine in the United States for contra purchase of arms. Bush was not alone in this: William Casey, CIA chief, was even more deeply involved. But, as the Panamanian dictator boasted, "I've got Bush by the balls . . . Bush is my friend. I hope he becomes president."[28] In the Iran-contra mess Bush supported Reagan, though he later denied it.[29] These spiritual prostitutions came back to haunt him later. He was useful to his Texas oil friends, convincing Reagan to retain a slew of tax preferences for the oil industry.[30] A wit summed up: "FDR had Fala, Nixon had Checkers. Reagan has George Bush."[31]

In October 1987 Bush announced his candidacy for president, the only formidable opponent in the Republican primaries being Bob Dole. Despite the liabilities of the Iran-contra fallout and his close association with Manuel Noriega, his obvious loyalty to Reagan—and Reagan's endorsement—made him a favorite of most Republicans.

Michael Dukakis, an effective governor of Massachusetts, was his all-but-certain Democratic rival in November. The Gallup poll in May showed Dukakis sixteen points ahead of Bush. And the race between the two men swung back and forth. Bush had to prove to hesitant conservatives that he was redivivus Reagan. He embraced polarizing language in a style that later became only too common. He was against any kind of abortion, against school busing, and for prayer in schools. He fawned on Jerry Falwell, founder of the Moral Majority and hero of the fundamentalist right, who promptly endorsed him. He was opposed to gun control and any new taxes, despite the crushing deficit. "The Congress will push me to raise taxes, and I'll say no . . . and I'll say to them read my lips: no new taxes," a statement that came back like a boomerang later. Why, Bush wondered, had Dukakis vetoed a bill mandating that school children recite the Pledge of Allegiance? After his acceptance speech before the Republicans, he told the enthusiastic audience to stand to chant together the pledge. Indeed, Bush's transformation was complete: he *was* Ronald Reagan, though in cardboard.

The glory of Bush's successful campaign came from research on Dukakis's background initiated by Lee Atwater, his political expert in hitting below the belt. Dukakis was a member of the American Civil Liberties Union. He supported gun control. He had also vetoed a Massachusetts death penalty bill. These were measures that did not arouse people in his home state, among the most liberal in the nation. But this was less true throughout the rest of the country, where Reagan had used the "L-word" in contempt, deeming the word "Liberal" too rotten to utter. Dukakis's positions were repeatedly used with disgust by Bush.

The crowning achievement of Atwater's burrowing was the case of Willie Horton. A black man, Horton, who had previously been jailed in South Carolina for assault, was then sentenced in Massachusetts to life imprisonment for the murder of a gas station attendant. He was one of four prisoners ineligible for parole who was given a weekend furlough while Dukakis was governor. Horton went down to Maryland, where he beat and stabbed a man and raped his girlfriend. The case became a national scandal. Dukakis initiatialy defended state furloughs as a process to reintegrate inmates into society but, under pressure from popular outrage, ended the program.[32]

The issue was test-marketed by Bush's campaign team with two groups of Reagan Democrats, whose reactions were monitored electronically and by watching them through one-way mirrors. The results were what was desired. Bush then agreed to an attack campaign and Atwater, delighted, vowed to "strip the bark off the little bastard [Dukakis]" and "make Willie Horton his running mate."[33]

The next step was a short film. A specially built gate was made at Utah State Prison, the revolving door showing men in prison outfits moving through the gate, in and out, and thus back into society. The speaker told the audience that Dukakis had vetoed the death penalty and had given furloughs to first-degree murderers not eligible for parole, as well as many others who had committed other crimes such as kidnapping and rape.

No mention was made of Horton's being black for fear of a backlash but the film didn't need to because the convict's identity was so well-known. Starting in October before the election the film was shown nationally. Then a commercial featured the girlfriend of Horton's Maryland victim, followed shortly thereafter by another that featured the sister of Horton's first murder victim. Listeners heard that the crimes were caused by Dukakis's "liberal experiments." A local Republican group contributed its bit by asking voters to inquire what life would be like with Jesse Jackson as secretary of state. All of these sponsors claimed, of course, that they had not thought of race as a factor.

The tide turned decisively for Bush. The Republicans took 53.4 percent of the popular vote and forty states. Bush went jogging with Lee Atwater the next morning before attending church. Abraham Lincoln's adage that "you can fool some of the people all of the time, and all of the people some of the time, but you cannot fool all of the people all of the time" might be simplified in American politics to "you can fool most of the people most of the time."

Bush's presidency was in many senses a third term for Ronald Reagan without his charisma, flavored by a verbal compassion for the underprivileged. It was accurately called "Reaganism with a human face." Like Carter, who had rewarded his Georgia backers, Bush appointed many old Texas buddies. Bob Mosbacher, the very rich financial backer from earlier days, headed Commerce. The Texan scion James A. Baker III became secretary of state. Baker's aide under Reagan, Dick Darman, led the Office of Management and Budget. Former Texas U.S. Senator John Tower, who flipped cartwheels to exonerate Reagan as head of the Tower Commission investigating Iran-contra, was named to head the Department of Defense. A bone was thrown to Bob Dole by naming his wife, Elizabeth, as secretary of labor. An appointment that he learned to regret was John Sununu, who engineered a key Bush primary victory in New Hampshire and now became chief of staff. Bruce S. Gelb of Clairol, an old friend from Andover and also a financial backer, was named to lead the U.S. Information Agency. Lee Atwater was rewarded by heading the Republican Party's national committee.

About a third of Bush's cabinet were former Reaganites in the same or similar positions. Marlin Fitzwater moved up from deputy press secretary to press secretary, Lauro Cavazos remained at Education, Nicholas Brady at the Treasury, Richard Thornburgh at Justice, and William H. Webster at the CIA. The deck was thus somewhat reshuffled but they were the same fifty-two cards. The only controversial appointment was Dr. Louis W. Sullivan, a black man who had expressed some support for abortion, to head the Department of Health and Human Services. Sullivan, however, atoned for his sin by staffing his department with antiabortionists.

Bush's main personality trait was loyalty, whether it led into a rose garden or into a bed of thorns. This loyalty was soon tested by his appointment of John Tower to head the Defense Department, which had to be confirmed by Congress. Tower was an incredible choice. He was a notorious adulterer and boozer. At the time of the nomination, in his third marriage, he was involved in a well-publicized affair with a rich Chinese woman. The FBI reported that Tower kept a Russian ballerina in Texas and described an incident where the two danced nude on top of a piano. He had often been seen drunk, weaving out of restaurants and bumping his way along. In the three years since leaving the Senate he had earned some $750,000 as a consultant for defense contracts due to his contacts made as a Reagan arms control negotiator. This was the man to represent the most powerful nation in the world at the Department of Defense!

Yet Tower was an icon of the right and Bush stood behind him like cobalt steel. He wrote, questioning the investigation, of "any individual, to say you have to be purer than the newly driven snow in order to serve . . . I will adhere to my high ethics crusade, but I don't want it to go so far that good people are kept from serving."[34]

Apparently Bush's idea of "good people" was not the same as that of the U.S. Senate because Tower's appointment was rejected by a vote of fifty-three to forty-seven. This was the first time a president's choice for a cabinet position had been turned down in thirty years. Its flavor lingered on, especially in the later behavior of the arrogant and autocratic John Sununu.[35]

Domestically, Bush was a caretaker—some might say an undertaker—for Reagan. The conservative policies instituted by Reagan—cutting corporate and personal taxes, doubling defense spending, and weakening government regulations—had been largely achieved. This left Bush, a prudent and cautious man by nature, little ground for initiative. Moreover, unlike Reagan's election in 1981, the Republicans had suffered losses in both houses of Congress in 1988, which put the president in the position of having to respond negatively to legislative proposals rather than to suggest new ones. For most of his term, following his campaign pledge, Bush dared not increase taxes. As a result, with no change of policy on military spending[36] and taxes, the national debt went from $2.8 trillion to $4.3 trillion and the annual federal deficit nearly quadrupled to $290 billion per year. Faced with catastrophe, Bush finally had to accede to a tax increase in 1990, a prudent measure indeed but one that made him a hypocrite in the eyes of hard-line conservatives and many ordinary Americans.

★

Bush, facing a hostile Congress, governed by "veto strategy." Ten of these related to the abortion issue; almost all of the others killed legislation involving social, regulatory, tax, and spending policies. He did support a few bills that followed his widely circulated promise to push for a "kinder and gentler society." One was the Americans with Disabilities Act, which prohibited workplace discrimination against the disabled. Another was a revision of the Clean Air Act, calling for some reduction of destructive emissions that caused acid rain, urban ozone, and toxic air pollution. His major triumphs, aside from blocking anything related to abortion, were some campaign finance reforms, the right of employees to receive family and medical leave, and a civil rights bill. It is doubtful whether one can establish a direct correlation between presidential actions or nonactions to economic movement up or down, but during the Bush administration overall growth in the number of jobs, in weekly wages, and in family income was lower than during any presidency since the Great Depression.

The policy of detente with the Communist powers of China and Russia—initiated by Nixon with China and by Reagan with Russia—continued to make strides with Bush. One might say that these Republican right-wing leaders propelled forward peaceful coexistence simply because, as known conservatives, they could advance this process in a way impossible for liberals. Yet the fact remains that all three of these presidents made progress toward a more tolerable world.

The continued Gorbachev "peace offensive," though regarded by hard cynics as just another Soviet Cold War ploy, met with Bush's cautious approval. Early in his term, Bush's speechwriter on his national security staff prepared a speech in which the president, after warning the Soviets to stick to their commitment to arms reduction, concluded: "In sum, it is the determination of the United States that this new doctrine [detente] has as its soul the reintegration of the Soviet Union in the community of nations."[37] A turning point in history, the United States officially buried the theme of the Evil Empire. It was thus possible to move toward more decisive steps.

Bush was helped not only by America's changed mood but the fact that he had assembled united national security advisers, unlike those under Reagan who fought against each other almost as much as the common enemy.

In his first year of office, Bush was still distrustful of Gorbachev's overtures for arms cuts, but after the Soviet leader allowed the collapse of the East German and Czech satellites, he pressed ahead with agreements that ended the Cold War. As to China, a country that Bush knew better than any other president due to his station there in earlier years, he refused to make other than token protests against the brutal repression of the students at Tiananmen Square for fear of endangering the new Sino-American relations. He also refused to revoke the most-favored-nation status that had led to important commercial investments. This view was attacked by liberals but its realistic premise was that if we didn't buy and sell to China other nations would simply step in instead, to our loss and their profit. Also, he felt that what has ironically been dubbed "Wall Street communism" would inevitably lead to more personal freedom.

A rather large war engaged the United States during the Bush administration. Operation Desert Shield, ostensibly about Iraq's invasion of Kuwait, a small sultanate carved out for oil control by Great Britain during its imperial days, was in reality a war over this oil. In 1980 Iraqi dictator Saddam Hussein invaded neighboring Iran, governed by his fellow dictator Ayatollah Khomeini, over access to the Persian Gulf. After the war Iraq was saddled with a debt of $90 billion, $17 billion of which was owed to Kuwait. Kuwait refused to forgive the debt, so Iraq invaded the sultanate both to wipe out the debt and to take over that country's huge oil deposits. This aroused Saudi Arabia's fears of a similar takeover, for Iraq had developed the world's fourth largest war machine. Such a result would have been to give Saddam Hussein control over international oil prices, a fearsome prospect for the United States, which imported nearly half its oil and was dependent on a stable, reasonably priced supply.[38]

In response, President Bush assembled a coalition of twenty-

★

eight nations. He demanded Iraq withdraw from Kuwait. With no money for the war effort because of the huge U.S. deficit, he convinced Saudi Arabia, other small Gulf states, and Japan and Germany—the latter two heavily dependent on oil imports—to pay most of the military costs. The Soviet Union, beset by its own internal problems, was no longer a factor in the equation. Operation Desert Shield became Operation Desert Storm as 700,000 allied soldiers, 500,000 from the United States, entered Kuwait and advanced into Iraq in coordination with a ferocious six-week aerial bombardment. Unlike Vietnam's jungle, Iraq was largely open terrain where air strikes could be devastating.

The war was quickly a rout. An estimated 100,000 to 145,000 Iraqis were killed during the bombings and combat, as well as the postwar devastation, while only 144 American soldiers died, about half through accidents (many due to that most ironic phrase "friendly fire") unrelated to the enemy. Allied bombers wiped out almost all of Iraq's civilian infrastructure and left its people starving.

The Gulf War was a great success. Its real aim, securing reasonable oil prices, was attained. Few American soldiers died. The war bill was mainly footed by other nations and it gave the U.S. military establishment a new reason to ask for more money to lubricate the war machine. The American people, believing it a combat to save a small innocent nation and now recovered from the psychological hangover of Vietnam defeat, were thrilled. Bush's popularity rose to unprecedented heights.

In the long run, however, nothing was settled. To maintain an equilibrium in the Gulf area, fearing the complete humiliation of Iraq as a counterweight to Iran, Bush did not push to its final conclusion the accessory aim: to destroy Saddam Hussein. The Iraqi dictator remained defiant, with growing sympathy in the Arab world. A possible detente between Iraq and Iran would be a greater threat to the area's stability than before the Gulf War. The U.S. decision to neutralize large areas of Iraq (the Kurds in the north and the Shi'ite religious groups in the south) with northern and southern no-flight

★

zones covering more than half of the country's total area, required constant and often massive air strikes. This, an intolerable affront to any nation's pride, is a combustion chamber. And the despotic Arab regimes, including Kuwait, are as far from any measure of democratic rule as they were before the war.

At the end of his term George Bush, remembering the Nixon tapes, was concerned with future judgment. The night before he left office he made a deal with the National Archives that left in his hands the computerized Bush records, a deal which contravened the law stating that all official records are public property. As a reward, he arranged that Don Wilson, head of the National Archives, was hired as director of the George Bush Center at Texas A & M University.

Despite erratic lapses, we still have a system of law in the United States. In 1995 Federal Judge Charles Richey in Washington ruled that George Bush had no legal right to the records and his action was a breach of the principle that "no one, not even a President, is above the law."[39] The 1978 law that Bush broke was passed specifically to prevent presidents from doing what Richard Nixon tried to do.

Seen in the larger frame of American history, the Bush family is another of that small ruling group that maintains eminence by a network of contacts, what has been called the Eastern Establishment although it is now percolating west. This power bloc starts with exclusive prep schools, moves on to the Ivy League colleges, marries into the same class, and then matures on Wall Street, Texas oil, real estate, startup technology, venture capital, and myriad contacts through politics, both domestic and international.

The family money background of two former generations of the Bushes has been discussed. This has continued. An example of George Bush's method of increasing income was his stock interest in Seacat Off-Shore Drilling, which operated as a British company and avoided paying American taxes. This device, though morally questionable, was legal and a common gimmick among the rich.[40] More questionable was the sale of his Houston house at the same time he bought more land at Walker's Point in Kennebunkport, Maine, and for tax purposes deducted the cost of the Houston sale against the new purchase. Bush claimed the Walker's Point property was a new home, although he already owned other property there. This reduced his adjusted gross income tax of 48.6 percent in 1981 to 24.2 percent in 1982. However, the federal government provides a home for vice presidents and the IRS ruled this was his residence. As a result, Bush was forced to pay a penalty of almost a $200,000 in back taxes and interest.[41]

Prescott Bush Jr., George's oldest brother, availed himself of this same prestigious network of interests. He organized his own company, which acted as a consultant for clients overseas, especially in Asia. His greatest success was in Japan, where a system of interlocking relations controlling the investment of capital is an enlarged example of the same tight-knit kinship of the Bush family. In 1989 Prescott Bush's firm was paid a $250,000 fee as consultant for Asset Management, a New York firm in which West Tsusho Company of Japan bought a large interest. Part of the agreement was that Bush would be retained by Asset Management as a consultant for three years at $250,000 per annum, thus guaranteeing $1 million for the president's brother. An aspect of this deal was that West Tsusho was reported by Japanese police as a front for a leading crime syndicate, which implied that Japanese criminals were creating an American foothold through the investment.[42] The Japanese police were also examining West Tsusho's investment in Quantum Access, another American company for which Prescott was a consultant. At the time, he was a director of Quantum, which was headed by his nephew. Prescott Bush was also one of three partners in an $18-million golf course development near Shanghai, which, according to a report in the *Los Angeles Times*, he received free of charge in return for introducing Japanese officials to acquaintances among their high-ranking Chinese counterparts. "George's rise to power had placed Prescott in the position of cashing in by arranging American deals for Tsusho."[43] And, as indicated, others as well.

A more serious problem involved the president's son, Neil Mallon Bush.

The S & L bank disaster the Reagan administration created by deregulation, then worsened by a compliant Republican Congress, made millionaires out of wheeling-and-dealing bank officials and their friends—among whom were both Democratic and Republican congressmen. The mathematics was simple: Invest in risky deals, mainly real estate, run by a group in which the organizer was a partner or from which he received a high salary or other compensation. Inflate the value with bogus evaluations to pass the scanty rules still in place. When the deal collapsed, the government would reimburse the bank depositors. No one would lose—except the taxpayers.

The resultant losses were staggering, amounting to over $500 billion by 1999. Six years after deregulation some twelve hundred savings institutions went bankrupt because of bad debts and fraud. Already within two years of the deregulation alarm bells were sounding, but nothing was done. Too many prominent people had their fingers in the pie.[44]

In 1985 Michael Wise, chairman of the Silverado Banking, Savings and Loan Association in Denver, approached the twenty-nine-year-old Neil Bush, son of the vice president, and asked him to join the Silverado board. Such a contact would obviously be very valuable for its political entrée, since all these deals depended on federal authority. Young Neil agreed, avid to imitate his father's early success in Texas.

Cronyism now took over. Bill Walters, a Denver real estate developer who had received more than $200 million in loans from Silverado, financed Neil. He helped the young man and two partners create an oil development and leasing company called JNB Explorations. Bush put in some $100; Walters, $150,000; and three banks extended Neil a credit line of $1.2 million.[45]

On November 8, 1988, George Bush was elected president. The next day federal regulators closed down Silverado, which crashed to the tune of close to $1 billion. Neil, without doubt forewarned, had resigned from the board shortly before. He also walked away from JNB, which turned out to be a dud.[46]

In May of 1990 an investigation by the U.S. House Banking Committee found that Neil Bush voted to approve $106 million in loans to Walters but did not file a required disclosure form showing that he had a business relationship with the borrower. Continuing investigation revealed that Bush was also silent when Silverado forgave $11.5 million in debts owed by Kenneth Good, another real estate developer, who had lent Neil Bush's JNB Exploration $3 million. On another occasion young Bush recommended a $900,000 credit line to Good for a venture involving JNB, and on still a third Good invested $100,000 for Bush, a debt which he then cancelled.

In April of 1991 federal regulators concluded that Neil Bush's business dealings constituted a conflict of interest and he was directed to refrain from such action in the future, not only the mildest penalty that could be imposed under the law, but also one less severe than those directed against the other members of the Silverado gang. President Bush defended his son's actions and suggested that the charges were politically inspired to embarrass him. No one involved in Silverado went to jail; the U.S. taxpayers, as usual, picked up the tab.[47]

Whether good or mediocre, it is hard to hold a man with the right connections down. Neil became involved in another oil venture, Apex Energy Company, also based in Denver.[48] He put up $3,000, and Apex received more than $2 million from investment companies backed by the Small Business Administration, with the federal government subsidizing part of these investments. The companies giving the seed money were controlled by a backer and friend of President Bush.

Neil Bush was paid an annual salary of $160,000 on his $3,000 investment, but was forced to resign in 1991 when it was revealed that he continued to benefit through a federally subsidized program. At last report he was working for a sports cable television company based in Houston, hired by a fund-raiser and longtime friend of the president.[49]

Two other sons of George Bush have become important political figures. John Ellis (Jeb) is governor of Florida. George W. Bush, the former governor of Texas, is now president of the United States. He will be discussed in chapter 10.

After his unsuccessful bid for reelection, the elder Bush was welcomed by big business as a convention speaker, his usual fee being $100,000 a speech. In 1998, advised by an old friend, Lodwrick M. Cook, former chief executive of the Atlantic Richfield Company, in lieu of the fee he took stock in a start-up company, Global Crossing Ltd., when addressing a telecommunications group in Japan. The *Wall Street Journal*, reviewing the deal on March 19, 1999, reported that the Bush stock was worth about $14.4 million. One might consider this a nice return, though it should be added that the stock has fallen considerably since the stock market debacle of the last year.

In 1927 a Frenchman named Julien Benda wrote one of the most important books on sociology—really on politics—of our time. Translated as *The Treason of the Intelligentsia*, this violent and bitter invective attacked men of talent and intellect who, knowing better, sell out their values because of hunger for power and money and thus serve as tools for rapacious persons, groups, or nations. We, too, have such men who range from low to high, and the brilliant denunciation of Julian Benda has its parallel in American politics.

George Bush was such a man. After Watergate, Nixon replaced Bob Dole with Bush as chairman of the Republican National Committee. According to H. R. Haldeman's *Diaries*, published in 1994, Nixon felt threatened by Dole and issued orders to "eliminate the politicians, except George Bush. He'd do anything for the cause." Haldeman added that Nixon wanted "good hacks."[50]

A code of honor, a value system, was given to Bush by his background and education. That they were upper class and noblesse oblige—looking down with commiseration—is not to condemn them. The two Roosevelts, Theodore and Franklin, came from this same class system. There are many honest conservatives of similar background. But Bush, one by one, changed his own values, ending against gun control, against any type of abortion, and then supporting corrupt and murderous governments. These are just the prominent examples. The result is that he "climbed to the top of the greasy pole," in the words of the astute politician Benjamin Disraeli.

Not, however, to the top of the pantheon of great presidents; but, rather, to rest among the ambitious figures whose names infest little-read histories of the American nation. Certain men from long-ago times who never became presidents, such as Alexander Hamilton, Henry Clay, and Daniel Webster, will be remembered after Bush is forgotten.

On the other hand, a cynic might reply that, given the present nature of our system, men of at least some integrity can only become president by accident. The Democrat Adlai Stevenson and the Republican Nelson Rockefeller were brought down by a relatively higher measure of uprightness than the men they ran against. This was also true of our most recent election. Unless we reform the system it will always be that way.

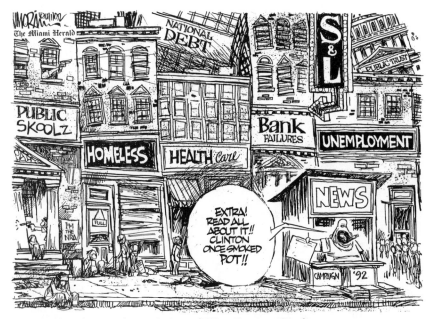

Reprinted with special permission of King Features Syndicate.

David Horsey, *Seattle Post-Intelligencer*. Reprinted with permission of North America Syndicate.

# CHAPTER NINE

# WILLIAM JEFFERSON CLINTON
## (1993–2001)

---

★

---

*"Everything is good or everything is bad, according to the votes they gain."*

Baltasar Gracian, *The Art of Worldly Wisdom*

*"In a Republican district I was a Republican. In a Democratic district, I was a Democrat. And in a doubtful district I was doubtful. But I was always for Erie."*

Jay Gould, chief owner of the Erie Railroad

Wi illiam Jefferson Blythe was born in 1946 at Hope, Arkansas, four months after his father was killed in an auto accident. In 1950 his mother married again, to Roger Clinton, and at the age of fourteen the young man adopted Clinton as his last name. The family moved to Hot Springs, where they were lower middle class in a town where almost everyone was on this same level; there is no indication of any internal conflicts over class distinction from Clinton's youth.

Even before high school Bill Clinton was an accomplished saxophone player, and he was soon chosen as First Chair Tenor Saxophone in the Arkansas All-State First Band, the highest honor a high school musician could reach. Winning trophies and awards, for a time he seriously considered a career as a professional musician. Free of racial prejudice, he organized an integrated musical group in his hometown, where this was still considered taboo.

Endowed by nature with an excellent memory and great energy, in high school Clinton was a National Merit semifinalist and president of the Beta Club, which stood for outstanding academic achievement. He also received the Elks Youth Leadership Award for Arkansas. Despite his bubbling self-confidence, high school friends recalled him as friendly and open.[1]

As a high school junior, Clinton decided on a political career. He was advised to go to the School of Foreign Services at Georgetown University in Washington, D.C., its proximity to the Capitol being a further inducement. At Georgetown—a Southern Baptist attending a Jesuit school—he was elected class president in his freshman and sophomore years. Receiving honors on the Dean's List in his first year, he also made Phi Beta Kappa. And on the side, he worked for the famous Arkansas Senator J. William Fulbright.

Graduating in 1968, Clinton was only the second Georgetown student to receive a Rhodes Scholarship, helped of course by his contact with Fulbright. He spent the next two years at Oxford, England, where he became close friends with Bob Reich, another Rhodes Scholar recipient, whom he later chose as his first secretary of labor.

After receiving a scholarship to Yale Law School, he met a fellow student named Hillary Rodham, with whom he took a semester off and moved to Texas. There, as part of a team, they managed George McGovern's presidential campaign in that state. Then they returned to Yale and, though they hadn't attended a single class for the period absent, passed their finals.[2]

After Yale, Clinton moved back to his home state, where he accepted a job as professor of law at the University of Arkansas in Fayetteville. In 1974, while still teaching, he ran for the U.S. House of Representatives but was narrowly defeated. Fayetteville is located in the northwest corner of Arkansas, the state's sole Republican voting stronghold. It was in this same year that Hillary Rodham moved to Fayetteville and also joined the University Law School as an assistant professor. They married the next year.

In 1976 Clinton ran unopposed for attorney general of Arkansas. From there on, with one minor break, it was always up. Only two years later, Clinton was elected governor of Arkansas; at thirty-two, he was the second youngest governor in U.S. history. The sole setback in his career came in 1980, when he lost reelection due to the national sweep for Ronald Reagan. That was also the year that Chelsea, the Clintons' only child, was born.

In 1982 the charismatic young man launched a comeback campaign and was reelected governor,[3] and then reelected again and again, every two years, for a total period of twelve years. In 1985 he was chosen as chairman of the Southern Growth Policies Board; in 1986 he was chairman of the National Governors Association; in 1988 he gave the Dukakis nominating speech; and in 1990 he was elected Chairman of the Democratic Leadership Council. The following year Clinton declared his candidacy for president, and in 1992 he gained a first-ballot victory at the Democratic National Convention in New York City. At forty-six he was elected president.

Governor Clinton's reputation in Arkansas mainly derived from the fact that his program was socially liberal and fiscally conservative, two positions usually not found in tandem. Because of his magnetic personality and intellectual force he developed a reputation for being a liberal Democrat, which he himself considered inexact: Clinton preferred the word "centrist" or, because it was more catchy and fuzzy, "New Democrat." Certainly he was not remotely radical and most of his positions might be defined as right of Franklin D. Roosevelt's New Deal.

Clinton's passion as governor (much due to his wife) was education, which he advocated equally for white and black children. He insisted that both students and teachers meet new and higher standards, taking an unpopular position by raising the sales tax to support the changes. Other changes along this line were improving school facilities, adjusting aid among the higher and lower income districts, and establishing programs for gifted students.

Part of this, however, was as much political rhetoric as real change. Despite the Clinton educational reforms Arkansas still was almost last in the nation in per capita spending for education, in the percentage of students completing high school, and in the proportion of persons with college degrees. During the Clinton years Arkansas was rated last in the nation for the effectiveness of its environmental policies. Governor Clinton passed no new civil rights or fair-housing laws: After eleven years, Arkansas still remained one of the only two states in the Union without a civil rights law. And the governor had to be sued by advocates of childrens' rights before he moved to reform Arkansas's child-welfare system. For those who cut through the surface charm, nothing much changed in Arkansas except that it became a trampoline for Clinton's larger ambitions.

To be fair, however, in a state that was a barony of a small, rich clique whose money dominated the primaries and news media, Clinton could never do much if any significant reforms required tax increases. In his first term he smashed head-first against these interests. He alienated the Chamber of Commerce when he altered its objective in order to focus on small business development. The Arkansas timber industry was angered when he opposed wholesale timber cutting. The medical community was aroused when he made extensive subsidy efforts to recruit physicians for poor rural communities. To bypass these opponents Clinton raised car license fees, which in a very poor state was a burning issue. And, of course, a rise in sales tax negatively affected those with less income.

These were factors in Governor Clinton's defeat in his first reelection. He learned and stopped struggling for real change, contenting himself with popular wallpaper issues. In fact, we can see in Clinton's years as governor of Arkansas the pattern of what would follow later as president. He became a fiscal conservative, compromising with the Arkansas monied interests as he later would compromise with conservatives in the U.S. legislative branch. His middle ground was largely defined by his opponents and thus led to an ad hoc character to everything he tried to do. Some might say he had no choice given his great ambition; others might counter he could

★

have tried harder. But to judge in abstraction is quite different than standing in the firing line, especially for a very ambitious politician.

Clinton was first elected president in 1992 by only 43 percent of the voters, exactly the same as Richard Nixon in 1968. Issues such as draft dodging, marijuana, adultery, and sexual harrassment drove 57 percent of the voters to prefer President George Bush or the independent candidate Ross Perot, who received 19 percent. In the 1994 interim election, which led to the rout of Democrats and the elevation of Newt Gingrich in the House of Representatives, only a little more than a third of those registered voted and only slightly more than half of them voted Republican; that is, in total about one-sixth of the registered voters went Republican. This was interpreted as a fundamental realignment, which was nonsense and proved to be so by the subsequent election. Relevant was that "the 1994 election was more of an assault on the political system than an affirmation of the Republicans."[4]

Clinton actually did better in his 1996 reelection, when he won 49 percent of the popular vote. His complete ideological shift, engineered by pollster Dick Morris, did the trick: tough on welfare, tough on crime, balancing the budget, and cracking down on illegal immigration, appeals that had no relation to his original stands before his first election. It may be pointed out, however, that the reelection turnout was also the lowest percentage of the voting population since 1924, and 7 million fewer people voted in 1996 than in 1992. The largest political party in the United States is now the nonvoters. Most Americans simply feel they have no voice in government, and they are right.[5]

That the republic indeed was safe in conservative hands was already apparent by Clinton's initial choice of cabinet members. His first secretary of the treasury, Lloyd Bentsen of Texas, had close ties to oil and gas interests and, as former chairman of the U.S. Senate Finance Committee, was so well identified with his financial supporters he had earned the nickname "Loophole Lloyd." Bentsen would have been just as comfortable, perhaps more comfortable, in

Bush's cabinet. After retiring, he was replaced by Robert Rubin, co-chairman of Goldman, Sachs & Co., a top Wall Street investment firm, a man whose net worth was reported to be at least $100 million. The secretary of energy, Hazel O'Leary, was an executive from a Minnesota power company. The initial choice for attorney general was Zöe Baird, holding a high position in a Connecticut insurance company; she was replaced by Janet Reno in a flap over hiring illegal aliens as household workers.

The other cabinet members were former governors, mayors, and similar figures of the political status quo. Only Secretary of Labor Robert Reich represented the shards of the New Deal, but he was a personal friend of Clinton's from Oxford days and knew Hillary even earlier, when she went to Wellesley before Yale Law School.[6] Besides, the secretary of labor is almost always a liberal figure. In sum, the cabinet was hardly distinguishable from the precedent Republican ones as well as that of John F. Kennedy. And when the éminence grise of orthodox conservatism, Alan Greenspan, reached the end of his term as chairman of the Federal Reserve Board— originally appointed by Ronald Reagan—he was immediately reappointed by Clinton.

The oligarchic element in Clinton's tenure was also apparent. Vice President Albert Gore Jr., hand-picked by Clinton, is the son of the very powerful Democratic former Senator Albert Gore Sr. of Tennessee. An earlier family member was Senator Thomas P. Gore of Oklahoma, a bitter opponent of Franklin D. Roosevelt. A cousin of the vice president was Gore Vidal, the vituperative writer who also had political ambitions. Andrew M. Cuomo, originally assistant housing secretary and then elevated to secretary of housing and urban development, is the son of former Governor Mario M. Cuomo of New York and is married to a daughter of Robert F. Kennedy. In December 2000 he issued a long report, paid for by the taxpayers, titled "Vision for Change," in fact the first shot in his campaign to become governor of New York. Harold M. Ickes, deputy White House chief of staff in Clinton's first administration (and forced out because he could not stand the rightist acrobatics of his boss), is the son of Franklin D. Roosevelt's interior secretary, Harold L. Ickes.

The only significant change from the past was more ethnic diversity, better reflecting the kaleidoscope of the American population. Clinton appointed four African Americans and two Hispanics to his cabinet, of whom four were women. This indeed accounted for his greater popularity in those groups than in the general population. His wife, Hillary Rodham Clinton, played a large role in his choices, to the disgust of more traditional groups whose members still psychologically perceive a woman's true place to be decorator of the home nest.

This break with the past was likewise true of his judicial appointments, where by the end of his second year in office Clinton appointed more nontraditional judges than any preceding president: Nearly one-fourth were African Americans, almost 10 percent were Hispanic, and about one-third were women. Sixty-five percent of these appointments were rated by the American Bar Association as "well qualified," a higher percentage rating than those appointed by Carter, Reagan, and Bush. Of his two Supreme Court appointments, Ruth Bader Ginsburg and Stephen G. Breyer, one was a moderate liberal and the other a moderate conservative. Both were Jewish, the only Jewish judges appointed since the presidency of Lyndon B. Johnson.

As in his early years as governor of Arkansas, Clinton tried to do too much too quickly during his initial period as president. The most important change he stressed was universal health care, a proposal first initiated by Richard Nixon. This was well received and even Newt Gingrich showed sympathy. But Clinton put the program in the hands of his wife, detested by many conservatives, both Republican and Democrat; she, without regard to legislative protocol and logrolling, tried to ram the program down the throats of Congress. What had been first seen as favorable by congressmen of both parties—the United States is the only advanced industrial country without such a program—became more tenuous and then impossible to pass as small businesses and insurance companies, as well as many doctors, viewed the health program a threat to their income.

If the Clinton administration had concentrated on this one issue, it could have been enacted. But it also put on the table at the same time other programs and pushed for wholesale change, invading the fiefdoms of various vested interests who then were alienated. The result was not so much cohesive pressure but a degree of chaos. The Democrats themselves did not present a united front: As George Stephanopoulos, a top man in the first administration, cleverly expressed it, "After forty years of dominating Congress, our party [the Democrats] had become a complacent feudal kingdom no longer dominated by fervent belief or fear of the king. Each member was a master of a barony; each chairperson, lord of a duchy. Our majority was more a tactical alliance of autonomous factions than a political movement based on shared values and a coherent governing philosophy."[7] And once this happened the lobbying groups, with their enormous sums of money, stepped in and reversed what indeed the majority of American people seemed to want.

Licking his wounds and always greedy for popularity, Clinton then switched to less divisive issues—and those usually involved positions contrary not only to his professed philosophy but also to his core support. Indeed, his major achievements—the deficit-reducing budget of 1993, the General Agreement on Tariffs and Trade (GATT), the North American Free Trade Agreement (NAFTA),[8] the crime bill, and welfare overhaul—were in the main contrary to the positions held by his liberal constituency. With the Democrats disorganized by Clinton's flip flops and lack of leadership, this gave the Republicans, a minority in the first two years of the Clinton presidency, an unprecedented opportunity to stop anything they considered liberal thinking. Senator Bob Dole of Kansas, leading the Republican minority, blocked Clinton legislation with twenty filibusters in two months, more than had been used in the previous two decades. And further disorganizing the Democrats, Clinton accepted defeat after defeat instead of fighting back.

There were, of course, exceptions. An increase in taxes to reduce the tremendous deficits caused by Reagan and Bush won by one vote; many of the decent legislators who knew of its necessity and voted accordingly were slaughtered in the 1994 interim elections—because the American people hate taxes, but at the same time they want more entitlements, a contradiction most do not seem to perceive.[9] The Brady Bill, calling for a waiting period before purchasing a handgun, was passed despite intense pressure from the gun lobby. A bill went through requiring employers to give their workers up to three months unpaid leave for a family emergency or severe medical problem. But the story of those early years was dismal: only three bills strongly endorsed by Clinton passed, the worst record of any post–World War II president. It was, as the *Washington Post* stated, "Perhaps the Worst Congress."[10] And Clinton didn't even get credit for successfully reducing the deficit by $500 billion—a deficit that turned into a surplus in the years that followed.

After the 1994 triumph of the Republicans and the signing of Newt Gingrich's Contract with America, the early failures seemed pallid by comparison. Clinton, desperate for reelection, proceeded to swallow the Republican platform. Riding in triumph, the Republicans went out to destroy the last vestiges of the New Deal. The president, preaching in the Republican pew, acceded in 1995 to drastic cuts in education and job training to bring the total under the level of 1992 during the Bush presidency. Now the only two basic objectives of his administration were the need to balance the budget and reduce the national debt, and any slashing of public services was laudable toward these aims. Newt Gingrich was left breathlessly hanging on a splintered limb with little to cushion his fall except, as it turned out, sex, sex, and sex. The Republican Congress, with its auxiliary arm, Kenneth Starr running the Star Chamber, played a nineteenth-century French bedroom farce. This, it may be added, eventually ricocheted, because these so-called political leaders forgot that ordinary citizens tend to side with a victim when stomped too viciously. But that was still in the future.

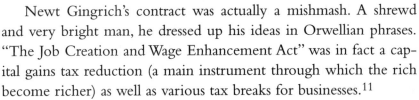

Newt Gingrich's contract was actually a mishmash. A shrewd and very bright man, he dressed up his ideas in Orwellian phrases. "The Job Creation and Wage Enhancement Act" was in fact a capital gains tax reduction (a main instrument through which the rich become richer) as well as various tax breaks for businesses.[11]

The "Balanced Budget Amendment," which Clinton embraced, was in reality a device to cut back or eliminate federal programs such as school lunches and food stamps for the very poor as well as reducing benefits for disabled children and legal immigrants. The welfare reform program was directed against illegitimate children— as if ignorant women will stop fornicating because they won't get more money. The Strategic Defense Initiative (SDI), the crackpot Reagan idea of a complete missile defense at a cost of untold billions, was resurrected (as it has been under George W. Bush, Clinton's successor in office). Gingrich was careful not to include in his contract such items as prayer in the schools, abortion, or a repeal of the ban on assault weapons, because these issues would divide Republicans. "Gingrich the history student in particular seemed to have a way of putting present battles into historical context, making them battles over principles even if they were really about feeding the lobbyists."[12]

The Gingrich contract had some affirmative aspects. It called for political term limits, soon discarded as the intoxication of power increased the desire for continued power. It attacked the corruption and stagnant bureaucracy created in many fields of welfare. But inherently it was self-contradictory, as had already been evident from the Reagan days. More money for the military, a staple of Republican thought, with tax deductions and credits, can only be possible by cutting social programs, and then cutting them again. And even the most rabid Republicans dared not meddle with Social Security and Medicare programs, the darlings of the middle class.

The president, hoping desperately to regain popularity after the Democratic defeat in the 1994 interim election, agreed to most of these measures.[13] Ironically, neither Clinton nor Gingrich could imagine the tremendous financial boom that soon followed, which made feasible budget balancing and debt reduction without further destroying still more government social programs.

The president's massive retreat on the social front was matched elsewhere. Clinton came to power on a pledge of open government, curbing the excesses of federal agencies and a more efficient but reduced military machine. His stay in office indicates the contrary.

One of the three articles of impeachment drawn up against President Nixon in 1974 was "He misused the Federal Bureau of Investigation. . . ." Actually, post–World War II presidents routinely "misused" their power—the practice preceded Nixon and went back to the 1950s—but, as in such matters, the question is one of degree and purpose. In 1996 it was disclosed that in late 1993, after the political furor caused by firing the government travel office staff and their replacement with Clinton supporters, the White House sought and obtained confidential material on Billy R. Dale, the fired director of the travel office. Then it was further disclosed that Clinton staffers likewise requested and obtained material on more than three hundred Republicans—a practice that was an important element in Nixon's fall.[14]

When this information became public, Louis J. Freeh, then director of the FBI, stated that he would no longer respond to requests from Clinton aides for confidential files. The White House immediately issued a statement that it was all a bureaucratic error. Freeh also announced new controls to prevent any repetitions. The White House stated that it would return to the FBI all the requested files—the new total was actually 408. A later investigation by an independent counsel concluded that the files were acquired by the White House Office of Personnel Security through the mistakes of a low-level employee there, and that there was no criminal intent.

Whether this was a whitewash or not, there was one laudable result. In reaction to this scandal, Congress passed legislation in 1998 making it unlawful for a president, a vice president, or any of their staff employees to request, conduct, or terminate an audit or investigation of a tax liability of any taxpayer, which helps solve the problem.

As to new "controls" on the CIA, Congress and the White House announced in late 1998 the largest spending increase for intelligence since the Cold War. In a speech the previous May, George J. Tenet, director of the CIA, stated that his agency had to "rebuild our field strength" in order "to stay in the espionage business" because American intelligence was "seriously eroding." The overall budget rose to an annual $29 billion, close to the figure at which it peaked during the height of tension with the Soviet Union. This amounts to about one-tenth of the total defense budget. Presumably our enemies are now as dangerous as when we were threatened with nuclear war by the Soviets.

In January 1999, sixteen years after President Reagan proposed the ridiculous Strategic Defense Initiative program—ridiculous because almost all experts said the project was not only unfeasible but the cost would break the nation[15]—President Clinton pledged $7 billion over six years to go back to a modification of SDI; this despite the fact that such a program would violate the Anti-Ballistic Missile Treaty signed by the United States and the Soviet Union in 1972. Clinton, however, cleverly arranged that work on the system would be postponed until after his term ended, so he would not be responsible. In the meantime, the Pentagon has included in its budget for 2001 the sum of $4.166 billion, oblivious to the cost and the failures of every attempt to create the system.

Also in January 1999, President Clinton proposed the largest increase in the Pentagon's budget since the Cold War buildup of the mid-1980s; as usual, a complete shift from his proclaimed priorities. Budgetary financing allocated for defense training and operations per capita was higher than that of the Reagan administration; the United States apportions more money on defense than all of its declared or potential adversaries combined. And this budget request was before the additional monies called for by the Kosovo War, which added $14 billion as an initial sum—with far more money likely to be spent in the future rebuilding what we have destroyed.[16]

However, certain of the accusations against the presidential family were malignant. When it was found that Hillary Clinton had made $100,000 over a period of nine months from a series of cattle future speculations suggested by a friend, there was a hue and cry. Political opponents claimed that the gains reeked of illegality. When on a speaking tour in Japan, as mentioned before, former President George Bush put his $80,000 lecture fee into the stock of a new company on the advice of a friend—Global Crossing, a proposed worldwide fiber optic network designed for Internet transmissions—the value of the stock rose to $14.4 million in a little more than a year.★ Mrs. Clinton's action was called a devious speculation; Bush's, an investment. Millions of dollars of taxpayer money was spent to investigate Mrs. Clinton's perfectly legal market gambles while nothing but praise met the tip-off that led to Bush's huge profits.

Wily as Bill Clinton may be, and shrewd as his wife may be, such charges are impelled by pure malice. G. Gordon Liddy, the infamous Nixon pal (whose own history should have taught him a lesson), suggested the use of cardboard cutouts of both Clintons for target practice. Reverend Jerry Falwell peddled videotapes accusing the president of murder because of his position on abortion. Crowds have carried signs: "Bill and Hillary are immoral homosexual communists." Kenneth Starr, during the Monica Lewinsky cross-examinations, demanded answers to personal questions—not only of Ms. Lewinsky but of her mother and friends—that were in many people's minds blatant intrusions into private habits unrelated to the investigation. This deportment is closer to psychotic behavior than reasoned analysis of presumed wrongs.

The media are also responsible for such piranha feeding. This great organ of democracy can at times be its worst enemy by spreading sensationalism in order to titillate the public and often, by slant or omission, to undermine matters of far greater importance. For example, when the Whitewater scandal broke—accusing the Clintons of illegal real estate transactions—the major network news-

★This stock has declined radically in value during the 2000–2001 market collapse of technology stocks.

★

casts devoted three times more publicity to this unproven charge than they had given to the rival health-care issue. And the whole country was convulsed by the journalism devoted to the Lewinsky sex scandal, during which time the fundamental issues facing America were thrown into a wastebasket.

Many, if not most, Republican legislators have shown what might be called a demonic hatred for the Clintons. This has been more psychological than political; try as they might, it was futile to point to the president as a leftist or even as a liberal in the New Deal mode. It was more than his loose morals, though some hooked their prejudice in that closet.

There were two main reasons. The first was that the Clintons represented the 1960s rebellion against old values: draft dodging and flag burning, rather than "my country right or wrong"; pot smoking; acceptance of abortion; and agreeing to gay rights being aspects of this revolt. The second was that Clinton was the first American president who could relax with, and regard as equal, those not deriving from European ancestry, rather than using them as window dressing.[17] Can one imagine George Bush or even Lyndon Johnson having an African American as a close friend and golfing partner? Yet this was natural to Clinton and it frightened conservative legislators in a deep, primitive way. Many of them still implicitly believed that the United States was formed by white, Anglo-Saxon presidents and is a fiefdom of their descendants. The changing nature of the U.S. population, and the changing social attitudes that have resulted, scares them. A corollary to this is a clash of generations: those who believe in what they feel as absolute values planted in traditional Christian ethics and those, like the Clintons, who see life in varied hues rather than black and white.

The Republicans were so unhappy in their failure to crucify the Clintons over Whitewater (which investigation, along with the subsequent sex scandal, cost the taxpayers $52 million), they created a new committee headed by Kenneth Starr, an exemplar of the opposite type from the Clintons. He, too failed to find any incriminating

★

evidence but, Eureka!, discovered something far more lickerish—
Monica Lewinsky.

The House impeachment of President Clinton, among the various Marx Brothers comedies staged in Washington, was the most farcical. This frolic made the United States a laughingstock of the world
and indeed should raise questions in the minds of intelligent persons
as to whether such a primate zoo called the House of Representatives
is fit to be considered a serious factor in world leadership.

The Clinton impeachment involved two charges. The first was
lying under oath about his sexual infidelity. The second was whether
this alleged perjury could be construed as a high crime or misdemeanor under the American Constitution.

Only one other presidential impeachment is on record previous
to this action and it was equally a farce.[18] President Andrew Johnson,
who took office after the death of Lincoln, was charged in 1868
with treating the defeated South with what might be called the
crime of charity. The die-hard, vindictive congressmen who hated
the South, and whose continued electoral success was often based on
the vitriolic spleen pouring from their mouths, succeeded in
bringing the articles of impeachment in the House but lost by one
vote when the charges were tried in the Senate, an outcome much
like the the Clinton case. A minor incident that stopped short of
impeachment occurred later, in 1929, when First Lady Lou Hoover
invited the wife of a black congressman from Chicago to the White
House, the first time an African American had ever been received
socially. This touched off a national controversy and the Texas legislature proposed impeaching President Hoover, an action not picked
up elsewhere.

In the Clinton impeachment, lying about sex was the initial
charge. The Republicans were very clear that this was a damnable
matter, as though no previous great statesman or president ever had
dreamed, let alone committed, a sexual act outside marriage. Perhaps
a brief review can be called forth.

Alexander Hamilton, the darling of American conservatives and our first secretary of the treasury under President Washington, was as deeply implicated in a sex scandal as was Clinton, one indeed involving possible government favors. In 1792–93 Congress investigated Hamilton for financial misdealings with James Reynolds, a convicted securities swindler. Hamilton initially stonewalled and then admitted to making secret payments to Reynolds, whose release from prison Hamilton engineered. Hamilton explained that he was trying to avoid public exposure of an adulterous relation with Reynolds's wife but that this blackmail did not involve government funds.

The congressional investigative committee, which included James Monroe, the future president, concluded that the matter was private and not public; and that as a result no impeachable offense had occurred.[19]

The icon of the liberals, President Thomas Jefferson, was accused during his administration of a sexual relation, which included fathering children, with Sally Hemings, one of his slaves. This was even more titillating in that Sally and Jefferson's wife were half-sisters, products of the lust of the same Virginia plantation owner. Sally indeed was not only a slave but very young at the time the relationship began, which would now be labeled statutory rape.[20]

Jefferson kept a studied silence before the charges and even most of the New England Federalists who hated him could not believe this intellectual southern aristocrat would indulge in such practices. The result was that the proof only arrived in our time, with DNA testing of the black descendants of Jefferson.

Thus, both the classical heroes of the American Revolution under Washington (who indeed was suspected of having an affair with Sally Fairfax, the wife of a close friend) were involved in evading or covering up charges of sexual escapades.

The record does not stop there. Many presidents of consequence have been involved with lesser or greater sexual adventures. Grover Cleveland had an illegitimate child, which disclosure caused him much trouble in his 1884 campaign; he was also accused of beating his young wife. Remarkably, similar to the Clinton charges, the press branded him with phrases like, "The libertine is the enemy of the family and, thus, a traitor to the Republic."[21] What saved Cleveland was an exposé of even a more scandalous past of his adversary, James Blaine.

Warren G. Harding (1921–23) was excoriated by the publication of intimate relations in the memoirs of a woman named Nan Britton, with whom he started an affair when he was forty-seven and she twenty. Nan had a child with Harding for whose adoption he paid. While president, Harding set up a divan in a large White House alcove, where they made love.

Franklin D. Roosevelt had longtime mistresses, first Lucy Mercer, twenty-two-year-old secretary to his wife; then Marguerite LeHand, called Missy, who Roosevelt chose as his personal secretary.[23] Though she never explicitly acknowledged it, Dorothy Schiff (director of the New York *Post*, at that time an important Democratic newspaper), with the approval of her husband, George Backer, was at FDR's beck and call; when she divorced Becker and married Ted Thackrey, the president sent an amusing message to the couple at the betrothal: "She ought to know how by now."[24]

Dwight D. Eisenhower was involved romantically during World War II with Kay Summersby, an English soldier, later promoted to captain, who was his chauffeur. Telling his superior, General Marshall, of his passion, Marshall threatened to throw him out of the army if he divorced his wife. At the end of her life Summersby wrote *Forgetting the Past*, in which she recounted that Eisenhower had serious sexual problems.

John F. Kennedy's licentious conduct is well known, amounting indeed to priapism. Among the better-known women with whom he slept were Jayne Mansfield, Rhonda Fleming, Angie Dickinson, Mary Pinchot Meyer, and Marilyn Monroe, who also was sleeping with the president's brother Bobby. One of his most notorious affairs was with Judith Campbell Exnet, who was at the same time the mistress of the Mafia head Sam Giancana. It is claimed that through the connection President Kennedy tried unsuccessfully to have the Mafia kill Fidel Castro, using Frank Sinatra as a go-

★

between.[26] Traphee Bryant, one of Kennedy's aides, wrote in *Dog Days in the White House* that naked men and women used to cavort together in the White House pool. J. Edgar Hoover, director of the FBI from 1924 until his death in 1972, had his agents collect salacious information on the politicians of his time, possibly to discourage them from replacing him. When the Freedom of Information Act was passed by Congress, researchers found several hundred pages devoted to the sexual exploits of Kennedy.

These same archives contain much information on the sexual infidelities of Lyndon Johnson. As vice president, Johnson had a torrid affair with the wife of a congressman; fearing disclosure because the woman was a "blabber," Johnson asked President Kennedy to offer her husband a prestigious post far away from Washington, which Kennedy did. Johnson and Kennedy used to gossip about the sexual goings-on of the U.S. legislators and Johnson, knowing these scandals, used them to force votes for his legislation as president. Particularly important was the arm-twisting of Senators George Smathers, Herman Talmadge, and Alben Barkley. Johnson's wife, Lady Bird, wanted to divorce him but the two were so entangled in their mutual private business ventures that she decided not to. Several other written memoirs attest to Johnson's attempts, often when drunk, to enter the rooms of women who rejected him. Because of his weak heart, Johnson was advised by doctors to discontinue these adventures; he refused, which, it is claimed, contributed to his final heart attack.

Richard Nixon also entered into the periscope of Hoover's agents. An FBI agent in Hong Kong reported to his boss that on a visit to the Orient Nixon had an affair with a Chinese woman.[27] Nixon's friends said this was impossible, but several years later the literary agent Scott Meredith revealed twenty-two love letters that Nixon had written to the wife of a Spanish diplomat. It may also be noted that when at the White House Nixon and his wife never spent the night together.

Gerald Ford was very attracted to women and even showed it in

★

front of his wife. He flirted openly, if not more, with such beautiful ladies as Raquel Welch, the actress; Vikki Carr, the singer; Elke Sommer, another actress; and Phyllis George, a former Miss America.[28]

Ronald Reagan, it appears, was unusual in this aspect, though it must be kept in mind that Reagan was seventy and already sickly when he became president. As to President Bush, rumors circulated as to one particularly close "friendship" with a woman for years.

A psychologist might state that the same enormous drive for power that leads to the presidency also shows itself almost inevitably in an equally powerful sex drive. It is rather amazing indeed that no complete study has been published on these peccadilloes of American presidents.

There are those who say sexual infidelity is a private subject, but lying under oath about it is another matter. Readers of this book should be reminded that president after president has lied publicly and under interrogation. A most notorious example is Reagan's shuffling and evasions before the Tower Commission's investigation of the Iran-contra affair. In fact, several Congressmen suggested an impeachment proceeding on this issue. Johnson's and Nixon's continued lying are also common knowledge.

The point can be carried even further. There are circumstances in which a president, aware of impending action against an enemy state but forced to testify before a hostile committee of the opposing political party, may be forced to lie for reasons of national security. It is not so much the lie but the overriding issue of national security involved. Western religions clearly separate what might be called the white lie from the black lie, or what the Catholic Church defines as venial (forgivable) and mortal (unforgivable) sins.

The Clinton impeachment proceeding was technically based on the meaning of "high crimes and misdemeanors" in the U.S. Constitution. The Republicans insisted that a consensual private intimacy, when lied about, fell within the government's power to investigate and punish. They then forced through an impeachment

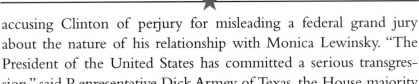

accusing Clinton of perjury for misleading a federal grand jury about the nature of his relationship with Monica Lewinsky. "The President of the United States has committed a serious transgression," said Representative Dick Armey of Texas, the House majority leader. "Among other things, he took an oath to God to tell the truth, the whole truth and nothing but the truth, and then he failed to do so, not once, but several times." To ignore this, Armey continued, is to "undermine the rule of law."

The constitutional phrase or question, to anyone with plain common sense, refers to offenses against the state that threaten the nation's security. A succession of legal scholars and historians had warned the House Judiciary Committee that Clinton's act in no way could be interpreted as "Treason, Bribery, or other high Crimes and Misdemeanors," the exact wording of the Constitution. But the House Republicans concluded that the president should be impeached. For what? For denying an oral sexual relation with an ambitious intern.

Let us analyze these House Republicans who followed their Holy Grail.

Almost two dozen of them, including the top leaders, have confessed to, have been convicted of having, or there is creditable documentation showing illicit sexual relations, violation of laws, or circumvention of congressional ethical rules. Two representatives have been caught employing prostitutes, two were charged with serial sexual harassment, four covered up knowledge of felonies in the Iran–contra scandal, and six attempted to use their influence to win favor for convicted criminals. Since 1971 thirty-nine members of Congress have been convicted and gone to prison.[29]

We can be more specific. Representative Robert L. Livingston, Republican Speaker-elect, resigned when it was disclosed that he had affairs with at least four women. Representative Henry T. Hyde, Republican chairman of the House Judiciary Committee—who pompously stated in the investigation that "no man or woman, how highly placed, no matter how effective a communicator, no matter how gifted a manipulator of opinion or winner of votes, can be above the law in a democracy"—was revealed by the Internet magazine *Salon* on September 17, 1998, to have carried on an illicit relation with the married mother of three, a five-year affair he began at age forty-one. Representative Dan Burton of Indiana, the Republican chairman of the Government Reform and Oversight Committee—who called Clinton a "scumbag" in a meeting with the editorial board of the *Indianapolis Star*—was forced to reveal, because of an impending story in *Vanity Fair*, that he was the father of an illegitimate child. Burton responded, "But this is private." Representative Helen Chenoweth of Idaho, who consistently criticized Clinton for his morals and sexual behavior, conceded due to forthcoming publicity that she had engaged in a long-term affair with a married man. Bob Barr, Republican from Georgia, the main sponsor of the 1996 Defense of Marriage Act,★ was divorced twice and is now on his third wife; it has been reported that at a celebrity fund-raiser in 1992 he licked whipped cream from the breasts of two women. Republican J. C. Watts of Oklahoma spent years covering up his out-of-wedlock children. Republican Ken Calvert of California was caught by the police in 1993 receiving oral sex from a prostitute; he was sued by his ex-wife for not paying alimony. The self-righteous Republican Dick Armey of Texas, as reported by the *Dallas Observer* in 1995, allegedly sexually harassed female students as an economics professor before entering Congress. Six women accused Republican John Peterson of Pennsylvania of sexual harassment; Peterson's answer was, "I may have have been an excessive hugger."[30]

Perhaps most interesting, the House Republican whip, Representative Tom DeLay of Texas—a driving force behind the effort to impeach Clinton on charges of lying under oath—himself gave a deposition several years ago in which he also lied under oath. In this deposition DeLay swore that he was no longer an officer of a Texas company, nor had he been for two or three years, where he was

★The Defense of Marriage Act defines marriage, for purposes of federal benefits, as the legal union of one man and one woman.

being sued; but DeLay had filed congressional financial disclosure forms saying that in those years he was the company's chairman. The discrepancy—if so it may be called—was reported by the *Houston Press*. Perjury charges could not be brought since there is a three-year statute of limitations in Texas.[31]

The Clinton farce reached its peak when it was revealed in mid-1999 that Newt Gingrich, the pope of the canting right, had been involved for several years (which is to say, long before the House impeachment of Clinton) in an illicit affair with a congressional aide twenty-three years younger than himself. Gingrich, who had announced in 1981 his desire to divorce his first wife when she was stricken with cancer,[32] stuck to his callous record by informing his second wife of the same decision by telephone in May 1999, while she was away visiting her eighty-four-year-old mother.

This is the man who in the hearings attacked the president in a celebrated speech: "We have had a thirty-five-year experiment in a unionized, bureaucratic, credentialed, secular assault on the core values of this country, and we should not be surprised that eventually they yield bad fruit because they are bad seed."

There is indeed not only bad fruit but also rotten fruit.

The conclusion for anyone not totally lacking in humor is that the Clinton impeachment, if it were not the act of the highest legislative body of the United States, was so farcical that one is reminded of the story of Susanna and the Elders in the Bible; the Elders in this matter being the largely upper-class, middle-aged congressman who preach virtue in public and practice vice in private.[33]

A good part of this sordid story was President Clinton's own fault. Any American who could read knew that he was a philanderer.[34] Denying under oath his relationship with Monica Lewinsky was a silly blunder, particularly since he had already admitted lying about his longtime relationship with Gennifer Flowers in Arkansas. Clinton should have realized that Special Prosecutor Kenneth Starr's investigation would force a confession from Monica Lewinsky. He was not chosen by the voters for his morals, but simply because they believed he would make a better president than his opponents. If Clinton had admitted to another transgression of conventional morality most Americans would have sighed in disgust or resignation but still favored him for his abilities. After all, Kennedy remains an icon for many people despite his far more outrageous sexual conduct. And the culmination was Clinton's sweeping together a group of Protestant ministers in an act of mea culpa that to many seemed to add hypocrisy to lack of credibility. Kenneth Starr's zealotry in his inquiries as he somehow slithered over from a Whitewater inquiry, in which no evidence could be found, to a sexual probe of the president was met by Clinton's grovelling.

A shabby face of the Clinton administration was that the young man accused of draft dodging in the Vietnam War, and in sympathy with others of like mind, turned out to be among the most militaristic presidents of the latter part of the twentieth century.

It was not so in Clinton's first years in office. In that period he was quite successful in avoiding actual strife, though there was an invasion of Haiti to overthrow a repressive regime and stop the flood of illegal aliens entering the United States—Clinton's envoy, former president Jimmy Carter, succeeded in persuading the country's military leaders to step down. The bombings of Iraq continued but this was a logical extension of Desert Storm. Negotiations with North Korea obviated the threat of invasion of South Korea. The signing of a land adjustment treaty between Israel and the Palestinians, though it turned illusory, was a plus. In fact, Clinton's foreign policy was far more successful than his domestic policy in this initial period.

Things then turned sour. Clinton stumbled into the internal struggles of Somalia and then stumbled out with nothing changed. He fired missiles at Baghdad in revenge against an unsubstantiated report that Iraq's dictator was trying to assassinate former President Bush when he visited Kuwait. Desperately seeking popularity because of his other problems, the president embarked on clumsy attempts to combat terrorism or to solve ethnic problems that had

★

been around for hundreds of years. He ordered missile strikes in the Sudan and Afahanistan without a shred of evidence indicating their justification. In the Sudan, a factory "producing nerve gas ingredients" (in fact a pharmaceutical plant manufacturing half of the Sudan's medicines) was destroyed, and the administration never produced proof backing its statements. We are now quietly paying the Sudan compensation. The missile strikes against Afghanistan designed to kill Osama bin Laden, a wealthy Saudi exile accused of sponsoring terrorist attacks against Americans, were ill-timed.★ Throughout the 1980s the Soviet Union threw every weapon it had against the Afghans but their rebel camps dug into caves and bunkers in steep mountains were impenetrable. Yet the American military decided that firing dozens of million-dollar cruise missiles at these Afghan camps in a one-shot deal would be more successful than nine years of unsuccessful Soviet occupation. For any thinking person, the Sudan and Afghan attacks smelled more of a popularity campaign for the president's image than meaningful foreign policy.[35]

U.S. foreign policy then went from bad to worse. Henry Kissinger's Realpolitik, basing strategy on America's vital interests rather than abstract ideals (actually the position of America's first great president, George Washington), was discarded in a world where nuclear warfare is still a possibility. Whether agreeing or not, the true aim of President Bush in the Gulf War, namely, reasonable and stable oil prices, was a legitimate national goal. To take a good example from the past of what happens when abstract idealism guides military action, Woodrow Wilson's insistence on dismantling the Austro-Hungarian Empire after World War I left a range of small chaotic nation-states in Eastern Europe as prey first for Hitler and then Stalin—all in the name of "self-determination." And Clinton's pontifications about the former Yugoslavia fell into the same class.

Ethnic cleansing is, of course, horrible. But it should be pointed

---

★The American response to the terrorist attacks on New York City's World Trade Center and the Pentagon in Washington, D.C., will be discussed in chapter 10.

out that the initial Kosovar "cleansings" were in towns from which the Kosovo Liberation Army operated: patriots or rebels, take your choice. After the Serbian defeat, a reverse ethnic purging by Kosovars took place, far more drastic than the initial Serbian violence, much by active gangs of organized criminals tolerated by NATO troops. There were some 300,000 Kosovar refugees from the areas where the original Kosovar resistance was entrenched; within a month after the NATO troops entered, there were about 850,000 new refugees. The final result was that Kosovo became a Western protectorate whose NATO guardians watched with little apparent concern, and no action, while half the province's Serbian population and nearly all the gypsies were expelled. And in Kosovo at the present time a Serb is eight times more likely than an Albanian to be the victim of ethnic violence.[36]

The victims thus became the oppressors. A wit stated that NATO's action was the disease for which it claimed to be the cure. And despite the chaos, loss of life, and the smashing of the Serbian economy by high-flying planes, the West still opposes Kosovar independence, which was the initial reason Serbia attempted to break the revolt.

America is hardly the paragon of virtue to argue against ethnic cleansings or the right of regions to secede from the mother country. The United States was created by a combination of murdering and expelling the Native American population, perhaps the greatest example in history of ethnic cleansing. The Civil War, one of the bloodiest conflicts ever, was fought by the North to prevent the southern states from seceding, which is exactly what Serbia tried to do in its Croatian and Bosnian parts, and then Kosovo. As late as the twentieth century Theodore Roosevelt fomented a revolt in the southern isthmus of Colombia, separating the area from the mother country. Now called Panama, this artificial state was created solely to build the Panama Canal.

Ethnic convulsions everywhere on the globe are known to all. There is constant tribal warfare throughout Africa, including machete beheading of hundreds of thousands of women and children. The death toll in the Congo's two-year war, from 1998 to 2000, was estimated at 2.3 million; earlier in Rwanda, tribal violence led to eight hundred thousand killings. No one outside those countries lifted a finger. In Asia, India occupied the provinces Kashmir and Jammu in the split with Pakistan despite the overwhelming Muslim population of the territories. Three wars resulted.

China swallowed up an entire country of different ethnic background, Tibet, and no effective action was taken after the initial screams of anguish from the West. Indonesia had put down the freedom fighters of East Timor, a small state annexed by that country after being freed from Portuguese rule, until an overwhelming vote for independence by its citizens in August 1999 led to the sacking of Dili, the capital, with a quarter of the entire country's population fleeing from Indonesian army hoodlums. Then Clinton showed interest, suggesting in this case an international force from the Asian region rather than sending American troops. "We are not the world's policemen," said Secretary of Defense William Cohen, a refreshing statement but wholly at odds with our behavior in Kosovo—or indeed in Somalia and in Bosnia.

The best proof of American two-faced dealings under the Clinton administration involves the long-standing desire of the Kurds for self determination. The Kurds are not a small group like the Kosovars or Timorans; there are between 12 and 15 million in Turkey and an equal number scattered through Iran, Iraq, and Syria. The Kurds, an ethnically distinct people from the Turks and Arabs, are murdered on one side by the Turks and on the other by the Iraqi Arabs. Kurdistan as a geographic fact in history has far more validity than Kosovo or East Timor.

Between 1987 and 1996 Turkish security forces cleared out at least twenty-five thousand Kurdish villages, displacing up to 2 million people.[37] Some thirty thousand Kurds have been killed by the Turks alone in the last two decades.

What has been the American reaction to this brutal ethnic cleansing? The United States, in gratitude to Turkey, which lets

★

American pilots fly missions over Iraq from a NATO base in Incirlik, aided the Turkish security forces in entrapping the Kurdish nationalist leader Abdullah Ocalan who, on information reportedly received through the CIA, was captured by Turkish commandos in Nairobi and has been condemned to death in Istanbul. By this time, Ocalan had already modified his demands from freedom to political representation but neither Turks nor the Americans responded.

One answer to such criticisms of American policy has been that Asian and African problems are not those of Europe, which at best is a statement tainted with racism. However, Europe, too, has its own ethnic and geographic tensions and internal wars. Prime Minister Tony Blair's vow to send ground troops to Kosovo sounded a bit hollow (putting aside Britain's disgusting history in Ireland) when one remembers that England seized Gibraltar as war bounty in 1704 and has refused all Spanish appeals to get back its territory. Spain backed NATO in its attack against Serbia while at the same time the Spanish government continues to crush the Basque separatist movement in its own country[38] and clings to Ceuta and Melilla, enclaves in Morocco. And if Kosovo is a European problem, why shouldn't Europeans, not Americans, solve it?

A point not made by President Clinton is that Kosovo was a useful testing ground for the stealth bomber and new technological equipment, all of which, one may add, failed miserably. It gave the U.S. Air Force a marvelous opportunity to see whether a "brush war" against a weak foe could be won by air without American ground troops. And this undeclared war also gave the U.S. legislative branch, backed by requests for billions of extra dollars from the Pentagon, the opportunity to vote more and more money for the war machine and to defer closing obsolete military bases in the bailiwicks of various senators.[39] But war money has not solved the ethnic tension in Kosovo, nor will international troops. The "success" has merely slipped a loose lid over the cauldron boiling below. President Clinton promised that our troops would be stationed there for a short period. They are still there, and probably will be there a long time. Before his election, our present president opted for their quick removal; he, too, now has changed his tune.

Perhaps the neatest summary has been made by Col. David Hackworth, U.S. Army (Ret.), and the most decorated living American soldier:

> Not using the military solution would have taken wisdom, statesmanship and patience. Traits never easily found among world leaders during the twentieth century, when over 160 million human beings have been killed in conflicts because shooting is so much more profitable for the weapon-makers than talking.[40]

As apparent from these various facets of his presidency, Clinton is not one person but rather a mosaic of persons, matching Richard Nixon in complexity. Former governor of Tennessee Lamar Alexander said of Clinton that he got up on both sides of the bed every morning. One quip was that he thought like an encyclopedia without an index. Another was that his lines of authority looked like a plate of spaghetti. From those who knew him well and have written books, we see wildly different portraits. Robert E. Levin regarded him as a saint. For Paul Greenberg he was a complete hypocrite, a view largely shared by Roger Morris. Robert Reich, whose friendship with Clinton went back to Oxford days, struggled to find the same person as president whom he knew as a young man. The struggle was too much and Reich retreated to academia, where no Greenspans defile the pure air. To George Stephanopoulos the president was intelligent, compassionate, public-spirited but self-destructive, lacking the grandeur of a tragic hero because of his capacity for denial.

But the Bill Clinton in presidential office was not that different in character from the Bill Clinton as governor of Arkansas. On the eve of his first election in 1992, the *Arkansas Democrat-Gazette* published an editorial, "Not for Bill Clinton."[41] This newspaper had followed his entire politial career as governor. Some of the remarks are prescient:

Finally and sadly, there is the unavoidable subject of character in a presidential candidate . . . it is not the duplicitousness in his politics that concerns so much as the political ease, the almost habitual, casual, articulate way he bobs and weaves. He has mastered the act of equivocation. . . . It is not the compromises he has made that trouble so much as the unavoidable suspicion that he has no great principles to compromise.

Our few great presidents stood for something whether one agrees or disagrees with their stands. President Clinton seemed like quicksand.

To be fair, politics is the art of the possible, and with a united Republican Party in control of the legislative branch most of the time, a conservative Supreme Court, and a divided Democratic Party (Clinton couldn't even depend on his two Democratic senators from Arkansas), the "possible" was very limited. The result was an administration not only centrist, his desire,[42] but one remarkably similar to traditional Republican standards in economic and military matters. On social issues, where the president felt through polls that the American people, ahead of Congress, approved a course of action— be it race relations, gun control, student loans, environmental issues, or whatever—Clinton did attempt to fight. But always all was subordinate to the main goal: popularity and reelection,[43] for the aphrodisiac of power is more potent than Viagra.

Many followed this centrist with a liberal rhetoric without regard to where he was going—namely, farther and farther from the ideals expressed in the New Deal of Franklin D. Roosevelt. In a historic sense, perhaps what Clinton will be remembered for—aside from the Lewinsky comedy—is that through court nominations he attempted to shift the judicial system back toward the center, which is to say, interpreting the Constitution more flexibly rather than from the rigid stance adopted by the Reagan appointments.

Like everything else in the high-flying acrobatics of the Clinton administration, it is difficult but still appropriate to put matters in perspective regarding the acts of his last year in office. The deluge of personal gifts—worth by the president's yardstick over $190,000, which included gifts promised in earlier years but not accepted before—is hardly a novelty. All presidents have accepted gifts; indeed President Eisenhower was politely reprimanded by the New York City Bar Association for accepting $300,000 worth of gifts while in office, which, when adjusted for inflation, amounts to many times the dollar value of those taken by the Clintons.

Related is the rumpus raised by Hillary Clinton, before she became a senator, receiving an advance of about $8 million for a book of memoirs.* Yet no one raised a fuss when John F. Welch Jr., chairman of General Electric, received $7.1 million for the North American rights to his story, which will without doubt exceed the amount gained by Mrs. Clinton after he sells the rights in foreign markets. It is also useful to point out that Mrs. Clinton has published three books already and given all the royalties received to charity.

President Clinton's pardon of Marc Rich, an infamous financier, is another act that has to be seen in the light of historical perspective, disgusting as it was. The fact that there is an indissoluble link between the pardon and Rich's former wife's gifts of some $1 million to the Democratic presidential campaign, as well as a $450,000 pledge to the proposed Clinton library, is without question. The pardon was engineered by Jack Quinn, recent chief of staff to Al Gore and Clinton's former White House counsel, obviously no coincidence. Shortly after the Rich pardon, it was disclosed that two felons were also pardoned by Clinton in his last days due to the intervention of his wife's brother, Hugh Rodham. As usual in such pardons, Clinton denied knowledge of any payments for services rendered.

Despite these revolting and apparently quid pro quo deals, President Clinton was following a common practice of presidents, most of whose pardons were never investigated with such microscopic zeal. We do know, for an example, that the elder President Bush pardoned Armand Hammer, a comrade in the oil business who was so close to the Soviets, not only in oil deals but also transferral of art, that he was accused of

---

*Her husband, the former president, has upped the ante, having received a contract in mid-2001 for $10 million.

being a Communist agent. To show the intimacy on these high levels, Armand Hammer also did business with Al Gore's father. In fact, President Reagan awarded almost the same number of pardons as Clinton. And the older Bush also pardoned six Iran-contra figures who had knowingly broken the law, including former Defense Secretary Caspar Weinberger. The most famous case is President Ford's pardon of Nixon, which cost him the subsequent election. From a humane point of view the Marc Rich imbroglio cannot be compared to Ford's pardon of Nixon, who not only organized a house burglary (a criminal act itself) but extended American bombings to Laos and Cambodia during the Vietnam War, killing thousands of innocent women and children.

In many such acts it is obvious that President Clinton lacks a normal moral sense. What is more pertinent is the ultimate question of how anyone in our system of elections can retain a moral sense. All presidents—excepting those rare cases in crisis times, as with Washington and Lincoln—have to sign a Faustian bargain to sell their souls, in theological terms, in order to suck to the top.

In the long eye of history, President Clinton's last year in office will be judged with greater justice and appreciation. With Theodore Roosevelt he may be considered one of the greatest champions of the American environment, to which perhaps more credit belongs to his mentor, Al Gore. These may be briefly summarized. Clinton extended by executive order protection against exploitation, including logging, to nearly a third of the national forest land, a move covering more than 58 million acres in thirty-nine states. He likewise sealed off the Arctic National Wildlife Refuge from oil drilling, which would, of course, involve huge pipelines, road building, and waste disposal of chemicals, contaminating the environment. President Bush has attempted to overturn these actions.

Within the contiguous national territory Clinton imposed rules to stop industry from disposing of poisonous runoff into our rivers, lakes, and bays. He thus thwarted a trick used routinely in Congress where, undoubtedly influenced by industry contributions, certain congressmen add riders to spending bills in order to bypass existing

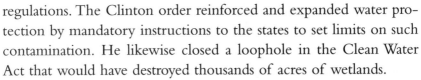

regulations. The Clinton order reinforced and expanded water protection by mandatory instructions to the states to set limits on such
contamination. He likewise closed a loophole in the Clean Water
Act that would have destroyed thousands of acres of wetlands.

In a very important executive order Clinton imposed regulations
to reduce air pollution caused by diesel fuel exhaust by more than
90 percent, preventing an estimated eighty-three hundred premature
deaths and tens of thousands of cases of bronchitis each year. To
offset the cost to oil producers and refiners, Clinton spaced these
regulations to take place over six years so that the expense could be
amortized. In this particular case the move was so salutory that first
the new Bush administration decided not to oppose it; and then,
under pressure from industry contributions, Bush killed the measure.

In sum, Clinton will be recorded in American history as among
the greatest presidents active in atempting to save the environment
from pollution and destruction.

There were other executive orders and vetoes of lasting importance. In November 1999 Clinton put into effect new regulations
protecting the privacy of patients' medical records, preventing their
misuse and peddling to private sources for profit in disbursement of
drugs and other treatments. The health-care industry has lobbied the
Bush administration to delay or change these rules, claiming they
would impose unfair burdens. But common sense dictates that a
patient's medical problems should not be used for private gain on the
part of doctors or hospitals.

In this same period President Clinton also vetoed a bill renewing
and enlarging the authority of the nation's intelligence agencies. The
bill contained a provision that would have made it a crime for a government official to disclose any classified information. This in effect
made government whistle-blowing a criminal act. Although without
question there is legitimate concern over leakage of important security matters, the practical fact is that federal agencies—not only the
CIA, the Pentagon, and the National Security Council but thoughout
government—routinely stamp as "secret" documents that are publicly

reported, discussed, and published. Furthermore, the vetoed bill would not only have applied to present government employees but as well to any and all former employees or private individuals with security clearance. Clinton did not find offensive the legitimacy of the bill's intent, but rather objected to its wide dragnet. Indeed, Clinton concluded in his veto message that he would not have objected if the bill were more carefully worded and not so overbroad.*

In September 2000 President Clinton also vetoed a Republican bill to repeal the federal estate tax because, as analyzed, it was mainly designed to benefit only the wealthiest 2 percent of Americans—mainly those whose campaign contributions put Bush into office. In fact, almost all the energies of President George W. Bush in his first few months in office were directed at undermining or scrapping the executive orders and vetoes of Clinton's last presidential year. On January 20, 2001, the day President Bush was sworn in, Andrew Card, the new White House chief of staff, ordered all executive departments to postpone for sixty days the dates of a wide range of regulations announced by President Clinton in this final year; the obvious purpose of this postponement was to devise strategies for weakening or killing the environmental protection regulations and building support to drill for oil in the Arctic as well as present mining and timber cutting in the western federal lands. Fourteen of Bush's top twenty-five financial patrons are in the oil and energy business—the president, the vice president, and the secretary of commerce all are from an oil background.

As reprehensible as the Clinton administration's practices of selling overnight stays in the Lincoln Bedroom and soliciting campaign funds from within the White House were—"It's now the Cheney Bedroom," commented House Democratic Leader Richard A. Gephardt, after similar disclosures surfaced about the Republican vice president—these are lesser abuses compared with the above-mentioned affirmative actions or stacked against the activities of

---

*In August 2001 the Republicans in Congress brought forward this bill again; a new, insidious version of the 1798 Alien and Sedition Acts.

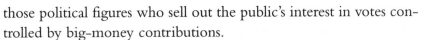

those political figures who sell out the public's interest in votes controlled by big-money contributions.

To sum up, the Clintons (she more than he) were outstanding products of a new generation, many formed by the turbulence of the 1960s, which traditionalists hate. With rising prosperity during the Clinton years, they peculiarly hated the Clintons even more because there seemed to be some devilish scheme at work to destroy the old hallowed values. The country's economic strength, which made the president popular,[44] only reinforced their zeal to destroy him by attacking his lax morals. Both Clintons, who symbolize civil and women's rights, sexual tolerance, and the right to abortion, are thus seen by them not as other Americans with divergent beliefs but rather as some kind of satanic force working to destroy the country. Only time, and new generations, will mute this view.

In 1996 Clinton ran successfully against Bob Dole, U.S. Senate Majority Leader and a congressman for thirty-six years. In his campaign, Dole tried to transform the issues from economic to ethical, stating that the American people had a sharp choice between his moral standards and those of the incumbent. Let us accept his statement and look at the facts.

Senator Dole, knowing where power resided in Washington, was made Senate Financial Committee Chairman in 1981, a position he only relinquished (though staying on as a committee member) when elevated to majority leader. He became an expert on the minutiae of the Internal Revenue Code because he realized that the tax code was so large and diffuse that one could put in multimillion-dollar tax giveaways without notice. A saying of this sardonic man was, "Who's gonna look at Section 2034, Section B, subsection C of the code?"[45] He was the supreme master at creating legislation to aid individuals and companies who then repaid him by aid in electoral campaigns and sometimes personally as well. Let us give several examples.

Archer Daniels Midland Company (ADM) produces about 70 percent of the nation's ethanol, a corn-distilled alcohol that is mixed with gasoline to create a fuel called gasohol. The Environmental Protection Agency has designated this product as a serious air pollutant. Massive tax credits for ADM amount in effect to a sixty-cent-per gallon federal subsidy for this company. The tax credits were scheduled to expire in 1992, but Dole succeeded in extending them indefinitely. Since 1978, the former senator sponsored more than fifty bills to protect gasohol, which the Treasury Department estimates as having cost the government the incredible sum of $5.9 billion in tax revenues.

Between 1980 and 1990 alone, ADM and the family of the company chairman, Dwayne Andreas,[46] contributed more than $80,000 to Dole campaigns. The ADM Foundation also gave $185,000 to the Dole Foundation, and ADM jets flew Dole around the country for free. Andreas further rewarded Dole in 1982 by selling him at a great discount a three-room apartment at the swank Sea View Hotel in Bel Harbour, Florida, the transaction being in the name of his wife, Elizabeth. The Doles, like the Lyndon Johnsons before them, have entangled financial affairs.

In 1981 Bob Dole opposed granting retroactive tax breaks to Chicago commodity dealers who used accounting techniques to indefinitely roll over their gains from trading. Then in 1984, when the traders gave Dole campaign contributions, he reversed his position and supported the tax breaks, helping pass a new tax bill that enabled them to continue avoiding taxes.

Ernest and Julio Gallo presided over the Gallo wine-making empire in Modesto, California, which bottles one-quarter of all the wine produced in the United States. In 1985 the two brothers, whose estimated combined net worth was about $600 million, had a problem. In their seventies, they wanted to avoid massive generation-skipping taxes in order to benefit their numerous grandchildren.

They went to Bob Dole, who immediately crafted a special exception, derisively dubbed the "Gallo Amendment" because it allowed the brothers to pass an estimated $80 million to their grandchildren without paying approximately one-third of that sum in taxes. The *Wall Street Journal* of October 31, 1985, called this one of the most made-to-order laws Congress ever passed.

Between 1985 and 1987 the Gallo clan gave $97,000 to Dole for his electoral campaigns and his specially forged "Campaign America" PAC.

Senator Dole helped write into the 1986 Internal Revenue Code a tax exemption applying to one specific company, the Ruan Trucking Company. The exemption—previously knocked out by the House but then creeping back into law by being craftily inserted in another obscure bill—saved Ruan taxes of about $8.5 million. John Ruan, the company's chairman, personally and through his company contributed $105,462 to Dole's political career through 1996, when the senator retired.

Elizabeth Dole, Bob's wife, put the family investments in a blind trust so that the Doles at least in theory did not know what happened with the money and could not be implicated. The trust assets doubled by 1987 to more than $2.3 million. In part this was due to real estate investments.

During an investigation it was disclosed that a former Dole aide had bought an interest in one of the properties from the trust. Ten months later his company was awarded a $30-million federal contract, with the help of Dole. The senator claimed that his backing was solely because the company was minority controlled. Further probing revealed that the business in question was a front for a white man who had been Dole's national financial director for one of his presidential campaigns and received a $54,000 "stipend" from the company when it received the $30-million contract, as well as $7,000 a month from another army contract given to a Kansas friend of Dole.★

In 1987 and early 1988, during Dole's losing bid for the Republican nomination, the Federal Election Committee (FEC), which establishes campaign financing rules, investigated him. The result

---

★Amusingly, these property disclosures came from George Bush (dredged up by Lee Atwater, Bush's political hatchet man) when running in the primaries against Dole in his successful campaign for president after Reagan's second term. Partly as a result, Bush gained in the polls against his most formidable GOP adversary.

established that the senator's run engaged in wholesale violations of the law. This led to a monetary fine of $100,000, more than any fine previously imposed. In addition, the FEC insisted that the Dole campaign committee refund all excessive and prohibited contributions, a total of $104,563. Dole also admitted breaking the federal spending limits by more than $600,000. In a "conciliation" agreement Dole conceded that his campaign had "knowingly accepted" these illegal contributions.[47]

Bob Dole, who started life as the son of a man keeping a produce and dairy product store in Russell, Kansas—whose peak population was 6,483 residents in 1950—is now, with his wife Elizabeth, a multimillionaire. Mrs. Dole was appointed to the Reagan cabinet as secretary of transportation and both she and her husband stand to collect federal pensions worth an estimated $4 million.

It is told that one night the famous philosopher and wit Voltaire and some travelling companions lodged at a wayside inn. In the isolated surroundings after supper they agreed to tell robber stories. When Voltaire's turn came he said, "Once there was a Farmer-General of the Revenues." He said nothing more, and they asked him to continue. "That," Voltaire said, "is the story."

As stated, the candidate Dole said the American people had a sharp choice between his moral standards and those of President Clinton in the 1996 election. The above examples give an indication of his moral character. Take your choice.

THE SPACE BELOW IS DEVOTED TO A PORTRAIT OF
PRESIDENT george w. bush
OF THE UNITED STATES OF AMERICA

# CHAPTER TEN

★

# GEORGE WALKER BUSH
# (2001–)

★

*"Gild the farthing if you will, yet it is a farthing still."*
Eighteenth-century English proverb

*"The common European perception is of a shallow, arrogant, gun-loving, abortion-hating, Christian fundamentalist Texan buffoon."*
A senior Bush administration official, commenting
on the president's first major overseas trip,
*New York Times,* June 6, 2001, p. 1

## BUSHISMS

"More and more of our imports come from overseas."

"One hundred percent of the people will get the death tax."

"We ought to raise the age at which juveniles can have a gun."

"Babies out of wedlock is a very difficult chore for mom and baby alike."

"Rarely is the question asked: Is our children learning?"

"Expectations rise above that which is expected."

"I know how hard it is to put food on your family."

"We ought to make the pie higher."

"Laura and I really don't realize how bright our children is until we get an objective analysis."

★   ★   ★

George Walker Bush, son of former President George Herbert Walker Bush, prefers to be called George W. Bush to escape the cloud of cloning that immediately comes to mind. He has further retreated to "Dubya," in Texan jargon standing for "W," his middle initial, to remove himself even more from the suspicion of a rare case of mitosis.

This superpatriotic Texan is actually a pure example in background and money of the Eastern Establishment. His father's ancestry in New England has already been discussed. On his mother's side he is likewise a direct descendant of President Franklin Pierce, also a New Englander. His standard political campaign talk while running for office was that he attended San Jacinto High School in Midland, Texas. The truth is that he was born in New Haven, Connecticut, went to San Jacinto for only one year, and, after a brief period of schooling in Houston, followed his father's footsteps to Phillips Academy, an exclusive prep school in Andover, Massachusetts, and then to Yale University in Connecticut, finishing his education at Harvard Business School in Massachusetts. Thus, the pure Texan.

The early years of George W. Bush are laced with fog. At Yale, accepted for family background rather than his mediocre marks (his grandfather sat on Yale's board of trustees), he was arrested twice for pranks before graduating in 1968.[1] Thereafter, he drifted for several years before returning east to attend Harvard, from which he graduated in 1975 at age thirty. The records show he had seven apartments, many girlfriends, and drank heavily. Apparently referring to rumors that he used drugs in this period, Bush excused himself with the statement that when young he was irresponsible. Up to the age of forty he was not only considered irresponsible but somewhat of a lost soul, though a happy-go-lucky one.

In a well-publicized Pilgrim's Progress, following a riotous drunken night after which it is claimed that his wife, Laura, threatened divorce, George W. Bush was "saved" in 1985 and became a born-again Christian, oozing such piety that he said only Christians could enter heaven. Rev. Billy Graham became his spiritual guru on things theological and presumably on things political as well—the same Billy Graham who stated to tumultuous cheers on Inauguration Day of 1969 that "In Thy Sovereignty Thou has permitted Richard Nixon to lead us at this momentous hour of our history." We now know where that took us. So far President Bush has not succeeded, as is his wish, in pushing through a constitutional amendment outlawing abortion, but as Texas governor he declared a state holiday, June 10, called Jesus Day.

The career of George W. Bush can be conveniently divided into two periods. The first is making money. The second is politics. The two are kissing cousins.

By conservative estimates President Bush is worth at least $20 million and is the richest president since Lyndon Johnson, whose financial hanky-panky has already been noted. The story of how he made his money is likewise well recorded. It came about exclusively through family connections.

Back in Texas, two years after graduating from Harvard Business School, the young man launched his own oil-drilling company called Arbusto Energy. His uncle Jonathan Bush, a Wall Street financier, put together a group, most of whom were friends of young Bush's father, that invested about $3 million.[2] The company, later renamed Bush Exploration Oil Company, did not do well and Bush had to be rescued. The generous benefactor was Philip Uzielli, a buddy of James Baker III, who was then serving as chief of staff in the Reagan White House while the elder Bush was vice president and being primed to run for president; Baker later became secretary of state in the elder Bush's cabinet. Uzielli paid $1 million for 10 percent of Bush Exploration when the entire enterprise was valued at $382,376—which, of course, made no sense from a business point of view.

In 1984 the company sank further and George W. Bush merged with Spectrum 7 Energy Corp., co-owned by other family friends.

★

Two years later, with oil prices still plunging, Spectrum 7 was on the verge of bankruptcy but Bush was saved again when Spectrum was acquired by Harken Energy Corp., with his shares being valued at over $500,000 and the receipt of a variable consulting fee that paid him up to $120,000 a year. Paul Rea, former president of Spectrum 7, knew very well why this seemingly unwise investment was made, for the Harken directors "believed having George's name there would be a big help to them."[3] Not so coincidentally, "George's name" was also the name of the president of the United States.

It was shortly thereafter that Bush learned through a former partner at Spectrum 7 that the Texas Rangers baseball team was for sale. The team was purchased for $86 million[4] in 1989, with Bush investing $606,000, almost all borrowed from a bank of which he had formerly been a director. The next year he cashed in his shares in Harken for $848,560, paying off this loan. Two months later Harken collapsed.

The matter was brought to the attention of the Securities and Exchange Commission (SEC), since Bush was a member of Harken's audit committee and, contrary to SEC rules on insider trading, he had not notified the government agency of his stock sale. The SEC concluded, however, that the action was not illegal. The SEC chairman at the time was an ardent loyalist of the elder Bush and the agency's general counsel was the same Texas attorney who handled the Texas Rangers purchase for young Bush and his partners in 1989.

The baseball team was sold by its syndicate for $250 million in 1998, at which time Bush was governor of Texas. The background of this sale is illuminating. When the syndicate had bought the Rangers almost a decade before, the ballpark was small, with limited parking space. The group of investors, all wealthy and well-connected, convinced the mayor and politicians of Arlington, where the baseball field was to be located, to subsidize the building of a much larger stadium with adequate parking by paying more than $135 million of taxpayers' money toward the $191 million total cost. They then got the government to condemn, through eminent domain, the property of private owners in order to build the new stadium.

The partnership that bought the Rangers did not even pay cash for its part of the stadium cost but contributed its share by a ticket surcharge. Even more outrageous, the franchise allowed the Rangers to take title to the $191 million stadium and 270 acres of surrounding land after the rental payments to the city of Arlington reached the ridiculously low sum of $60 million.[5]

Bush's piece of the sale netted him $14.9 million.[6] Most of this tremendous profit went into government bonds, though he also bought 1,583 acres in Crawford, Texas, for almost $2 million and built a palatial ranch, with a man-made lake stocked with fish, as a vacation house. In 1998, the year of the sale of the Texas Rangers, Governor Bush and his wife, Laura, reported an income of $18,405,524, the larger part from the sale. In 1999 their income fell to the deplorable level of $1,610,400; in 2000, to 894,880, on which they paid only 26.9 percent in taxes, presumably because of the tax-free bonds.[7]

During the presidential campaign of the younger Bush, little publicity was given to his Vietnam War record, which, however, has some intriguing aspects. It is filled with ambiguities and, considering the flap over Bill Clinton's evasion, is rather remarkable in that it did not cripple his political ambitions. The story of how George W. Bush got into the Texas Air National Guard, which amounted in practice to escape from active service overseas, is relevant. It is the son's only serious deviation from his father's route to power, Bush the elder having been a true war hero.

At the height of the Vietnam War there was a waiting list of some one hundred thousand men trying to get into the Texas guard, for obvious reasons. These included 150 pilot applications, some of whom had to wait eighteen months to be considered for flight school. Bush jumped over the waiting list and was assigned one of the last two pilot slots, after scoring the numerical minimum on the qualifying test. The story of how this happened has since been revealed.

In 1968 a close family friend of the Bushes got in touch with Ben Barnes, then the Speaker of the Texas House, informing him of the need to get young Bush into the guard. This, he said, was done at the request of the elder Bush, at that time a Texas congressman. Barnes called the general in charge of the Texas Air National Guard and recommended Bush, who was immediately accepted. Once in, even his attendance at guard duty is filled with holes: there seem to be several months where no records or even verbal testimony indicate he did his minimum service.[8] When Bush ran for Congress he claimed active duty in Vietnam. Pushed for an explanation, his press secretary said that time spent at flight school plus two weeks each year with the National Guard was the same as active duty.

A civil suit[9] many years later, and an interview with a former Texas officeholder, detailed the true events. There was an undercover chain that moved sons of privilege from Selective Service offices into the safe haven of the Texas guard units. The unit that accepted Bush also included the son of Lloyd Bentsen, the son of the former Texas governor John Connally, and a raft of other rich men's progeny. In an amusing twist, Ben Barnes, later elected Texas lieutenant governor after serving as House Speaker, cited legal precedents from Richard Nixon to argue executive privilege, giving him immunity from having to testify about these dealings.[10]

It should be noted that this preferential treatment in Texas was common elsewhere as well. The executives and legislators screeching war wanted other men's sons killed, not their own. Barry Goldwater's son did "alternate service" in the U.S. House of Representatives, safely anchored in Washington, D.C. Approximately 234 sons of senators and congressmen came of age after the United States got involved in Vietnam. More than half—118—received deferments. Only twenty-eight went overseas and of that group only nineteen "saw combat"—the word "combat" not defined—while none were killed and only one was wounded. Six senators' sons flunked their physicals and were rejected, also not defined—records in certain matters can be curiously obscure or misplaced. And not one person serving on the House Armed Services Committee had a son or grandson who went to Vietnam.[11]

It might be revealing to compare this verbal patriotism of our political leaders during Vietnam with the families of the signers of the Declaration of Independence during the American Revolution. Twelve of their homes were ransacked and burned. Two of their sons were killed while serving in the Revolutionary Army. Another had two sons captured. In total, nine of the fifty-six fought and died from wounds or hardships during the Revolution. But George W. Bush and Barry Goldwater Jr. watched and applauded while others with less influence and money died.[12]

Back in Midland at age thirty, the younger Bush married Laura Welch, a librarian whose hometown was Midland, and also filed as a Republican candidate for Congress. Here he replicated his father's early lust for power, as well as his failure. Given his happy-go-lucky life style and constant partying, his friends were startled at his political ambitions. He explained, "They were a little confused why I was doing this, but at that time Jimmy Carter was president and he was trying to control natural gas prices, and I felt the United States was headed toward European-style socialism."[13] His claim that Jimmy Carter was leading the country toward socialism gives one the flavor of Bush's political opinions in this early period.

Bush won the Republican primary but lost the election to a Democrat, Kent Hance, whose similarity to Bush can be seen by the fact that soon afterward Hance renounced his party and turned Republican. Bush at this date was still burdened by his New England background and education and Hance portrayed him as an elite Yankee carpetbagger. Pious churchgoers were also aroused against Bush by an ad in which he offered free beer at a political rally. Though he raised more than twice the money of his opponent in the campaign, the vote went against him 53 to 47 percent. However, he learned two important lessons from this failure. The first was to emphasize his local background, even to the point of exaggerating the droll Texan accent. The second was never again to be out-Christianed.

The defeat only increased Bush's political ambition, which a Freudian psychologist might find not difficult to analyze. He spent the next years as the front man for the Texas Rangers, building his presence and currying favor with the rich and powerful during a period in which the Lone Star state, out of resentment over the drive for black voting equality, was turning Republican. He was the obvious choice of the political right both because of his famous name and personal convictions, being antigay, antiabortion, pro-guns, Clinton-loathing, and in favor of school vouchers whereby the taxpayers would finance education at parochial schools—which, in Texas, meant fundamentalist Protestant schools.

After his initial slip, the political stars rose for George W. Bush. In his 1994 campaign for Texas governor against incumbent Ann Richards, a popular Democrat, everything fell into place. Certainly the defeat of Richards was not due to Bush's strong personal candidacy. Actually, he was artfully kept out of sight as much as possible. It was the avalanche of money from vested interests, not merely for political favors, patronage, or favorable legislation, but looking ahead to the greater prize of a possible presidency. The name Bush was magic in Texas; another native son—or one so considered—would be a strong Republican presidential candidate if he could win the state governership.

The year 1994 ushered in the great Republican revenge, when the hatred for Bill Clinton—the draft dodger who raised taxes, had close black friends, supported gay rights, favored reproductive choice, disliked the spread of guns, and had a bumptious wife—swelled into an avalanche that wiped out the Democratic legislative majorities in most of the country. It was the Newt Gingrich triumph, and its groundswell was especially strong in Texas. To many Texans Ann Richards, who was pro-choice in the matter of abortion, seemed a state Clinton type and money poured in to defeat her. Richards's self-autopsy after defeat is probably a good summary: ". . . we underestimated the Christian right, which probably reached its zenith that year. We underestimated the NRA [National Rifle

Association] and its money. That cost me the male union vote, the good ol' boy vote. I lost over guns. . . . He is governor today because of guns."[14] The latter reference is to her refusal to sign legislation allowing all residents of Texas—where it has been estimated that there are five times as many guns as citizens—to carry concealed weapons.

The Democratic Party, now a minority in most of the southern states, has been particularly undermined in Texas. Bush is by all reports a difficult person to dislike: a "good ol' boy" who tells jokes, slaps people on the back, and is cheerful and verbally compassionate. The years 1994 to 1998,when he ran for reelection, were prosperous and jobs grew in Texas as elsewhere. Just as Bill Clinton was given credit for the national prosperity, so Bush was credited in his home state. And the money behind him swelled even more. In 1998 he received $20 million in campaign donations; the Democratic candidate received only $3.5 million. The result was a great victory, over 60 percent of the vote, sending a nationwide message to the Republican Party that with the detested Bill Clinton forbidden to run again after two terms in office, George W. Bush should be their favorite son in November of 2000.

It is useful to review the actions of George W. Bush during his two terms as governor of Texas. They may be briefly summarized under the categories of criminal justice, health care and welfare, and education.

Perhaps the most serious charge to be made against Bush as a two-time governor is the operation of the abominable Texas justice system. Much of it was in place before his election, but he did nothing to improve the system and by several acts actually made it worse.

Texas has the largest state prison system in the country. Counting those in the various jails and on parole, there were at the end of 1999 some 545,000 persons in the prison system, almost double the national average. Since 1976, Texas has executed more than one-third of all prisoners put to death in the entire nation. Bush himself had signed one hundred death warrants by autumn of 1999, more than any previous governor.

George W. Bush, who has admitted to "youthful indiscretions" and avoided, mindful of a boomerang, attacking Al Gore during the presidential campaign for his use of marijuana, has left intact a system where 21 percent of Texas prisoners are in jail on drug-related charges, many merely for possession of a marijuana cigarette. In an exaggerated case that shows the system at work, a woman was sentenced to ninety-nine years in prison for possessing one-tenth of a gram of cocaine.

What was the governor's reaction to this draconic system? In 1997 he signed a bill making the drug laws even harsher. The old law required a judge to give probation for possession of less than a gram of cocaine; his new law gave judges the arbitrary right to sentence such offenders to jail. In 1999 Bush vetoed a bill that would have made it mandatory for each county to appoint attorneys for poor defendants. Now it is left up to the judge to decide in the matter. And those lawyers appointed are so indifferent in many cases that it is the same as no representation. In one well-documented case the lawyer appointed by the judge was so bored he slept through the trial, which resulted in his client receiving a death sentence.[15]

Welfare reform was high on Bush's agenda when running for governor. The results were apparent after his terms in office. According to a September 1999 Census Bureau study, Texas had the highest rate of people with no health insurance in the entire United States, some 25 percent. In another study done in October 1999, the health-care action group Families USA found that the number of Texas children enrolled in Medicaid declined by 14 percent between 1996 and 1999, the largest decline in the twelve states studied. In fact, Governor Bush fought for a plan that would have excluded two hundred thousand of more than four hundred thousand children eligible for the federal Children's Health Insurance Plan, but reluctantly signed the bill when Texas legislators insisted on a more expensive plan.[16] And this is only part of the picture.

"Is the air cleaner since I became governor? And the answer is yes," George W. Bush stated in May of 1999.[17] This is patently false.

★

According to the trinational North American Commission on Environmental Cooperation, a division of NAFTA, Texas pollutes the air more than any other state or Canadian province, a statement that covers both air and water pollution. And according to the Environmental Defense Fund, Texas is also number one in overall toxic releases, carcinogens in the air, and cancer risk.

Of course all this is not due to Bush, but during his six years in office the problems grew worse. Since 1988, Boston Harbor, the air in Los Angeles, and the water in New York's Hudson River have gotten better—all under Republican governors. In 1998 and 1999 Houston had the highest single recorded ozone levels of any U.S. city. And between 1993 and 1998 fifty-six of the ninety-six cities categorized as having filthy air were removed from the list—but not one of these cities was in Texas.

This is no accident, and it is not merely a hangover from former administrators. After coming to power in 1994, Bush insisted on the resignation of all three of the Texas board members equivalent to the Environmental Protection Agency and appointed men controlled by the industries it was established to regulate—foxes guarding the chickens. He beat back every legislative effort for mandatory controls, insisting on a "voluntary" program.[18]

The Texas Gulf Coast, from the edge meeting Louisiana to Corpus Christi, contains the largest concentration of refineries and chemical plants in the United States. Cleaning up the filth belching into the air and stopping the runoff into rivers and the ocean would call for great sums of money, and it has been a lot cheaper to buy politicians through campaign contributions than to eliminate this pollution. Actually, Bush is merely the latest recipient of this legal bribery; the practice went on long before his election. But the greater the outcry to solve the problem the larger have been the sums given to block cleanup, and Bush has been very much the eager taker. The pollution companies that designed Bush's voluntary program—rather than a mandatory one that could be enforced—gave $260,648 to his 1998 gubernatorial campaign as a thank-you gift.[19]

In his two Texas elections Bush received $41 million, an all-time record there.

It used to be that Texas elections were won by ballot stuffing, a habit so common that Lyndon Johnson joked about it. It is now said that nobody there bothers to steal elections; they are paid for in advance.

An area for which one can give credit to former Governor Bush, partly due to his wife, Laura, a former librarian, is education. In the matter of public schools he did try, with an energy and interest unusual in his personality, to make a difference.

A satirist stated that Texas ranked forty-ninth out of fifty states in public education for so long that it was believed the only reason for Mississippi to be a state was to prevent Texas from being last all the time. This is starting to change, though some of the change was prior to the election of Bush. The problem at bottom has been how to fund more money for poor schools without taking money from schools where the richer children go. A related problem is that many Texans believe that schools exist mainly for their football teams, and by raising minimum standards, good athletes might be disqualified because of their poor marks. And as one of the states with the lowest tax structure, there has been bitter opposition to raising taxes no matter how laudable the purpose. The result is that, despite progress, only 50 percent of minority students in Texas progressed from grade nine to high school graduation since Bush was elected in 1994, and recent SAT scores rank Texas in the bottom four of all fifty states.[20] This is inexcusable since, unlike Mississippi, Texas has the eleventh-largest economy in the world.

After much screaming the Texas legislature passed new laws reducing class sizes and leveling school funding, measures that, in practice, meant a fairer share for schools with minority students. It should be noted that the improved test scores predated Bush's first campaign; but after becoming governor he was both helpful and instrumental in continued progress, including an unsuccessful effort to close loopholes in the tax laws in order to increase school funding. In attempting to popularize further his political appeal, Bush has emphasized a sympathy with the educational problems of the growing numbers of Mexican workers flowing through our border with that country. He has learned some Spanish; at the appropriate times and places these Spanish phrases issue forth with enlivening monotony. He rarely forgets as well to tell the proper audience that his brother Jeb, governor of Florida, is married to a Mexican woman.

It may added that Bush, being far shrewder than usually judged, pumped for school vouchers, a die-hard principle of the ardent religious right, but never intensely followed through his verbal support on the political level. In such matters hypocrisy can even be seen as a virtue. And, ironically, the Republican Party, which he now heads, is opposed to educational reforms—such as smaller class sizes and prekindergarten programs—that he favored in Texas.

When Governor Bush made the decision to run for president, the groups backing him were the same phalanx that backed him throughout his political career. They were the oil and gas interests; the right-wing extremists who consider it government "socialism" to aid the weak; those who want Christian values (as they conceive them) built into the system through school prayers, prohibition on the teaching of evolution, vouchers for religious schools paid for by the general taxpayers, and total prohibition of abortion; those favoring the uncontrolled sale of guns; those desiring tort reform (i.e., restricting lawsuits against large corporations); and the super-rich who salivate at the thought of the elimination of all death taxes on family inheritance. Though separately, each of these groups is a rather small minority of the total American people, they collectively represent a significant percentage and, most important, one that never fails to vote.

Opponents of George W. Bush define him in amusing and often crude ways. Ralph Nader, to whom Bush owes his election for siphoning off votes from Al Gore, summed up this general attitude by saying, "He's no more than a big corporation running for president disguised as a human being." But this is only a partial truth, because those supporting Bush also include many people with modest incomes who hold sharp opinions. In certain areas of the

★

country, such as the South and Southwest and the Rocky Mountain states, these people are clearly a majority. That Bush often speaks fractured English; doesn't like to read serious books; hates long, intense meetings; and is reportedly contemptuous of intellectuals, are factors that still appeal to many Americans.

Al Gore took all the New England states except New Hampshire (where he lost by only 1 percent), the entire Northeast, and all of the Midwest except Ohio and Indiana, as well as all the Pacific Coast. Bush received less than 9 percent of the black vote. It might be said tongue in cheek, therefore, that the South finally won the Civil War.

But not in votes. On the basis of "one person, one vote," Al Gore won the election by over a half million votes.

The Bush-Gore contest will go down in American history as a classic example of how politics at the highest level can be twisted for partisan reasons. Dozens of books will explore this issue and one beneficial result shall undoubtedly accrue: namely, the modernization of machine voting to eliminate future confusion and fraud.

Cutting through byzantine explanations, the presidential outcome depended on the Florida Electoral College vote. Varying irregularities were reported and the state's political machine, controlled by Governor Jeb Bush, the Republican candidate's brother—feeling that a recount would result in a Democratic victory—attempted to stop this recount while George W. Bush was a few hundred votes ahead. Then the Florida Supreme Court authorized a return to the recount, but gave a specific cutoff date. The Bush lawyers thereupon appealed to the U.S. Supreme Court, still dominated by the Ronald Reagan appointees, which issued a stop order long enough that the recount cutoff date would expire, assuring the Bush victory.

This action was so extraordinary that 554 law professors at 120 American law schools from every part of the country, and of different political beliefs, stated in a full-page publicized newspaper analysis that the five justices in the five-to-four decision of the U.S. Supreme Court "were acting as political proponents for candidate Bush, not as judges" and that "It is Not the Job of a Federal Court to Stop Votes From Being Counted," stating further and even more clearly that, "by stopping the recount in the middle, the five justices acted to suppress the facts."[21] In plain English, these nationwide legal authorities stated the election was almost surely won by Al Gore but the Supreme Court, by a political and not judicial decision, over-turned the will of the voters.★

Elections in the United States are often "stolen" on the local and even the state level, but never by the country's highest court. It will probably take decades before the stench of this legal fraud wafts away. As Justice John Paul Stevens, one of the dissenters, wrote, the Court's action "can only lend credence to the most cynical appraisal of the work of judges throughout the land."[22]

The ironies of the situation are many. Some can be reviewed. While governor of Texas, George W. Bush signed a bill authorizing ballot recounting in questionable cases, the exact opposite of the position he took in Florida. In New Mexico, when it seemed that a recount in one county might throw the election to Bush, the Republicans asked the district court to authorize a hand recount, using the same arguments that Al Gore's lawyers used in Florida. And in New York, when State Senator Roy Goodman, chairman of the Manhattan Republican Party, lost to his opponent in the initial count, the Republican governor held up the decision for six weeks to settle disputed and absentee ballots, the final result being a razor-thin Republican victory.

Perhaps the supreme irony is that a rock of Republican Party philosophy is states' rights against federal intervention. Yet when the Florida Supreme Court authorized a recount, a matter entirely within its statutory authority, the Republicans immediately dis-carded this principle and rushed to the federal Supreme Court. In a further contradiction, those same federal judges who have repeatedly

---

★A final, complete recount disclosed that if only the ballots disputed by Gore in four counties had been counted, Bush would have won; but that if all the disputed ballots statewide in Florida had been counted, Gore would have won.

★

ruled in favor of states' rights at this point then did an about-face—solely because of their personal preference for one candidate over the other.

We can now look forward to an ersatz president who, as some of these tottering federal judges retire, will appoint a new round of similar-minded judges in what might be called facetiously a pro tem U.S. Scalieme Court, dominated by Justice Antonin Scalia, who without doubt has one of the finest legal minds of the seventeenth century.★

To taste the flavor of the "compassionate" president George W. Bush, it is helpful to look at the record of Dick Cheney, the man he chose to be his vice president; or, to be more precise, the man preferred by Daddy and to whom Bush immediately agreed.[23]

Dick Cheney, White House chief of staff under President Ford and a U.S. Congressman from Wyoming for ten years, has had a record so conservative that Newt Gingrich admitted it to be more so than his own. Cheney was consistent in his voting: consistently against everything that even Republican diehards accepted. The record is so bleak that it may be listed nay and aye.

*Nay:* A seven-day waiting period to buy handguns in order to check the purchaser's background; a ban on "cop-killer" bullets that even the NRA supported; a ban on plastic guns that couldn't be detected by airport security, also supported by the NRA; funding subsidized school lunches for poor children; funding student loans; funding the Older Americans Act, which offered nutrition to the elderly poor; grants to states to fund insurance for the unemployed; funding the Safe Drinking Water Bill, being one of only twenty-one House members to oppose; funding the Clean Water Act, one of only eight House members to oppose; creating Head Start, giving educational opportunity for poor children, a measure supported by

---

★The Bush administration has picked Eugene Scalia, son of Justice Antonin Scalia, as solicitor of labor, the top legal position in the department of labor. This would have been a "payoff" headline in Clinton's time; it only appeared as a small box when reported in the *New York Times* on May 8, 2001.

★

then-President Reagan; passing the Equal Rights Amendment, guaranteeing equal rights to women; creating a Department of Education; creating a federal hate-crimes bill; passing the Endangered Species Act; laws strengthening bans against discrimination in housing; abortion even in cases of rape, incest, or when the mother's life would be at risk; a nonbinding resolution condemning the apartheid regime in South Africa; the release of Nelson Mandela after twenty-three years in prison; creation of a House committee enquiring into the role of Ronald Reagan in the Iran-contra affair.

*Aye:* Cutting Medicare monies; cutting AIDS research, one of only thirteen House members in this matter; drilling in the Arctic Wildlife Refuge; covert spending to aid guerilla forces fighting left-wing regimes, even when limited or condemned by Congress; a constitutional amendment to ban busing for school desegregation; and, most of all, more and more money for the military.[24]

There are some who, in retrospect, reflect about the wisdom of former actions. Not Dick Cheney. Appearing on CNN's *Larry King Live* program in July 2000, Cheney discussed his voting record and said, "I'm proud of it."

In 1995, four years after helping win the Persian Gulf War and establishing close contacts with our Arab allies in the oil-rich countries, Dick Cheney, secretary of war during that conflict, became chief executive of Halliburton Company, a Dallas oilfield services company that received almost 70 percent of its business from these Arab nations. He received an annual salary and bonus of $1.3 million to $3 million along with stock options and Halliburton shares.[25]

When Cheney arrived this stock was trading at around $21 a share. Within two years the value nearly tripled, and Halliburton soon became the world's largest provider in its field. Furthermore, business with the U.S. government increased; Halliburton, with American as well as Arab contacts due to Cheney's former position as secretary of war, grew to become the nation's fifth-largest military contractor, having previously absorbed along the way Brown & Root, the firm made famous (and very rich) through its intimate and mutually beneficial activity financing the career of Lyndon Johnson.[26]

To be more specific, in the five years Cheney ran Halliburton, the company and its subsidiaries received $2.3 billion in U.S. contracts, almost double the amount received in the previous five years. Halliburton also received $1.5 billion in guaranteed or direct loans from the Export-Import Bank and the Overseas Private Investment Corp.; but in the five years before Cheney took command, Halliburton only received about $100 million from these same agencies.[27]

It is hardly a coincidence that in these same five years Halliburton, under Cheney, gave $1.2 million to both political parties and to members of Congress. It also increased its Washington lobbying from $280,000 in 1996 to $600,000 in 1999.

As is obvious, Cheney's political contacts were the key. "When we brought Cheney in, it really wasn't to run operations, it was to make the proper strategic decisions, and to establish relationships," said his predecessor, Thomas Cruikshank, in a discussion of Halliburton's business history.[28] It was indeed a wise decision.

In late May of 2000 Cheney sold one hundred thousand shares of Halliburton stock at its yearly high of $50.97 a share, thus netting over $5 million. This took place just before the stock price began to tumble. His income over the previous decade was almost $21 million, in which period he gave 1.01 percent to charity, which, in answer to questions, he defended as "appropriate."[29] It may also be mentioned that he did not vote in fourteen of the sixteen state and local elections held since he moved to Dallas—including the Texas primary that selected George W. Bush.[30]

Halliburton, like many companies, has an employee contract condition known as "golden handcuffs," which states that early retirement means forfeiture of certain compensation. In Cheney's case this was age sixty-two. Five days before Bush announced his selection of fifty-nine-year-old Cheney as his running mate, the Halliburton board voted to rescind this condition in his case and permit him to retire with a full package worth an estimated $20 million. About 50

★

percent of this package would have been forfeited if the normal rules of retirement had been applied. Under pressure due to publicity in this matter, Cheney was forced to give up certain stock options worth about $3.5 million, retaining the rest of the package. Cheney's income in 2000 was stated as $36,086,635.[31]

It may also be pointed out that, aside from firing thousands of Halliburton workers to "economize," as Halliburton CEO, Dick Cheney also reduced retirees' medical benefits.[32]

Aside from his choice of Dick Cheney, President Bush dropped a bucket into the well of his father's old-time Republican relics and dredged up as many of those unrusted as he could find for his cabinet, indeed going as far back as Nixon's regime. Their names and backgrounds may be summarized.

**Colin L. Powell, Secretary of State.** Former chairman of the Joint Chiefs of Staff in the elder Bush's presidency. Considered a moderate.

**Paul H. O'Neill, Secretary of the Treasury.** In the Office of Management and Budget under president Nixon and Ford. Former head of Alcoa, world's largest manufacturer of aluminum. He earned $56.4 million in 2000;[33] at the end of the year O'Neill still owned more than two million Alcoa shares, worth about $80 million.

**Donald H. Rumsfeld, Secretary of Defense.** Held the same post under President Ford. Former top executive of the large pharmaceutical firm G. D. Searle & Company.

**John Ashcroft, Attorney General.** Former U.S. Senator from Missouri and ultraconservative, voting at times to the right of Newt Gingrich.

**Gale A. Norton, Secretary of the Interior.** Former attorney general of Colorado and top antienvironmentalist.

**Ann M. Veneman, Secretary of Agriculture.** Former deputy secretary of agriculture under the elder Bush's presidency.

**Donald L. Evans, Secretary of Commerce.** Best friend and fund-raiser for Bush; in the oil industry at Midland, Texas.

**Elaine L. Chao, Secretary of Labor.** Deputy transportation secretary in the elder Bush's presidency, wife of U.S. Senator Mitch McConnell, foremost foe of eliminating soft money.

**Tommy G. Thompson, Secretary of Health and Human Services.** Governor of Wisconsin who overhauled the state's welfare system with dubious success.

**Melquiades R. Martinez, Secretary of Housing and Urban Development.** Republican Party chairman of Orange County, Florida, and a close ally of Jeb Bush, the president's brother.

**Norman Y. Mineta, Secretary of Transportation.** The only Democrat; briefly secretary of commerce under President Clinton. Former vice president of Lockheed Martin, a major government contractor.

**Spencer Abraham, Secretary of Energy.** Defeated U.S. Senator from Michigan; introduced a bill to abolish the department he is now heading.

**Rod Paige, Secretary of Education.** Superintendent of the Houston, Texas, school system; raised school marks by throwing out students who appeared unable to make the grade.

**Anthony J. Principi, Secretary of Veterans Affairs.** Hangover from the elder Bush's presidency.

The following were also chosen for strategic positions:

**Robert E. Zoellick.** Former under secretary of state for the elder Bush, also worked for President Reagan. The country's top trade negotiator, he will be retained.

**Christie Whitman.** Governor of New Jersey, head of the Environmental Protection Agency (EPA). Considered a moderate in the Bush administration.

**Mitchell E. Daniels Jr.** Served in the Reagan White House and then a senior executive of Eli Lilly & Company, the pharmaceutical firm, now director of the Office of Management and Budget.

**Andrew M. Card.** Veteran of the Reagan years and secretary of transportation for the elder Bush's presidency. Now to be chief of staff in the White House. He was a General Motors lobbyist.

In summary, the eighteen listed Bush administrators consist of fourteen hard-line conservatives, several being extremists and four being from America's top 500 financial companies; two moderates; and one Democrat who is a conservative tied by background to an important government contractor.

Aside from advocating a ban on abortion, his so-called National Missile Defense System, and oil/gas drilling as well as timber and mineral permits for work on federal lands as well as offshore—all core desires of the ultraconservative right—the Bush years will most likely resemble those of his father's presidency. What had been an evenly divided U.S. Senate, now tipped toward the Democrats after the switch of Vermont Senator James Jeffords from Republican to independent, makes this comparison even more striking; the elder Bush also faced a Congress with a Republican minority.

The knowledge that his political party may face a rout in the 2002 midterm elections if he shows too much contempt for public opinion will also stop President Bush from pushing too hard for some of the extreme measures desired by the ultraconservative right. It very well may be that drilling in Alaska's Arctic National Wildlife

Refuge and the "Star Wars" ballistic plan will both be modified, if not doomed. What increases this possibility is the national recession ballooning in late 2001.

What President Bush accomplished in the early days of his presidency—namely, sharp tax cuts and estate tax elimination for the very rich—is also not certain, because these measures are only phased in over many years and during that period may be modified. Many of his antienvironmental initiatives can also suffer the same fate. The one certainty will be his pick of die-hard conservatives for the Supreme Court to maintain its Reagan flavor.

If, however, Bush succeeds in completely weeding the estate tax, this will create a new United States, one moving from a flexible plutocracy, where merit is still a major propulsion, to an out-and-out caste system, where the upper 2 percent of the population will resemble the hereditary aristocracy of Europe before the French Revolution.[34] However, it is striking that some of the richest Americans—men such as David Rockefeller, George Soros, William Gates Sr., and Warren Buffett[35]—have publicly opposed this extreme move which, among other drastic results, would severely dampen charitable donations. Like most measures, the weight of upper-middle-class opinion will bring this proposal back to a centrist way of thinking—that is, to the center for the more civilized rich.

The recent terrorist attacks against New York City's Twin Towers and the Pentagon in Washington, D.C., have provoked a hysteria that in some ways resembles that during the early years of the Vietnam War. Whipped up by a mixture of genuine patriotism and extreme statements from Washington—in such times the more a president folds himself in the flag, the more popular he is—a majority of the American people seem willing to war against not only the perpetrators of these crimes but also against whole nations that appear to be in sympathy.

As in the case of Vietnam, time will dissolve this hysteria into more reasoned thinking. Terror is nothing new; it has existed from the start of civilization. The word "assassin" actually comes from an early medieval Islamic cult that practiced murder as an arm of policy, deriving from the Arabic "hashish," which was fed to the assassins before they were sent out to kill. In Europe, the prolonged wars between Roman Catholic and Protestant nations led, among other results, to the 1572 Saint Bartholomew's Day massacre in France, a general slaughter of Protestants; and in Germany, civil strife that ended with the butchery of one-third of the population. Russian history is dotted with the murder of czars. In the United States, two presidents were shot during the latter part of the nineteenth century. World War I was set off when a Serbian nationalist killed the heir to the Austro-Hungarian throne. After World War II and through the 1960s and 1970s, Red brigades and anarchists in Italy, Germany, and France abducted and assassinated top politicians and terrorized the general population. In England, the fight by the IRA for Northern Irish independence has led to so many bombings that a general camera surveillance has been set up at the street corners of major cities. Little more than six years ago, an American bombed a federal building in Oklahoma City, with dreadful consequences.

Not one of these countries in recent times went to the expense of placing National Guard units at the mouths of all airports, of scrutinizing tickets bought for railroads, of police checking the trunks of cars entering major cities, or of mobilizing more than twenty thousand members of the National Guard and reserves—as ordered by President Bush—because of a handful of terrorist lunatics.

It is salutary to recall that Israel never had an airplane hijacked or destroyed despite being surrounded by enemies. The technique used is quite simple: a rigid inspection of baggage and passengers at airport gates, and an armed guard on every flight. This elemental strategy is more effective than swarming cities with soldiers or inspecting the contents of every moving vehicle. With an enormous corps of U.S. Army troops standing idle at bases throughout the country, a simple assignment of an armed soldier to every airline flight would be effective and cost no more money to the taxpayers.

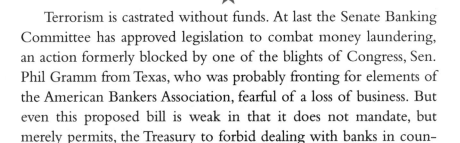

Terrorism is castrated without funds. At last the Senate Banking Committee has approved legislation to combat money laundering, an action formerly blocked by one of the blights of Congress, Sen. Phil Gramm from Texas, who was probably fronting for elements of the American Bankers Association, fearful of a loss of business. But even this proposed bill is weak in that it does not mandate, but merely permits, the Treasury to forbid dealing with banks in countries that hide money laundering behind a smoke screen. Sealing off money to these countries will stop them.

Most of all, efforts should be concentrated on reducing our oil dependency. If one-tenth of the billions spent on our armed forces was devoted to creating alternative energy sources, especially a cheap electric battery for cars, the economy of the Arab nations that openly or surreptitiously support terrorism would collapse in a short time, with no money available for international thugs. We have a historical example of this: Because of the gold and silver looted from the New World, Spain—with its Inquisition—bestrode the world in the sixteenth century. Once the precious ores were exhausted, Spain fell on its face. The same would happen with the oil-rich Arab nations.

The side effects of this, our national tragedy, have enabled President Bush to trot out some major themes that normally would have great trouble passing Congress. The most obvious is his request to abolish permanently the corporate alternative minimum tax, which forces individuals and corporations to pay at least some taxes. The president has also requested an acceleration of the package of income tax reductions he won from Congress, which favor high-income Americans. The more simple truth is that Congress should reject permanent tax cuts and—especially with a proposed $100-billion package to stimulate the sagging economy—should roll back rather than speed up the president's ten-year tax-reduction plan, which will inevitably require dipping into the Social Security surplus.

Perhaps most frightening is the excuse given by the crisis to throw many civil liberties into the ash can. Attorney General John Ashcroft, undoubtedly with the approval of the president, wants the right to detain immigrants indefinitely without recourse to law, as well as the right to wiretap ordinary citizens. The idea of national identification cards, raised by members of Congress, reeks of fascism. Rather ironically, the opposition to these measures is voiced not only by civil-rights liberals, but also by right-wing Republicans who oppose all extension of government controls.

The need for nearby ground bases to attack Afghanistan requires some modification of our hostility toward totalitarian regimes, but it should be kept in mind that three nations we have embraced— Uzbekistan, Turkmenistan, and Tajikstan—are among the world's worst violators of human rights, while the huge nation of Pakistan is a rigid military dictatorship. Our fight against terrorism should not involve a repetition of the United States' sorry history in Latin America, where not only were dictators supported by the CIA, but our government was actively involved in the repression of democratic movements.

Above all, we must deal not just with the symptoms but also with the root of terrorism, which is totalitarian fanaticism versus our secular culture, a fight which in Christian Europe took two centuries to win. Patience, not hysterical patriotism; steady resolution, not hasty action; and the realization that our fight for freedom to think differently from others without repression took many years, with many casualties, but was achieved at last. And this cornerstone of civilization was won not by armies of soldiers on the battlefield but more by the conquest over rigid thinking through example, constraint, and education.

IN
MEMORY OF
FRED FRIMKIN

BORN: DOW 147
DIED: DOW 10,715

David Brown, P.O. Box 481, Orillia, Ontario, Canada L3V 6K2

# CHAPTER ELEVEN

---
★
---

# — DEMOCRACY/PLUTOCRACY —

---
★
---

*"The punishment which the wise suffer, who refuse to take part in the government, is to live under the government of worse men."*
    Ralph Waldo Emerson, paraphrasing Plato

*"The death of democracy is not likely to be assassination from ambush. It will be a slow extinction from apathy, indifference, and undernourishment."*

    Robert M. Hutchins

DEMOCRACY: *Government in which supreme power is vested in the people and exercised by them or their elected representatives.*

PLUTOCRACY: *Government by the wealthy; a ruling class of wealthy people.*

The destruction of the ideals of Franklin D. Roosevelt's New Deal by Ronald Reagan, a process that continued without stop up to and including President Clinton, has made the United States the most economically stratified of all the industrial nations. Even Britain, with its centuries-old class differences, now has greater economic equality than the United States.[1] The last Federal Reserve figures available show that the richest 1 percent of Americans own more than 20 percent of all America's wealth; the richest 5 percent own over 40 percent; the richest 10 percent own over two-thirds;

while the poorest—almost half of Americans put together—own little more than 3 percent of the total. Some one-fifth of our population, about 70 million households, has a net worth close to zero. In effect, we have economic apartheid.

And, one may add, former South African apartheid in a concealed form. The net worth of the thirty richest families in America is about $500 billion; these thirty have assets greater than the gross annual earnings of the thirty-five million black people in the United States.

Since the 1960s the household incomes of the rich have risen faster than those of the poor. The economic boom under President Clinton, a fact that the 2000 presidential candidate Al Gore avoided in his appeals to the unions, was a period in which the income gaps widened even further. Indeed, in 1999 the poorest 20 percent of Americans earned a smaller percentage of the total U.S. income than they did in 1967. From 1973 to 1998, in an economy that almost doubled in real terms, the wage of the typical worker in production and nonsupervisory jobs (some 80 percent of the workforce) actually declined by 6 percent.[2]

In 1948 there was only one American, Henry Ford, who was definitely a billionaire. By the 1970s there were more than ten billionaires; by 1980 there were ninety-four; and by mid-1999 this figure zoomed to 268. To put this sum into perspective, a billion dollars invested at an interest rate of 5 percent creates an annual income of $50 million; invested at a tax-free 3 percent, $30 million.

Millionaires are common, ordinary garden flowers. Although statistics vary, the generally accepted figures are that in 1997 there were 11 million millionaires, with the group growing by three hundred each month. At its height the Internet was making sixty new millionaires each day. As of the start of 2000, one in fourteen American households had a net worth of $1 million or more. Young professionals from good schools now start with a salary of $75,000 in our major cities; young lawyers begin at $125,000 at major firms, with a guaranteed $25,000 annual bonus.

The five most wealthy Americans plus the seven Walton heirs of

Wal-Mart have a total worth of over $300 billion, a sum so astronomical that it exceeds the total gross national product of more than forty-five of the least-developed countries, with a total population of 600 million people. The net worth of the thirty richest Americans is about $500 billion. The last "Forbes 400" list of the four hundred richest persons in America—an annual analysis of *Forbes*—stated that the total worth of this group was $1.2 trillion, an amount larger than the worth of the total population of China, where one-fifth of all the world's people live.[3]

American chief executives are paid many times more than those elsewhere. Japanese executives make an average of ten times the pay of their workers, while in the United States they receive twenty-five times as much.[4] This gulf is increasing. In 2000 the annual pay package of chief executives continued to soar and now exceeds $10 million among the largest public companies, having more than doubled since 1995. Much of the increase is in stock options, now accounting for 60 percent of the compensation packages, an increase of almost 30 percent from 1999.[5]

The following figures show the total compensation from 1995 through 1999 of the top most highly paid U.S. executives, the figure in each case representing salary, bonus, realized gain in stock options, vested stock grants, and miscellaneous goodies. It is to be emphasized that these figures do not include the market value they hold in stock of their companies.

- Charles B. Wang, Computer Associates, $713 million
- Michael D. Eisner, Walt Disney, $674 million
- Sanford I. Weill, Citigroup, $619 million
- Stephen C. Hilbert, Conseco, $392 million
- Stephen M. Case, America Online, $334 million
- Jack F. Welch Jr., General Electric, $262 million
- Reuben Mark, Colgate-Palmolive, $208 million
- Louis V. Gerstner Jr., IBM, $185 million
- John T. Chambers, Cisco Systems, $165 million
- Richard M. Scrushy, HealthSouth, $146 million.[6]

"Minor" figures are Henry A. Silverman of Cendant, paid $134.5 million, and Ray R. Irani of Occidental Petroleum, who netted $125.5 million.

Some of these men with enormous salaries have done poorly in their jobs, but stockholder revolts are very difficult to engineer and the company directors are often hand-picked. Even when CEOs are asked to leave for doing poorly, they often walk away from the cosy enclaves of Wall Street and Silicon Valley with huge parting gifts. Frank Newman of Bankers Trust was eased out by acquirer Deutsche Bank with $74 million in his pocket. David Coulter left BankAmerica after trading losses but was consoled with $29 million. Compaq crashed but its chieftain, Eckhard Pfeiffer, got $10 million on leaving, with a $150-million stake in options. In fact, a study by Monitor Group Corporate Finance Practice, based in Cambridge, Massachusetts, found almost no correlation between annual changes in pay and shareholder returns. As that financial wit John Kenneth Galbraith remarked, "The salary of the chief executive of the large corporation is not a market award for achievement. It is frequently in the nature of a warm personal gesture by the individual to himself."[7]

The power of these CEOs is stupendous. They can—and do—buy political offices. They dictate the flow of cash to our presidents and their staffs as well as to U.S. congressmen, and thus control to a large extent the democratic practice, or what used to be known as the democratic practice. Billionaire Howard Hughes was quite blunt in his self-appraisal: "I answer to no one, can do what I want, and wield more power than presidents, whose authority is limited and tenure is brief."[8]

The rich run the United States; the battle for political control is not grounded in different ideologies but is simply a personal contest among them. A brief review of several examples of this big-money contest for the purchase of U.S. senatorial seats during the last decade will be illustrative.[9]

In 1992 Michael Huffington, son of a Texas oil and gas operator worth some $300 million, spent $5.9 million to win a House seat in California. Unknown, and with unknown opinions, in 1994 he went

★

all out in an attempt to defeat California U.S. Senator Diane Feinstein, who herself has a family fortune estimated at $50 million. Huffington spent close to $30 million trying to beat Feinstein, who was forced to spend more than $14 million to win. In 1996 Republican Senator John Ashcroft, an heir to the Ralston-Purina fortune, waltzed to victory in Missouri and, though defeated in 2000, he was appointed attorney general by President George W. Bush immediately thereafter. New Jersey Senator Frank Lautenberg, cofounder of Automatic Data Processing, in that same year spent $7.4 million to defeat his opponent, whose war chest was "only" $4.4 million. In Ohio, Joel Hyatt, son-in-law of the Democratic Senator Howard Metzenbaum, was defeated by Lieutenant Governor Mike DeWine in a clash of millionaires; and in Tennessee, Republican Dr. William H. Frist, whose family cofounded the Hospital Corporation of America, spent $2 million in a small state and won. He spent a similar sum in 2000 to be reelected.

In the 1996 Virginia U.S. senatorial election, Oliver L. North, the idol of the extreme right wing because of his Iran-contra role, raised $20 million and was defeated only because an independent took 11 percent of the vote. In Wisconsin, Democratic Senator Herb Kohl, the owner of the Milwaukee Bucks basketball team as well as shopping centers and real estate, spent $6.3 million to win in 1988 and then, secure, smashed to victory in 1994 over a weak candidate by reducing his expenditures to merely $2.5 million. In 1998 Peter G. Fitzgerald, Republican senatorial candidate in Illinois and scion of a very wealthy banking family, spent $12 million of his own money to defeat his Democratic opponent.[10] In this same year New York Senator Charles E. Schumer spent $8.1 million to be elected, though in this case it was not all his own money.

The 2000 election reached new heights in campaign spending. In Minnesota, Mark Dayton, a Dayton-Hudson department store heir, beat Rod Grams, the Republican senatorial incumbent. The four rivals to Dayton in the Democratic primary were all multimillionaires and he had to spend about $11 million to overcome his Democratic, and then Republican, adversaries.

The senatorial campaign in New York was the most expensive ever wagered in that state. Republican Rick Lazio garnered $33 million from all the Clinton haters in the nation. Hillary Clinton, who spent $26 million, prevailed nevertheless.

In Michigan, Democratic U.S. Representative Debbie Stabenow edged out the Republican incumbent, Spencer Abraham, who was then rewarded by President Bush with an appointment to his cabinet. The two candidates together spent more than $16 million.

An unusual upset occurred in a very close election in the state of Washington, where Democrat Maria Cantwell edged out incumbent Senator Slade Gorton, a strong ally of Microsoft in that company's fight against the U.S. Justice Department. Cantwell spent $10 million of her own money—the most money ever spent in that state's history—which she had made creating and expanding a software video company.

The most astonishing election occurred in New Jersey. The writing appeared on the wall when Republican Governor Christine Whitman decided not to run for the U.S. Senate. Whitman is a very wealthy woman, both from family and marriage. But her decision was based on the fact that Jon S. Corzine had announced he would run as a Democrat and stated that he would spend "whatever is necessary" to win.[11] Whitman acknowledged that the prospect of outdueling Corzine's great fortune was a significant fact in her decision.

She was right. Corzine's successful campaign is perhaps the best example of how to buy an election. At fifty-three, the former cochairman of Goldman Sachs & Company, a completely unknown figure in his home state of New Jersey, spent over $60 million—outspending every other senatorial candidate in U.S. history—to purchase the position. He could easily afford to do so: Corzine's income from 1996 through 1999 was $144.5 million; his fortune is claimed to exceed $400 million. First he knocked out former Governor Jim Florio in the Democratic primary, spending $36.7 million to his opponent's $1.9 million, also a first nationwide in primary spending. In a state with a large black population, he first concealed and later had to admit making a donation to a group of black ministers who later endorsed him. He hired unemployed blacks from Pennsylvania, busing them into urban centers like Newark to canvas for him.

A reporter visiting eight polling places on election day found three workers at each electioneering for Corzine. At one, the pollsters, bearing Corzine stickers, were also openly campaigning for him. Two men threw out the reporter, threatening him if he did not leave.

The result was a great victory.[12] It might be mentioned that Corzine took over for retiring Senator Frank R. Lautenberg, also a multimillionaire. And Whitman was rewarded by President Bush, who made her head of the Environmental Protection Agency.

These are examples. It could be said that we should label and seat our U.S. senators and representatives to indicate the business they represent—or the major businesses subsidizing their elections—rather than their political party.

If the general public were decently fed, housed, and clothed, these election purchases would have less significance, for a person with money in a free country can spend or waste it as he or she likes. But with the great fissures in American life, where a significant percentage of the population is poorly nourished, undereducated, and without health care, the issue is moral as well as economic.

The huge gap between the rich and poor was created by the radical declines of the ordinary tax rate and the capital gains bracket plus a vast series of measures designed to give special tax breaks to those who buy our politicians. This process, which started with Ronald Reagan and has continued, can be clearly shown in the political arena.

Until the 1970s one could run for Congress for $100,000, even less in some states. Then the cost started to rise radically. Media compaigning—the consultants, poll takers, radio and television spot ads, private detectives to uncover dirt on the opposition—ran into the millions. In 1960 John F. Kennedy spent a little under $10 million to win the election; his opponent, Richard Nixon, spent slightly more. Twelve years later, in 1972, Nixon spent six times that amount,

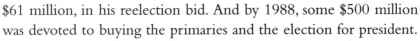

$61 million, in his reelection bid. And by 1988, some $500 million was devoted to buying the primaries and the election for president.

Even the cost of running for the House of Representatives has shot through the roof. By 1998, one out of six House candidates expended more than $1 million on the race. A record laid out for a House seat was set by Newt Gingrich in 1996, when he spent $6.3 million.[13]

The result was obvious. As contributions poured in from pressure groups—business, labor, farm, and mining interests—legislators no longer represented the people of their states but rather those of private interests. And zealots such as the Christian fundamentalists and the opponents of gun controls, rather small groups in the total population, gained great leverage as a result.

With rare exceptions, one has to either be very rich or sell one's vote to special interests to run successfully for public office. Congress is now a club of millionaires. Back in 1994, when fewer than 1 percent of Americans were millionaires, 14 percent of House members and nearly 30 percent of senators were millionaires. In 1998 the percentage of millionaire senators rose to almost 40 percent. And a survey in 1998 indicated that in 94 percent of Senate races and 95 percent of House races the candidate who spent the most money won. Almost all the incumbents were reelected, more than at any time in the last decade. These are the individuals who receive the largest cash contributions from those seeking favors.

As more money is spent in recent elections, fewer people vote. It used to be that when important issues were debated, the public came to hear. Now almost no one comes to the Senate chambers to listen; the likes of Henry Clay and Daniel Webster, who dealt in ideas, have vanished. The level of incivility has also increased: "You're with me or against me" has more and more become the rule, as though party members come from different countries rather than trying to legislate for the common good of the same nation. Raising money, obsessive reliance on polls, and loss of dignity are common characteristics. Edmund Burke, perhaps the greatest British conservative thinker ever, said in Parliament in 1777 that a representative "is in Parliament to support his opinion of the public good and does not form his opinion in order to get into Parliament, or to continue in it." This would be considered laughable today.

In July 2000 the GOP delegates to the national convention that nominated George W. Bush were actually more conservative than their candidate. They were in favor of large tax cuts, school vouchers, and a full-speed-ahead ballistic missile plan; they opposed gun control, environmental safeguards, abortion rights, prescription drug subsidies for the elderly, and campaign finance regulation. One in five belonged to the National Rifle Association (NRA) and more than half owned a gun. Only 4 percent of the delegates were black and 2 percent were Asian. Almost one-quarter were millionaires. Thirty-five percent were women.

This contrasts with the Democratic convention. Forty-two percent were women, 19 percent black, and only 12 percent called themselves millionaires. Thirty-one percent of these delegates belonged to a labor union, compared to only 4 percent among the Republicans. Whereas almost two-thirds of the GOP delegates were in favor of soft money contributions,★ only 44 percent of the Democrats favored them. While 86 percent of the Democrats opposed tuition vouchers, to the contrary, 71 percent of the Republicans favored them. And the Democrats supported only a limited ballistic missile program.[14]

As a summary statement one could conclude that the Democratic delegates were to the left of the general public while the Republicans were to the right. This follows history, for when elected almost all the presidents move to the center regardless of party. Clinton is an excellent example. George W. Bush will almost surely follow the well-known dictate of Richard Nixon for Republican candidates: cultivate the right in the primaries and move to the center when president. In fact, since both parties owe allegiance to their financial backers—who often give large sums to both parties in order to hedge their bets—this is the likely outcome.

---

★The issue of soft money will be discussed further in chapter 12.

The presidency is a great prize. With a salary of $400,000, an expense allowance of $50,000, travel expenses of $100,000, plus an entertainment allowance of $19,000, the basic intake is $569,000. But this is only the start, for the influence the president wields leads to much greater income later through honorary sinecures and book publishing. Former President Bush is worth some $20 million from speaking fees, corporate directorships, and so on. Clinton receives $100,000 a lecture; his wife signed a book contract with $8 million as an advance—reduced, of course, by the payment made to a ghostwriter. There are more ghosts floating among top politicians than in the cemeteries on All Saints Day. Indeed, almost all the former presidents of the twentieth century have published their memoirs for many millions in payment.

The sinecures flow down to the lesser fry. Jack Kemp, the Republican vice-presidential candidate in 1996, made $6.9 million in three years, mainly in speaking fees. Back in 1995 Colin L. Powell and Henry Kissinger were already commanding more than $50,000 a lecture; and Mario M. Cuomo, Barbara Bush, and Gerald R. Ford make between $25,000 and $50,000. General Powell's lecture fee has jumped to $80,000; and in 1995 he received a $6-million advance for his autobiography. As secretary of state under President George W. Bush, his wealth is now reported to be well over $28 million.[15]

With the possible exception of Senators John McCain and Russell Feingold, the general public is not stupid in their thoughts about these so-called sincere politicians. In May 1997 a poll was taken inquiring as to whether people believed congressmen and President Clinton really were honest in what they said about backing reform. Only 27 percent thought the legislators were sincere; only 30 percent believed the president. And about 40 percent of Americans said in a July 2000 poll that they had no desire to watch any of the national political conventions.[16] Perhaps the final critique came from a poll of pollsters. Among twenty-five professions they ranked members of Congress twenty-fourth in honesty. Probably the presidency would have come in twenty-sixth.

Contrary to the impression created by some movies and popular novels, most top businessmen—though obviously hungry to get high salaries and stock options—are basically honest. *Business Week* in April 1997 surveyed the attitudes of four hundred leading American executives regarding the pressure put on them to contribute to political candidates. About 70 percent said they had contributed money to various 1996 political campaigns, but 68 percent of them said they felt shaken down and wanted to end the corporate and individual contributions known as soft money. And in October 2000 a survey of business leaders by the Committee for Economic Development found that three out of five CEOs were resentful of being pressed to give campaign money in exchange for access and wanted a soft-money ban.

There is nothing new about this nefarious practice. The well-known writer Henry Adams, who saw these practices more than a century ago, wrote in *Democracy*: ". . . for democracy, rightly understood, is the government of the people, by the people, for the benefit of Senators."

A parallel practice is the more recent fad of searching for dirt on the opponent, waiting until just before the end of the campaign, then exploiting it through the media. Many candidates hire private detectives to smear their opponents. In an interview a leading private detective named Ernie Rizzo provided details of his work:

> Politicians are the easiest people in the world to set up. They're all whores. You stay with them for a week and you'll catch them doing something—women or money or something. Forget about the millions spent in political contributions. You don't need that. Everybody got to the top by stepping over somebody. Find the weakest link and attack it.[17]

Rizzo is only partly right. Perhaps the majority are indeed whores. But there is some leaven in the sour dough and, therefore, hope for the country. And he is wrong about the role of political contributions, as will be shown.

Reprinted with special permission of King Features Syndicate.

# CHAPTER TWELVE

★

## CAMPAIGN FINANCE
## AND PRIVILEGE

★

*Politicians spend half their time making laws and the other half
helping contributors evade them.*

American maxim

*POLITICS, n. A strife of interests masquerading as a contest of prin-
ciples. The conduct of public affairs for private advantage.*
Ambrose Bierce, *The Devil's Dictionary*

After the Watergate scandal there was a huge public outcry to
curb money going to influence political activity. The
dilemma facing politicians was how to divert the public's disgust
with a corrupt system while retaining this flow of money. They
resolved the problem by creating two sets of campaign finance laws.
The first placed strict limits on individuals and corporations giving
money directly to candidates. The second bypassed the first.

Individuals and corporations are permitted to set up or contribute
to Political Action Committees, called PACs, up to $5,000 each. This
allows them to pool the money and give it to favored candidates. In
addition, they can give up to $20,000 a year to a national party com-
mittee, another $1,000 to a candidate for a primary campaign, and
another $1,000 for the general election, with a total limit of $25,000
to all candidates combined. The amount doubles to $50,000 for a
married couple. These limitations do not include volunteer work.

★

However, the catch is that there were no limitations placed on campaign contributions of individuals or corporations for state propaganda and indirect political activities, phrases vague enough to effectively invalidate the above limitations. This "soft money" can support candidates indirectly, through staff salaries, mailings, consultants, lobbyists, television ads asking people to vote for one party or the other (but not a specific candidate), and so on. The reforms thus are largely a joke.

The result was that almost nothing has changed. Huge amounts of contributions stream through these artifices into both political parties seeking and obtaining a bonanza of favors and subsidies. The final coup de grâce was the Supreme Court decision that—equating "money" with "free speech"in the 1976 decision *Buckley* v. *Valeo*—decided that individuals could spend as much as they wanted, without any limits whatsoever, to run for political office.

This money controls the actions of both the executive and legislative branches of our government on the federal and state levels. The payments made to U.S. legislators are obvious because they involve public records. The average House member as early as 1996 took in $275,000 in campaign money—more than half his or her budget—from PACs. Most of this money went to incumbents the giver knew could be counted on, rather than to challengers whose vote might be uncertain. Since the PAC contribution would be withdrawn if the vote was not "right," this determined in almost all cases the result—which explains, for example, defeat after defeat for gun control despite the desire of the majority of the American people. The gun lobby contributed $2,394,444, mainly to Republicans, in the last election cycle.[1] The nation's military contractors, smelling the enormous sums to be spent on antiballistic missiles, have donated $51 million to Washington politicians.[2]

In effect, campaign contributions can be called campaign bribes. What is the difference between the Mafia demanding money for protection and the threat to withdraw a PAC or soft-money contribution if the legislator's vote doesn't protect or enhance the giver's interest? What is the difference between a whore who sells her body and a government official who sells his vote?

A study by the Center for Responsive Politics found a direct correlation between monies received from special interest groups and the resultant vote. For example, the sugar industry poured money into the campaigns of sixty-one senators and 217 House members. This industry receives a subsidy that adds an extra fifty cents to every five-pound bag of sugar. The study found that the sixty-one senators who voted to continue the subsidy received an average of $13,473 in the several years before, while the thirty-five senators who voted against received only $1,461. The 217 House members voting for the subsidy each received an average contribution of $5,994; the 208 members voting nay received an average of $853.[3]

An even better example is the pressure exerted by America's pharmaceutical companies, fearful of the expiration of their patents or governmental limitations on their monopolies. The top fifteen of these companies spent $78 million a year over the last three years hiring former government officials as lobbyists, now amounting to 297 persons, to fight government price controls. In 1999 the industry trade group created Citizens for Better Medicare (another doublespeak title straight out of George Orwell), which has been running a $50-million advertising campaign against government-controlled drug benefits. A similar organization specializes in coordinating groups of patients, doctors, minorities, and business associates to pressure legislators not to control prices and profits.[4]

Each group of corporations, such as the pharmaceuticals, has its own lobbying bloc, other examples being oil and gas companies, cattlemen, mining, and timber interests. These lobbying pressures are not limited to organized groups but include individual companies and individuals as well. An excellent example of the power of a single company is that of Lockheed Martin Corporation, which led the legislative campaign for NATO expansion[5]—because the company could sell its military products to the newly admitted countries. Not incidentally, the Pentagon then announced it would establish a $15-billion fund to guarantee loans for the sale of arms to these countries.

As has been noted many times in the study of various presidents and their associates, individuals profit greatly from this system of legalized corruption. Some more recent cases can be noted.

Floyd Spence, the South Carolina Republican who was chairman of the House National Security Committee, sent out a request to military contractors for campaign money. This rather typical act was exposed when one of his staff members forwarded by accident a copy of the request to the Washington bureau of the Associated Press, which promptly published it. How can a defense contractor say no to such a request from the man who oversees his business?

Western Republican Senators Larry E. Craig of Idaho, Slade Gorton of Washington, and Ted Stevens of Alaska (Chairman of the Senate Appropriations Committee) have inserted measures into spending bills for the great benefit of logging and mining companies as well as ranchers, such as eliminating a rule that limited mine dumps on federal and Indian land, or a rider for an open-pit gold mine where operators will crush, leach, and dump nine million tons of rock that can wash into streams and rivers. Since 1991, these three senators have received more than $850,000 in campaign contributions from the companies and individuals involved.[6]

Former Chairman of the Republican National Committee Haley Barbour, working with Newt Gingrich, designed the Republican campaign to cut the growth of Medicare, stating in 1995–96 that it was heading toward bankruptcy. Then he was hired as a lobbyist for a dozen large nursing home companies in April 1999 and promptly turned 360 degrees, insisting that Medicare should increase its allowance to adjust for inflation and pay more money to sicker patients. "There's concern that nursing homes will close. It's resulting in harm to senior citizens," he said in an initial interview.[7] Not, however, to his pocketbook. From the other side of the same fence this was also true of Karen M. Ignagni, a Democrat, veteran trade union advocate, and former enthusiast for universal health insurance. Hired as a lobbyist for the American Association of Health Plans (Americans love doublespeak names), she argued the contrary. With appalling hypocrisy, Ignagni stated, "I've never had a sense that I was advocating something I didn't believe in."[8]

Sometimes the advocacy is trivial, but at other times it is hurtful to the nation. As an example of the former, Republican House Speaker J. Dennis Hastert in the 1998 budget won a $250,000 subsidy for the maker of a caffeine-laden chewing gum in his home district.[9] As an example of the latter, the push for campaign finance reform died in the Senate chiefly due to the filibustering of Republican Senator Mitch McConnell of Kentucky, who was heavily funded by the tobacco industry, one of the largest distributors of largess to the legislators.

An especially amusing case is the arm-twisting of Trent Lott, the former Republican Senate majority leader who, while preaching budget restraint, pushed through the Senate a bill to build for $720 million a DDG-51 Aegis-class destroyer at Ingalls Shipbuilding. The ship, of course, would be built at a shipyard in Lott's home state of Mississippi. This is not a first: He did the same with a half-billion-dollar contract to build another ship, the LHD-8, even though the Navy said it did not want the ship.[10]

Bill Gates of Microsoft has about sixty representatives in Washington, pressuring policies beneficial for the company—Microsoft had none in 1995. This is because his company was attacked in a successful lawsuit by the federal government for its monopolistic practices. In September 1999 it was disclosed that full-page newspaper ads published by the *New York Times* and the *Washington Post* in the previous June, in the form of a letter signed by 240 academic experts supporting Microsoft's position in this antitrust trial, were actually paid for by Microsoft.[11]

Bush's presidential campaign, which Microsoft backed with large sums, was far less favorable to the Clinton government's court-ordered remedy to break the company into two parts. To aid the view of a benevolent corporate director, Bill Gates has run a series of television commercials describing the company's value to the economy, Gates appearing in a blue sweater, open collar, sitting at a desk with a coffee pot—just a guy like you and me.

Gates won. The Bush administration announced in September 2001 that it would no longer seek a breakup of Microsoft. A variation of Julius Caesar's famous remark, "I came, I saw, I conquered," is more applicable to Bill Gates: "I came, I paid, I conquered."

Despite lip service to reform, Democrats and Republicans play the same money games. House Democratic leader Richard Gephardt of Missouri persuaded President Clinton not to tax beer to finance his proposed health-care plan; over the past ten years Gephardt had received $318,950 in campaign contributions from Anheuser-Busch Companies, the country's largest brewer.[12] Sometimes the route is more direct. Robert Rubin, cochairman of Goldman, Sachs & Company, gave Clinton's initial campaign more than $100,000; Rubin gave $25,500 directly to the Democratic National Committee and its congressional campaign committee; and he and his wife gave another $275,000 from a personal foundation to the New York section of the DNC.[13] Rubin was appointed secretary of the treasury after the incumbent secretary retired.

In the 2000 presidential election it has been estimated that in the total picture the two major candidates spent twice as much money as in 1996. According to the "official" figures posted by the Center for Responsive Politics after this election, the Bush camp spent almost $192 million and the Gore camp almost $133 million. But this might be called the tip of the iceberg. The Republicans set up an exclusive donor club, the Republican Regents, membership in which was limited to those giving $250,000. By the end of 1999, almost a year before the election, there were already 139 members. To counterattack, the Democrats set up their club, Leadership 2000, for those who contributed $350,000. But by the end of 1999 they had only garnered eighteen members. They then upped the ante with the "Chairman's Circle" for contributors of $500,000. Several unions and three individuals were the inaugural members.

In exchange for these contributions both parties promised private access to congressional leaders; that is, in vulgar terms, to be paid back through special subsidies and perks. Senator Russell D. Feingold of Wisconsin, the Democratic cosponsor of campaign finance reform with Republican Senator John McCain of Arizona, referring to his own party's calling for campaign reform while acting exactly as the Republicans, bluntly said it was "a system of legalized bribery and legalized extortion."[14]

By November 16, 2000, the soft money contributed to both parties, all of which was not included in the above official figures, was estimated at $500 million, again twice that of 1996, with the Republicans maintaining a two-to-one advantage. Though due to certain methods of burying contributions no one can ever know the true figures, it was estimated that the total spending on the congressional and presidential races, soft and hard money (the latter being the smaller donations), plus groups such as the Sierra Club, the U.S. Chamber of Commerce, the National Rifle Association (NRA), and the labor unions, probably exceeded $3 billion.

In the business community, three of the largest ten Republican donors were Philip Morris, the NRA, and Microsoft, all of which faced legal and/or legislative action by the Democrats. Enron, the giant Houston energy corporation, was the second-largest donor, having backed Bush from his political start, not only mounting a million-dollar campaign but circulating a letter to its executives and employees, suggesting "voluntary" contributions and detailing the amounts to be contributed in accordance with the person's position in the company. The Arctic Circle, where President Bush is pressing for oil drilling, may be far from Texas, but it is not far from the pocketbooks of top Texas executives who contributed to Bush.

As has been pointed out previously, some companies judiciously distribute money to both parties in order to reach their goals. Florida's sugar-growing industry's subsidy group, whose purchase of votes has been noted, is led by the Fanjul family. In July 1999 President Clinton attended a $1-million fund-raiser at the home of Alphonse Fanjul. But the sugar-sweet money still goes to both parties. Some of the ten top 2000 election soft-money donors also contributed to both major parties. AT&T gave at least $1 million to each of the national conventions; the company is resisting federal efforts to open its lines to other Internet providers. Time Warner renounced soft-money giving in 1999 but, needing federal approval for its merger with AOL, backtracked, its executives neatly dividing gifts of over $1.3 million between both parties in the 2000 election. Time Warner also sponsored a lavish party attended by almost a thousand lobbyists, House staff members, and journalists at the Republican National Convention in Philadelphia in August 2000.

Money flows in the largest amounts to those who offer the best payoff. For years the Democrats in power were the major recipients. Following the 1994 Republican sweep, in the first six months of 1995, Republican fund-raising committees more than doubled their intake of the year before; the amount Democrats received declined and was only about half that received by Republicans. Before Labor Day of 1994, House Democrats had received 61 percent of all campaign contributions from corporate and other special-interest PACs, while in the five months following the election, Republican House members received 78 percent of such contributions.

We have a system that might well be called, in some ways, socialism for the rich. In 1994 the Democratic Leadership Council published a list of such subsidies totalling more than $100 billion a year. They included: $2 billion to oil, gas, and mining companies; $4 billion to pharmaceutical companies; $2 billion for life insurance companies; $400 million to Christmas-tree growers, windmill makers, and shipbuilders; $500 million to corn-based-ethanol refiners (i.e., Archer Daniels Midland Company); $900 million for timber companies; $700 million for the dairy industry; and $100 million for companies to advertise abroad. Private corporate jets don't pay landing fees at airports as commercial jets do; corporations deduct the cost of entertaining at sports events, theaters, concerts, and golf resorts; wealthy ranchers pay a fraction of the cost of grazing cattle on public lands.

The farm subsidy is the biggest racket of all. In 2000 the government distributed $28 billion in direct payments, accounting for half of all the money made by farmers. Direct payments to farmers have tripled since 1996, when Congress passed a bill setting up new aids, not only for farmers in what are called the corn and wheat belts but also to new groups like apple growers in the state of Washington and rice farmers in California. Some farmers receive up to $280,000; the worse the year, the more money they get, aside from being paid not to plant. And many of these "farmers" are actually corporations.[15] The supreme irony is that some of the lawmakers who push for these subsidies also receive them. As two examples, from 1996 to 2000 Marion Berry, a Democrat from Arkansas, got $649,750; and Blanche Lincoln, also a Democrat from Arkansas, got $351,085.[16]

Lobbying creates these tax breaks. "Lobbying" simply means paying into the pockets of executive and legislative persons through one gimmick or another in order to buy their votes or administrative decisions. These subsidies are often packaged in the American flag, which is saluted sharply as the recipients pocket the money. In 1998 there were 11,500 registered lobbyists in Washington; in 1999, including consultants who perform functions on a slightly different level, the two categories involved 20,512 persons, or about thirty-eight persuaders for each five Congressman. They spent $1.42 billion in 1998 and have developed the art of ventriloquism to the most refined degree, disappearing from the act while leaving only the legislators on stage. And a recent study disclosed that 23 percent of former members of Congress joined the lawyer-lobby complex, which influences present congresspersons through monetary contributions.[17]

That they are successful cannot be disputed. Goodyear, Texaco, Colgate-Palmolive, MCI WorldCom, and eight other large corporations earned more than $12.2 billion in profits in 1996 through 1998, but not one of these companies paid any corporate income taxes over these years; indeed, as a group they received $535 million in credits or refunds. The biggest beneficiary was General Electric, which saved $6.9 billion in three years, reducing its income taxes to a rate of only 8.1 percent.[18] A significant reason, among a package of others, was the gimmick whereby stock options given to top executives are allowed as an expense for tax purposes, thus sharply reducing taxes.

It may be added that the Democrats controlled both the House and Senate in 1993 when the first beneficial laws were passed in this

★

matter, while later additional relaxations were passed in 1999 when the Republicans were in control. Both parties played the same game and for the same reason—lobbyists swaying votes by pledging campaign contributions.

Lobbyists and presidential aides are biological freaks, Siamese twins separated. There is a constant flow back and forth between the two groups, as has been shown in the specific history of various presidents. In the Clinton administration this not only continued, but increased. Howard Paster, former chief Clinton lobbyist (and purportedly a liberal), made hundreds of thousands of dollars each year at Hill & Knowlton, a public relations lobby firm, for such corporations as banks, defense contractors, oil companies, and even the National Rifle Association. Roy Neel, the Clinton deputy chief of staff, resigned to head a Washington telephone company lobby group. As Dee Dee Myers advanced in the Clinton White House staff to the position of press secretary, offers for her services increased, including a large jump in salary from CNN's *Crossfire*, Warner Brothers, and the talk television network CNBC.[19]

A few of these individuals with more delicate stomachs or sensitive consciences got fed up with the Washington rat race. Jeff Eller, a press aide for Clinton, was told he could command an annual salary of at least $300,000 as a lobbyist. Anxious to get away, he finally settled for an Austin, Texas, public relations consulting firm which, however, with salary and a performance bonus, doubled his $100,000 annual pay at the White House.

The change of administration from Clinton to Bush has flushed new quarry for the top businesses. The prizes from the Clinton administration are national security adviser Samuel R. Berger; Deputy Treasury Secretary Stuart E. Eisenstat; and John Podesta, Clinton's White House chief of staff. With their intimate contacts, because they know the main legislative committee heads and members of the House and Senate, they without doubt will be offered very plush jobs as lobbyists. The biggest prize, Defense Secretary William S. Cohen, is looking for a larger slot. Bypassing private offers, Cohen, emulating Henry A. Kissinger, hopes to strike it richer still and has set up the Cohen Group, a new consulting firm. He, with several other former government officials, will use inside contacts to land government contracts for a well-paying clientele.[20] From the near past, former Senator Bob Dole is already a lobbying powerhouse, as is former Senator George J. Mitchell. Million-dollar salaries go to these top names.

This is likewise true for brand-name senators now out of the legislature. Two very desirable men are available from the 2000 election. Foremost is former Republican Senator William V. Roth Jr. of Delaware, for whom the Roth IRA is named, and who held the position of chairman of the Senate finance committee.* The other is retired Republican Florida Senator Connie Mack, who served on the banking committee. Mere congressmen will be paid less, between $200,000 and $400,000 annually, depending upon which committees they served and how influential they can be in turning tricks as lobbyists for their new employers.[21]

Joel E. Klein, the former head of the Justice Department's antitrust division under President Clinton and in charge of the successful lawsuit against Microsoft, has already been hired "as a strategic adviser" by Bertelsmann, the huge German media company which, among many other divisions, owns Random House, the largest English-language publisher in the world. The hiring of Klein brought to Bertelsmann a man not only well connected in the United States but one who also worked closely with European antitrust regulators, the beating ground for the company's aggressive expansion. We can be sure that Klein's salary is not a measly sum.[22]

The military also enters into this caravan of post-service jobs, as has been discussed in earlier chapters. In a most recent example, the secretary of the navy and leading members of Congress are pushing for the DD-21 destroyer, an electric-powered stealth ship designed to attack enemies hundreds of miles inland from ocean water. The

---

*The eighty-year-old Roth is now an adviser to the influential law firm Reed Smith.

★

defense contractor General Dynamics is in charge of this proposed program. Kendell Pease, the vice president of General Dynamics, is its passionate advocate. He is a former rear admiral.

The post as chairman of the Federal Communications Commission has always been most coveted for the contacts created. Reed Hundt took a large pay cut to take this position in 1993, fully aware of the future advantages. Since he left in November 1997, six telecommunications companies have seated him on their boards of directors. Three were start-ups, giving him tens of thousands of cheap stock options. As of mid-1999, these stocks enriched him by about $20 million,★ multiplying nearly tenfold (at least on paper) the $2 million in assets Hundt reported after leaving the FCC less than two years earlier. Similar enrichment has come to former chairmen Richard Wiley, Mark Fowler, and Dennis Patrick, while dozens of other former FCC officials lobby the agency on behalf of the companies they once regulated.[23] The "Lyndon Johnson technique," using a high post as an official of government for great private profit, has now proliferated to the point that Johnson might be considered as having been a piker.

We are now reaching a new level in political-industrial relations, of which the best example is the Carlyle Group, a Washington-based private equity firm that specializes in using political influence to make deals. The earlier example was the consulting firm set up by Kissinger, which, though it made millions, is relatively insignificant when compared to Carlyle. Frank C. Carlucci, chairman of Carlyle, was secretary of defense under President Reagan. The four managing directors of Carlyle all had top positions under the elder President Bush: James A. Baker III, as secretary of state; Richard G. Darman, as director of the Office of Management and Budget; Jerome H. Powell, as undersecretary of the treasury; and Robert E. Grady, another deputy assistant. Senior advisors are former President Bush and William A. Long, undersecretary of defense for President Reagan.

Foreign advisors include John Major, former British prime min-

---

★These paper profits have probably greatly declined due to the recent stock market technology downspin.

ister; Lord Howe, former British deputy prime minister; Karl Otto Pöhl, former president of the German Central bank; Fidel V. Ramos, former president of the Philippines; and Anand Panyarachun, former prime minister of Thailand. Adding to the powerhouse are John M. Shalikashvili, chairman of the Joint Chiefs of Staff under President Clinton; and Daniel R. Coats from Lear Siegler Services, former Republican senator from Indiana.

The Carlyle Group, which until 1989 had done little of import, then took on the very influential Frank C. Carlucci as chairman. He promptly channeled its range of purchases into defense industry acquisitions and global telecommunications. He then extended the golden clasp to directors and advisers with intimate contacts in bureaucracies that control government contracts in these fields, who hopped on board.

The result is that Carlyle owns so many companies that it has now become the eleventh largest defense contractor (note the former positions of the directors and advisers) and, as is apparent, Carlyle invests largely in companies that do business with governments. Former President Bush is their expert on Asia; after he met with the top officials of South Korea, Carlyle won control of KorAm, an important bank there. Carlucci is an old college classmate of Donald H. Rumsfeld, President Bush's secretary of defense, which will without doubt be a very productive relationship.

With $12 billion from investors, Carlyle now claims to be the nation's largest private equity fund, with fingers throughout the world. The flow of politicians to top positions in industry based on government contacts is old hat. However, the Carlyle Group now is playing the game on a global level, and with fantastic success. It has been calculated that, with a current market value of about $3.5 billion, Carlyle's partners are already worth (assuming equal stakes) about $180 million apiece. Advisers, as distinct from partners, are compensated by receiving a piece in Carlyle investments where they close, or facilitate, the deal. This type of intimate network is another example of what might be called state capitalism, American style.[24]

The George W. Bush administration, still in its infancy, has swabbed the decks for its own financial voyage. The Federal Aviation Administration (FAA) skipped competitive bidding and, in March 2001, chose the Lockheed Martin Corporation, at an undisclosed price, to design and build a replacement for its long-distance air traffic control system. This work will run into hundreds of millions of dollars over the next decade.

Lockheed Martin was the main contractor in an earlier failed automation project for the agency, which was partly abandoned in 1994 at a cost to the government estimated at $500 million.

Norman Y. Mineta, the new secretary of transportation under President Bush, runs the FAA. He became a vice president of Lockheed after leaving Congress in 1992. His deputy secretary, Michael P. Jackson, was vice president and general manager for business development at a Lockheed subsidiary. Lynne V. Cheney, the wife of the vice president, was a member of the board of Lockheed from 1994 until she resigned after Bush's election.

All these individuals have announced that they disqualified themselves from the decision to give this enormous contract to Lockheed Martin, though it is admitted by the FAA "that it was a departure from normal practice."[25] Not at all; it is now becoming the norm in our cozening system of government.*

As for U.S. Senators and Representatives, they get not only high salaries—reaching an average of $133,600 a year all the way back in 1996—but, as noted, huge slush funds from PACs and soft money. They also get immense perks: life and health insurance, per diem travel expenses, subsidized food at dining facilities, and good pensions that go on for life regardless of how long they serve. The year that Bob Dole vigorously campaigned against health insurance, he himself received over $61,000 worth of free medical care. Con-

---

*In late October 2001 the Pentagon announced an award of $200 billion to Lockheed to build a new fighter jet. No figures on competitive bidding were presented. Lockheed's mfg. base is in Texas, and Lockheed "has said the contract will provide as many as 9,000 jobs, mostly at its plant in Fort Worth." (*New York Times*, October 27, 2001).

gressmen use government planes to go round the world with their wives on "fact-finding investigations." In late 1995 Representative Arlen even had the State Department wire ahead to set up squash partners for him in air-conditioned courts.[26]

Fighting government programs for the poor, legislators belligerently seek federal monies for pet projects such as federal highways and Veterans Administration hospitals in their home districts or states. Democratic Senator Robert Byrd of West Virginia is such a genius at grabbing huge sums that his state should be renamed Byrdsville.[27] Pious free-market speeches from Midwest senators are matched with unending efforts to maintain and increase farm subsidies. Hard right-wing Republicans from upstate New York insist on continuing price supports for milk; even Hillary Clinton, when campaigning for her seat as a Democratic U.S. Senator from New York, did the same. And on and on it goes.

The executive branch has similar perks in our bloated bureaucracy. Marilyn Quayle, wife of former Vice President Dan Quayle, had a government staff larger than that of President Truman. George Washington lived in a modest home while president; Vice President Al Gore had five offices, including one in his home state of Tennessee. Hillary Clinton, when preparing to run for the U.S. Senate, made use of Air Force jets for months to start her campaign.[28]

In turn, the American people are often paid with simple neglect. Busy raising money elsewhere for themselves, time members of congress put in at their Washington offices is minimal. Rarely there on Mondays, representatives leave early on Fridays. Many sessions start in the late afternoon and long vacations are the order. Some, such as John F. Kennedy when in Congress, rarely show up at all. When Dean Acheson resigned as secretary of state at the beginning of the Eisenhower administration in 1952, he said, "I will undoubtedly have to seek what is happily known as gainful employment, which I am glad to say does not describe holding public office."[29]

Not only is there neglect but also wrongdoing. In the election year of 1992 more than three hundred present and former members of the House wrote bad checks at the House Bank. Representative Robert Mrazek of New York had 920 overdrafts. House Majority Whip Tony Coehlo of California, who from 1981 to 1986 headed the Democratic Campaign Committee, had 316 overdrafts in one year. A private citizen could never do this. Despite this record, in 1998 Coelho was the first campaign chairman hired for Vice President Al Gore's unsuccessful bid to succeed Clinton.

Various attempts, all fruitless so far on the federal level, have been made to get rid of this money disease, the most noted being the McCain-Feingold Bill. This indeed proposed important changes: It eliminated PACs, cut down on soft-money contributions, and required that 60 percent of all monies for a candidate come exclusively from his own state. The bill, however, set very high limits on how much could be spent based on the population of the state of the candidate, in many cases so high it exceeded what candidates had spent so far. In 1997 the campaign financing bill was not only defeated in both branches of the federal legislators but received even fewer votes in the House than two years before.

Gaining new support over repeated revelations about how PACs and soft money corrupt the electoral process, Senators McCain and Feingold have received added support in the 2001 Congress, where the finance reform bill will be fought over again. President Bush, sensing that a majority of the legislators, including those of his own party, are moving in the direction of reform, has endorsed elements of the bill and may even support a modified version. Though it may pass in the near future, without doubt some clever amendments will dilute its force.

Oddly, the net effect of this law, if passed, would restrict the field even more to very rich candidates and incumbents, who can spend unlimited sums. This, of course, presumes that the horde of Washington lawyers—the District of Columbia Bar Association grew from some one thousand members in 1950 to sixty-five thousand in 1996—will not create new and ingenious tricks to siphon large sums of money to our legislators.

There is one favorable omen. While Congress defeats attempt after attempt to eliminate legalized corruption, since 1996 about half of the states have instituted campaign money reforms. Four states—Arizona (home of Senator John McCain), Maine, Massachusetts, and Vermont—have gone all the way, adopting public financing. The bloated federal bureaucracy has lost touch with the people; some states are starting to show them the way. That the United States is so retrograde in this matter can be seen by the fact that among twenty Western countries it is the only one that places no restrictions on the total amounts that can be donated to candidates. Canada, France, New Zealand, and Britain all limit campaign spending.[30]

Reprinted with permission. © Kirk Anderson.

# CHAPTER THIRTEEN

# — POLITICAL REFORMS —

*"It could probably be shown by facts and figures that there is no distinctly criminal class except Congress."*

Mark Twain

*"The backward quality of Congress is readily apparent: so also are the reasons. It over-represents white farmers, hardly bothers with Southern Negroes at all, and makes a joke of affording fair representation to the 70 percent of the population which is politically so misguided as to live in cities and suburbs."*

David T. Bazelon, *The Paper Economy*

## THE ELECTORAL COLLEGE

It might be said with some truth that the Founding Fathers created the Electoral College to thwart democracy. To understand this, a brief review of the men creating the U.S. Constitution is necessary.

The Constitutional Convention met in the spring of 1787 to prop up the toothless Articles of Confederation. Delegates from twelve states attended; Rhode Island refused to go. Thirty-three of the fifty-five men, or 60 percent, were plantation owners and/or land speculators; it thus became a kind of national real estate convention. Thomas Jefferson, minister to France, was out of the

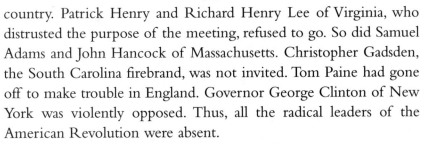

country. Patrick Henry and Richard Henry Lee of Virginia, who distrusted the purpose of the meeting, refused to go. So did Samuel Adams and John Hancock of Massachusetts. Christopher Gadsden, the South Carolina firebrand, was not invited. Tom Paine had gone off to make trouble in England. Governor George Clinton of New York was violently opposed. Thus, all the radical leaders of the American Revolution were absent.

In September of 1787, after months of bickering, thirty-nine, little more than half of the original delegates invited, signed the Constitution. Edmund Randolph, then governor of Virginia, and George Mason, author of Virginia's Bill of Rights, refused to sign. Two of the twelve states present would not go on record as being officially in favor; South Carolina split; and New York did not vote. The final result was thus ratified by nine of the thirteen states.

The resultant Constitution was mainly an instrument of the southern landed gentry and the northern land and currency speculators. It defined the form of the new republic and had little to do with democracy; that is, it organized a national entity in which the sovereign power was exercised by representatives elected by the people or chosen by the state legislators, differing from democracy in which the people exercise power directly.

Indeed, the Constitution was created specifically by the moneyed minority to prevent the general mass of people from exercising this power. Alexander Hamilton wrote in *The Federalist* that the one great advantage of the Constitution—which he initially opposed, suggesting that George Washington be crowned king—was that it would protect persons of property "against domestic violence and the depravations which the democratic spirit is apt to make on property." In large part both John Adams and James Madison agreed in their writings; and, always prudent, George Washington wrote nothing but by his enormous prestige swayed the very divided Virginia state convention to support ratification.

Because democracy was as much loathed by these men as tyranny, even within the thirteen colonies those who could vote were few. The definition of "people" was very narrow. Native Americans, slaves, and women were, of course, excluded. Many of the states excluded Catholics and Jews as well. Almost all limited the vote to men of property. In general it may be stated that suffrage was restricted to propertied white Protestant males.

The Electoral College must be seen in this context. The well-to-do elite who created the Constitution did not trust the people to select the president directly. Twice the convention voted down by wide margins this proposition. Five other variants were also voted down. Finally, a compromise was reached whereby voters would choose people known as electors who would then make the decision; or as an alternative the state legislatures would choose the electors, whose members they felt would be more in sympathy with their narrow views. As John Jay, the first chief justice of the Supreme Court, stated succinctly, "The people who own the country ought to govern it."

Each state accordingly was assigned a number of electors equal to the total of its representatives and its two senators in Congress and the state legislatures were directed to decide how they would be chosen. There was no necessary correlation between a state's popular vote and the choice of its electors; they would be selected in whatever way the state legislatures decided. If no presidential candidate received a majority of the electoral votes then the House of Representative would choose the president, with each state representative having one vote.

Only gradually did the view prevail that the point of elections was to reflect directly the people's vote, following of course the practical extension of the idea of "one person one vote" regardless of religion, color, or property. This process took a long time. Until 1824, electors in some states were chosen by the legislatures rather than being bound by voter preference. It was only after 1832 that every state but South Carolina held direct elections for electors. Since then, electors were to vote in accordance with the will of the voters. Actually, in accordance with Article II of the Constitution a state legislature even in our time has the constitutional power to choose the state's electors, but no legislators today would dare exercise that power.[1]

The problems created by this archaic system can be shown by a brief history of Electoral College crises long before the recent Bush-Gore election.

In 1800 Thomas Jefferson was elected by the House of Representatives because of a tie in the electoral votes. This result was due to Alexander Hamilton who, hating Aaron Burr (though of his same political party) more than he did Jefferson, cast his influence to elect Jefferson; and it may be added, signed his death warrant by that act, as he was later killed in a duel with Burr.

In 1824 John Quincy Adams was elected by the House of Representatives because no candidate polled a majority of the electoral votes despite the fact that Andrew Jackson had won a plurality of the popular vote. The hatred for Jackson by the monied class caused this result; Jackson, however, was elected four years later.

In 1876 Rutherford B. Hayes in a joint session of Congress was declared the winner over Samuel J. Tilden, though the election results were disputed in Florida, Louisiana, Oregon, and South Carolina.

Grover Cleveland had more popular votes in 1888 than Benjamin Harrison, similar to the Bush-Gore contest, but Harrison garnered 233 electoral votes against 168 for Cleveland.

Even in the twentieth century, some electors have refused to vote for the candidates for whom they were pledged. In 1956 an Alabama Democrat elector broke ranks and voted for Eisenhower; in 1960, when John F. Kennedy was elected, fifteen Democratic electors voted for Senator Byrd of West Virginia; at Nixon's election in 1972 a Virginia elector voted for an obscure figure, libertarian John Hospers of California; in 1976 a Democratic elector from Washington voted for Reagan; and in 1983 when the elder George Bush was elected, Senator Lloyd Bentsen of Texas received one vote from a West Virginia elector. It should be emphasized that no federal law forces electors to vote in compliance with the popular vote; those who fail to do so are called "faithless electors," but subject to no legal penalty.[2]

It may be noted that there is no necessary correlation between the popular and electoral votes. The following examples refer only to relatively recent times. In 1960 John F. Kennedy received 49.7 percent of the popular vote, Richard Nixon, 49.6 percent; yet Kennedy got 303 electoral votes to 219 for Nixon. In 1968 Nixon received 43.4 percent of the popular vote to 42.7 percent for Hubert Humphrey; but Nixon shellacked Humphrey with 301 electoral votes against 191. And in 1976 Jimmy Carter received 50.1 percent of the popular vote while Gerald Ford got 48.0 percent; but Carter overwhelmed Ford in the Electoral College by 297 votes to 240.

An odd aspect of the Bush victory over Gore in the Electoral College during the 2000 presidential election is that it functioned precisely in accordance with its original purpose. James Madison of Virginia was worried at the Constitutional Convention that direct elections would not only threaten the propertied class but also that the South, outnumbered by the North, would be hurt. Part of the resulting Electoral College deal was to allow the southern states to count slaves, with a two-fifths discount, in computing their share of electoral votes, even though the slaves could not vote. Thus Virginia, with its huge slave population, got more than a quarter of the electors needed to elect a president and vice president. As a result, for thirty-two of the Constitution's first thirty-six years, white Virginia slaveholders occupied the presidency.

The recent Bush-Gore contest was a replay of the same theme. Bush swept the Old Confederacy and the western areas that became slaveholding states after the American Revolution. Gore decisively won the North and Midwest, as well as the votes of blacks and women. We thus have reenacted the earlier period of American history, giving undue power to the South and financial control of the country to many of its richest citizens.

The obvious response to the archaic eighteenth-century system is to get rid of the Electoral College, an appendix in the Constitution like the appendix in the human body—with no real function and a constant possibility of infection. The president and vice president should be elected directly by a plurality of the national popular vote.[3] After all, every other office in the United States is filled by the person who gets the most votes.

However, this is more easily said than done because the change would require a constitutional amendment that would be blocked by the small states. The reason goes back to the original compromise that created the institution, namely, that every state regardless of size and population gets an additional elector for each of its two U.S. senators; this gives disproportionate weight to the smaller states, i.e., two more electors are given to states like Alaska and Delaware exactly as two more for states like New York and California. Several states with one representative have their electoral vote tripled by the additional two senatorial votes while New York's electoral weight, for example, is increased by only 6 percent. Nineteen million people in New York get twenty-nine electoral votes, while fewer than fourteen million in a collection of small states also get the same amount.

The result of this discrepancy can be seen in the November 2000 election. Bush captured seventy-three electoral votes in twelve small states whose combined population equaled that of California, where Gore received only fifty-four for that single state.[4]

Since a constitutional amendment requires the approval of three-quarters of the states, such an amendment is unforeseeable because of the unfair benefit—which they will not give up—conferred on these smaller states. Mining and agricultural interests, for example, carry inordinate weight in sparsely populated states and their politicians would fight with all their might not to give up this benefit from which they receive campaign monies, personal favors, and power.

An argument often used against a uniform national polling system is that the small states would be ignored as a result. But why should they get preferential treatment? Does anyone propose that, as farmers in these states get money for not planting due to their influence, landlords in the major cities should be paid by the federal government if they lose tenants? Or that store keepers or other businesses should be subsidized when their income drops?

Another argument against this change is the difficulty of eliminating defective voting mechanisms, which problem falls into the prerogative of states' rights. But whether federal or state, it is ridiculous to assert that the richest and most technologically advanced nation on earth cannot develop a foolproof machine—such as a standard ATM—to state quickly and accurately its voters preference.

In many places, votes are still recorded by antiquated methods. Local officials are responsible and each state has a patchwork of county-selected voting devices. Some levered machines during the November 2000 election were invented in 1890. New Yorkers still cast their ballots on machines in use for almost forty years that have been out of production for the last two decades, with parts difficult to obtain. In New York City, Mayor Rudolph Giuliani had to wait nearly forty minutes before he could vote because of the back-up caused by problems with these machines. In St. Louis and Detroit, polling stations were so overwhelmed by prospective voters many angry citizens gave up and went away without voting. In Wisconsin, precincts ran out of paper ballots.

Many ballots were discarded not only because of antiquated machines and long lines, but also because instructions were confusing. An additional factor was that the less efficient punch-card systems to register choice were more common in poor districts— where no money had been assigned to upgrade—while the more affluent districts had modern equipment. In fact, Kweisi Mfume, president of the NAACP, delivered to the Justice Department after the 2000 election a three hundred-page document listing "voting fraud, intimidation, and irregularities," and these were not limited to Florida. The Committee for the Study of the American Electorate reported that at least two million votes were invalidated throughout the nation in the Bush-Gore election.[5] The culprit in most cases was the punch-card ballot (poking out small holes, or chad, in the ballot) still used for almost one in three voters.

There is finally a rush to modernize voting equipment. Within a month after the 2000 election, Wisconsin banned punch-card voting. The speaker of the California Assembly proposed spending

$300 million to upgrade the state's voting machines. Michigan's secretary of state wanted the same machine in every voting booth. Connecticut officials suggested using part of the state's projected budget surplus to buy an electronic voting system. Georgia and Maryland passed legislation to overhaul their voting equipment. And in May 2001 Florida lawmakers from both parties (with the endorsement of Governor Jeb Bush, brother of the new president) reached an agreement on a bill to ban punch-card ballot machines and give counties the money to purchase modern voting machines.

The problem of modernization is, of course, money. Until the 2000 Florida scandal, new machines were a low public priority, far below roads, hospitals, health care—or where executives redecorated their offices or hired political friends. The top equipment, such as the touch-screen SVS system, which confirms votes with an X next to the candidate's name on a large color screen, costs around $35,000 for each unit. Since one machine is recommended for each 500 to 700 voters, the cost for Palm Beach County in Florida alone would amount to $2.6 to $4.6 million. A less expensive machine, an ATM-type device that has buttons on the side of a monochrome screen, sells for $1,500. Optical machines, where voters fill in dots on ballot cards that are counted by optical scanning, are already in limited use and sell for $5,700. Their advantage, despite the higher price, is that each machine can be used by far more people. But no matter what equipment is chosen, the costs are very high.[6]

The great advantage of the strong emotions aroused in the dubious victory of President George W. Bush is that now there is almost universal acceptance that the status quo cannot continue and that machinery to correctly record voter preference must be used. Although elimination of the senile Electoral College probably lies in the distant future, a modernization of voting machines will at least wash away most of the present problems.

★

## TERM LIMITS

Partly because Franklin D. Roosevelt, sick and edging toward dotage, sought and won a fourth term as president—and in that physical condition gave away Eastern Europe to the wily manipulation of Stalin over the strong objections of Winston Churchill—the Twenty-second Amendment to the Constitution was passed, limiting presidents to two terms. Many states have also attempted to apply term limits; some have been thrown out by the courts. But if there is any one overriding need, greater than curbing the power of lobbyists and limiting PACs and soft money, it is term limits.

From the day a person gets elected—any politician, from the local dog catcher to the president—this person's supreme aim is to be reelected. Power is the greatest drug and very few can resist its appeal. Though a president may rationalize his actions, and former President Clinton was a master of this art, the overriding goal is remaining in office as long as possible.

All offices, extending up to and including Congress and the chief executive, should be limited. This ought also to include the Supreme Court, where some judges have actually presided in their late eighties.[7] Those in the legislature should be limited to a maximum of two terms. The president should serve for one. Two presidential terms is too much. An extended term of six years, which could be done by a constitutional amendment, would solve the problem. This is not a vague delusion; the majority of American people are so disgusted with our legislators and presidents after their election that they would most probably support such a measure. And, one might add, our representatives would benefit as well, at least in the eyes of history. Knowing what measures are needed, often against the short-term views of the public, they now tend to ride the popularity wave. Voting according to transient poll figures, which are often manipulated, is not reasoned democracy but demagoguery.

Furthermore, this change would reduce the appeal of the independent voters for third-party candidates, who often are no better than those of the two major parties. Over one-third of Americans now call themselves independents. This leap in independents is a 50 percent increase in the last eight years, indicating the disgust of many people with the major parties. Presidents and legislators, knowing they could not be reelected, would tend to be more honest and effective; and the faith of the people would be renewed in their offices.

Of America's last seven presidents before our current one, only two stayed in office for a second term. Gerald R. Ford, Jimmy Carter, and George Bush were defeated in their second-term bids. Richard M. Nixon was forced to resign over Watergate. Lyndon B. Johnson declined to run again because of the Vietnam War. Only Ronald Reagan and Bill Clinton were elected to a second term: Reagan with the help of tax reductions that created prosperity at the cost of saddling the American people with a colossal national debt; and Clinton, whose reelection would have been doubtful if the public had known of his shady methods to raise campaign funds.

The people are very skeptical, if not cynical. The Founding Fathers in their wisdom divided power among three branches, knowing from bitter experience how power corrupts; a mistake they made, however, was not realizing that to continue in office creates, through desire for reelection, similar corruption. A truly great man, George Washington, reluctant for a second term, declined to run for a third. But there are very few Washingtons.

A century ago, when issues were debated rather than put behind a smokescreen, turnout usually exceeded 80 percent of eligible voters in presidential elections, almost 90 percent outside the South. Today, with all the massive media hokum, turnout has dropped to a half. In the 1998 Congressional elections (although not a presidential election year) the overall turnout was only 26 percent. This tells best what the public thinks.

The real solution to the lies and dirty acts of the executive branch would be to set up a permanent and independent oversight board drawn from the professional and educational world. This group would, at stated intervals, review the acts of the president, his cabinet, and his staff and would have the right to subpoena anyone and compel testimony under oath. This was attempted after Watergate but was suborned by political infiltration, i.e., the Starr Counsel. The overseeing body should be sealed off from political contamination by its nonpolitical choice of members. Investigation would be limited to true insubordination of office, not personal affairs. It should also be not only permanent but a revolving body so that bureaucratic dry bones, the curse of most organizations, would not disintegrate into partisan motives.

The United States originally had a meritocracy for the highest political posts. President Andrew Jackson then initiated the "spoils system," which gave most posts to sycophants. All attempts, though, at creating a truly effective merit system have since failed when it comes to top positions. The White House staff, cabinet members, and ambassadors are chosen for their political or financial contributions to the success of those elected, and legislative courtesy most often means automatic confirmation. In a great many cases they are totally unfit for their jobs. Many are political hacks or very rich persons trained in making money but nothing else. Business trains for competition; politics is more a matter of compromise. As to rewarding those who won the campaign by slogging the election trail, the functions of winning elections and governing are very different. Elections are won or lost by public relations and manipulating images. Governing is the creation of programs and their effective implementation. No one in business would dream of hiring the company's advertising agency personnel to run policy, and yet in practice this is often the way of Washington.

It is also absurd to send ambassadors to foreign countries who know neither the language nor the customs but receive the positions as payoffs. It is equally ridiculous to pick as cabinet members persons who represent the interests of special groups with whom they formerly had close financial relations. Unless a merit system is adopted the United States will continue to be led by individuals who, although competent for the most part in previous activities, are ignorant in the world of diplomacy and political wisdom.

## PRIMARIES

Three-quarters of the states hold primaries to determine which candidates will face off in the general election. But each state has its own rules. To control the primary is to pick the candidate. As has been shown, parties and politicians have the ability to rig primaries through packing the electorate with selected voters, or buying through future promises or gratuities, as well as distorting the results through the media. These were major factors in the elections of Kennedy and Carter. This clumsy technique, whose results have little relation to the true wishes of the majority of the electorate, is "surely the most idiotic method of choosing national leaders ever invented in a free society."[8]

An excellent example is the 1996 national election, in which Bob Dole became the Republican nominee. A tremendous fight was waged in the states of New Hampshire and Iowa, the two earliest states voting and therefore the ones that could profoundly influence the future of the competing candidates. Nine Republican candidates slugged it out through these two states, the prize being a total of forty-one delegates to the Republican National Convention—or only 2 percent of the total delegates.

The nine contenders spent about $40 million. Yet this relatively small sum in today's political arena tipped the scales for the leading contenders. New Hampshire, whose total population is only a little over a million—and with a minority of Republicans voting in the primary—thus influenced the national picture. Furthermore, in New Hampshire those not registered in a party also have the right to vote in any primary they choose, which distorts the results even more. In this same year in Iowa, only one in six Republicans voted but this, too, strongly influenced the national choice.

The various state rules on primaries further contort the results. In New Hampshire the final vote is proportionately divided among the delegates. In California—a very densely populated and key state—however, the winner takes all. If the top candidate wins by only 1 percent, that person gets all the delegates.

New York has its own machine-controlled racket. There is a direct primary, but the system has been rigged by rules that limit access to the ballot. In 1996 Bob Dole was chosen by the bosses. Other candidates were so restricted that in practice they could not enter their names. The trick employed was a rule that an alternate candidate had to have 5 percent of all registered Republicans in each of the state's thirty-one congressional districts. Then every technicality was used to void ballots of Dole's adversaries: a wrong letter in a name, leaving out the middle initial, a misprint in address, and so on. Pat Buchanan, for example, had enough signatures but the Dole-controlled Board of Elections knocked out about a third of the signatures, eliminating his candidacy. Only a lawsuit by Steve Forbes succeeded in opening the New York primary to others than Dole.

The result of those rules is simply that restrictions and influences in the primaries can nominate a presidential candidate who, as in the case of Jimmy Carter, is barely known. John F. Kennedy's father spent large sums in West Virginia and Wisconsin to influence the few voters in those states' presidential primaries. The successful results gave significant momentum to the Kennedy campaign. The smaller the state, the fewer the number of primary voters, and the easier it is to influence them, and thus propel a candidate forward with little relation to the general desire of the voters of the entire nation.

In the last five presidential races, each party nominated the candidate who raised the most money in the two years before the elections. By February 1999, long before the November 2000 election, the campaigns of both major parties had spent more than $138 million preparing for the primaries; four years earlier the sum was $23.2 million. In the 2000 state primaries, Super Tuesday consisted of fourteen states where the organizational and tremendous financial advantages of George W. Bush and Al Gore enabled them to eliminate their opponents before voters in more than thirty states (i.e., more than half the states) even had a chance to cast a ballot. A survey shortly thereafter indicated that 74 percent of Americans believed that party leaders and big contributors had a larger voice than the voters in the selection of the nominees. And a majority of polled voters checked affirmatively the statement that "politics in America is generally pretty disgusting."[9]

The obvious solution to this ridiculous system is to have a national presidential primary on the same day, obviously adjusted to the differences in the time zones, where all the registered voters of each party could then express their choice. No one who was not a registered party member would be allowed to vote in these contests. In case of a very close vote, where the top two candidates were nose to nose, the other similar-party candidates would be eliminated and a second election then would decide the issue. This would truly confirm the real popularity of the winning candidates.

## UNITED STATES SENATE AND HOUSE APPORTIONMENT

When creating the legislative branch of government, the United States Constitution provided that two senators represent each state. The result has been ludicrous, as can be shown.

There were over 281 million Americans in the fifty states of the Union, excluding the District of Columbia and Puerto Rico, as recorded in the 2000 Census. The eight largest states—California, Texas, New York, Florida, Pennsylvania, Illinois, Ohio, and Michigan, with a total population of some 136 million persons—had sixteen U.S. senators. The eight smallest states—Wyoming, Vermont, Alaska, North Dakota, South Dakota, Delaware, Montana, and Rhode Island, with a total population of less than 6 million persons—had the same sixteen U.S. senators. Put simply, these eight smallest states had little more than 4 percent of the population of the eight largest states— but wielded the same power in the Senate. The two senators from Wyoming (one of whom had been Vice President Dick Cheney), whose population is less than 500,000 persons, are equal in power to the two senators from California, where the population is almost 34 million people—almost seventy times more people than Wyoming. Thus, a very small minority of the population can block the needs of the very great majority, or, conversely, extract disproportionate privileges. An excellent example of how this operates is in the state of Montana, where the total net farm income in 1999 was subsidized by government assistance; in eight of the last nine elections the citizens, living in the equivalent of a socialist system, voted Republican.

It is doubtful that the Founding Fathers deliberately built this feature into the Constitution. At that time some 90 percent of Americans were farmers, and they believed the farming population would be distributed more or less equally as the people moved West. Cities were few and not greatly peopled; they could not conceive enormous urban centers such as New York and Los Angeles, whose citizens are effectively disenfranchised in comparison with Cheyenne, Wyoming, or the many small towns in Alaska. And this discrepancy is becoming ever greater as the general population shifts west and south, to such states as California, Texas, and Florida, while states like the Dakotas and Wyoming lose population.

The same disproportion is true for U.S. Representatives. The apportionment of the 435 seats in the House takes place every ten years following the official federal census. The shift in seats is based on a complex formula that takes into consideration population gains relative within the state—not to a percentage basis calculating all states. Thus, for example, Montana would gain an extra seat on the basis of some ten thousand persons because of its very small population, while California would get another seat only if it gained over three hundred thousand persons. Nothing less democratic can be imagined.

Furthermore, it has been calculated that the average census misses close to 12 million persons, most of them minorities living in the big cities. At the same time, again according to the Census Bureau, more than 8 million people are counted twice, many of them in more white and affluent areas. A change has been suggested in the counting method: Rather than trying to count through questionnaires and door-to-door visits, the census would attempt to reach 90 percent of households in each neighborhood and then estimate the rest. This is strongly opposed by Republicans because they feel the change would apportion more seats to poorer areas and, since the poor tend to vote for Democratic candidates, this would adversely affect the number of seats Republicans hold. The resolution of this problem, however, should not be political but factual.

Other than the sheer undemocratic nature of the legislative branch, the serious problem is that it permits a handful of determined members of Congress from states with small populations to dictate policy to the whole country in matters such as peanut, sugar, grain, and mining subsidies. The power of the farm bloc, as illustrated by the example of Montana, is too well known to warrant discussion. As a rather recent example in another industry, the Democratic senators from several mining states went to then President Clinton, who needed their votes elsewhere and killed several environment measures. These senators were motivated by campaign contributions from mining companies—and, ironically, most were not American but foreign companies.

A change in the law regarding U.S. senatorial apportionment more closely related to the number of people in each state would require a constitutional amendment, difficult to achieve. But in a nation that amended the Constitution to give the vote to African Americans, to women, to residents of the District of Columbia, to the poor, and to young people,★ it seems not impossible to pass an amendment to provide a more equitable system of voting for the general population. As to the House, this would be simpler. The formula to distribute seats could be altered to more fully reflect national population changes. It is certain, however, that retaining the present system gives various small groups great power over the will of the general public.

★The Fifteenth, Seventeenth, Nineteenth, Twenty-third, Twenty-fourth, and Twenty-sixth Amendments, respectively.

"SO WHY ALL THE FUSS WHEN I SAY
THOU NEEDN'T LOVE THY NEIGHBOUR?"

# ——————CONCLUSION——————

*"A decent provision for the poor is the true test of civilization."*
Samuel Johnson

*"He gave it for his opinion, 'that whoever could make two ears of corn, or two blades of grass, to grow upon a spot of ground where only one grew before, would deserve better of mankind, and do more essential service to his country, than the whole race of politicians put together.'"*
Johnathan Swift, *Gulliver's Travels*, II

This is a glorious America for the alert and resourceful, particularly those of white native stock. Its riches reach deep into the pockets of people, and is paradise indeed when compared to much of the rest of the world. Two-thirds of all its citizens own their own homes, though heavily mortgaged, and fewer than 1 percent of these homes are without refrigerators. As of 1999 an estimated 45 percent owned equities in some form or other, up from 14 percent in 1980, although it is likewise true that the richest 1 percent owned over 50 percent of stock shares. By the 1960s nearly 90 percent of all houses had at least one television set. And by 2000 more than half of the households in the United States had at least one computer, with more than 40 percent connected to the Internet.

This is an unhappy America for the disadvantaged, the weak in body or mind, those born without close family ties, and many of those who are not white. It is a strange and contorted land whose contradictions are often little noted because the underbelly of society is mute.

Very expensive apartments stand cheek by jowl with the shelter-less sleeping in the streets and on church steps, now amounting to some seven hundred thousand homeless throughout the nation. Fashionable and very expensive restaurants sit alongside soup kitchens. By the 1990s the largest single private employer was an agency for temporary help,[1] since by hiring such employees corporations avoid insurance and pension obligations. Immense fortunes are made by stock speculation while manufacturing declines and is sent overseas. Opulent art collectors pay $50 to $55 million for a Van Gogh or Picasso oil painting and $29 million for a Degas pastel while homeless men and women beg in the streets.

Fraudulent manipulation of savings and loan associations have saddled the taxpayers with an obligation of over $500 billion. Crooks pay off politicians and escape jail sentences. The national trade deficit has skyrocketed to $1 billion a day and is only held up by foreign investors; foreigners now own 38 percent of outstanding Treasury notes and 20 percent of corporate bonds, which leads to the ominous possibility of a national collapse if markets such as Japan or the Euro bloc would stabilize and offer higher interest rates. A feather in this wind is the Iraqi announcement that the country would price its oil in Euros and not American dollars. And Americans themselves are no help: Their savings rate as a percentage of disposable personal income in 2000 was literally zero. A good number of them live on credit cards with high interest rates. And U.S. bankruptcies have shot up to unprecedented heights.

Americans have the highest rate of poverty-stricken single mothers and children in the developed world, a disproportionate number of whom are black and urban. Forty percent of our children are now born out of wedlock; in cities the figure is much higher. In Hartford, Connecticut, in 1998 it was 80 percent. The child poverty rate in 2000, after almost two decades of prosperity, was still higher than it was twenty years ago. The U.S. rate was the highest among the eighteen most advanced industrial countries;[2] in New York the ratio was one in four; in California it was one in six. The child poverty rate stands at 22.7 percent in the United States, compared to 19.9 percent in the United Kingdom and 8.7 percent in Germany.

Nearly a million low-income parents have lost Medicaid coverage since 1996 because of President Clinton's pandering to Newt Gingrich. In the fifteen most affected states the decline was 27 percent, according to the consumer group Families USA.[3] In mid-2000 the World Health Association (WHA) issued figures ranking health-care systems in each of the 191 nations that are members of the WHA. The United States came in a dismal number thirty-seven, outperformed by the European nations. The five best nations caring for the health of their citizens were France, Italy, and the tiny countries of San Marino, Andorra, and Malta. America outspent the world but distributed the cost unfairly, one of the report's measuring sticks: Native American children, for example, look forward to a life span of only fifty years on average.[4]

In fact, we are the only advanced industrial nation without some form of comprehensive health plan. Our levels of income inequality and relative poverty are triple that of other wealthy nations. In 1999 it was found that 33 percent of Hispanic people, about 21 percent of African Americans and Asian Americans, and 11 percent of non-Hispanic whites had no health insurance.[5]

Related to the question of health is our way of life, what is called the couch-potato culture of contemporary American society. The combination of little physical exercise and fast food is ruinous for the health. The fast-food business is now a $110-billion industry. The typical American eats almost three hamburgers and four orders of french fries a week. Diabetes, little regarded as a problem compared to AIDS, is a looming epidemic in America, and this in turn is directly linked to the problem of obesity. The Centers for Disease Control and Prevention reported in early 2001 that diabetes increased one-third nationally between 1990 and 1998 and, with approximately eight hundred thousand new cases reported each year, it is the seventh leading national killer.

The link with obesity is strongest among minorities. Over one-quarter of blacks and one-fifth of Hispanics are obese (defined as 30 percent overweight), compared to 17 percent of whites. Not only diabetes but asthma, heart disease, and hypertension are directly related to being overweight. There is a vicious chain connecting these conditions. The obesity of these two groups in turn relates to the flood of television commercials advertising candy, snacks, and junk food.[6] These products are produced by powerful national corporations that, through political contributions, avoid scrutiny by federal agencies to curtail such sales or, minimally, to post their negative effects. It was a European boycott that forced Monsanto to give up its genetic alteration of food products, not any U.S. supervisory agency.

As last reported, America's rate of imprisonment was five times that of western Europe. We have more people in prison than did Stalin, percentage-wise. The number of jail beds has quadrupled in the last twenty-five years. The prison population has tripled since 1980. About 16 percent of the inmates are imprisoned because of mental illness since the wholesale closing of public mental hospitals in the 1960s. The Justice Department reported that from 1950 to 1993 alone, the percentage of drug offenders in state prisons rose to 60 percent from 25 percent. The poor, deprived of any system of social protection as in western Europe and therefore not feeling any inner identification with society (especially true for nonwhite minorities), have turned to drugs and crime.

By 1999 the number of prisoners—including county, state, and federal prisons; those locked up but not yet convicted; and those on probation—rose to over 6 million persons, or about 3 percent of all American adults.[7] The solution endorsed by major sectors of both parties, including the assent of former President Clinton, was to give longer sentences and build more prisons. New York State spent some $4 billion building prison cells in the past two decades. Newt Gingrich's Contract with America called for providing billions of dol-

★

lars in federal financing for state prison construction if states would lengthen the required time inmates had to serve.

George W. Bush, then governor of Texas and now president, greatly increased the prison capacity and number of inmates in his state, 85 percent of whom, it has been stated, are jailed for drug use. Bush himself denied using cocaine in recent years, refusing to comment on younger days, which he described as "foolish and irresponsible." Those foolish and irresponsible young cocaine users in Texas who lacked money and political pull went to jail under Bush; he became president. Clinton was damned for a marijuana cigarette in his mouth which he childishly claimed not to have inhaled; presumably Bush only exhaled, which of course is quite different.

It costs about $25,000 a year to keep an inmate in jail.[8] American prisons (along with the military) have in effect become our form of social security, replacing welfare, for the urban poor minorities. Instead of trying to educate, we jail. Instead of modifying our harsh drug laws, some states have increased them. And the rich seek more tax relief, which can only result in cutting back the minimal social safety net we have.

Jerome G. Miller, the director of the National Center on Institutions and Alternatives, said the criminal justice system is turning the majority of impoverished minorities in the inner cities into criminals. Almost three-quarters of prison inmates are now African American or Hispanic, and if the prison trend continues, by 2010 "we will have the absolute majority of African American males between ages 18 and 40 in prison and camps."[9] It should also be mentioned in states where studies have been made, such as California, more than two-thirds of parolees land back in jail; almost one-quarter have AIDS, and more than a third have tuberculosis. The majority are also functionally illiterate.[10] For these citizens the United States is no longer a land of opportunity but rather a police state, a Soviet-like gulag.

Unfortunately, another aspect of this same problem is that more than 60 percent of young American males—almost twice the World War II level—were rejected in 1999 when volunteering for military

★

service because of poor health, past drug abuse, or a record of trouble at school or with the law.[11]

Not unrelated, according to the Center for Media Education, an average child will witness more than one hundred thousand acts of violence on TV, including eight thousand murders, by the time he or she completes elementary school. The numbers double by the end of high school. As for commercials, that same person by the age of twenty-one will see one hundred thousand advertisements for drinks involving alcohol.[12] Violence sells movies and television programs, and alcohol is also big business. When Tipper Gore, Al Gore's wife, spoke against violence on such public media the Democrats seeking Hollywood money shuddered, and she was forced to shut her mouth. The Democratic phalanx on the West Coast was liberal until their pocketbooks might be affected.

The Federal Trade Commission, after a yearlong study in 1999, reported that the vast majority of the best-selling restricted movies, music, and video games, were deliberately marketed to children as young as twelve. The ratings on movies are voluntary and the industry reaction to this study could have been foreseen, ranging from statements that it was impossible to keep promotion of products away from the eyes and ears of children to a more frank admission of one top executive, who requested anonymity, that "everyone's hands are dirty."[13]

And what is seen often goes beyond the limits of even tolerant people opposed to censorship. The rapper Eminem stated on a CD that he'd like to have sex with his mother. In his music, all women are whores and he's eager to rape and murder them. For this nauseating work he was given a Grammy Award as the best rap soloist in February 2001. The top album to receive this prestigious award at the same time was devoted to incest, statutory rape, threesomes, and drugs.

Aside from the filth and violence on television and in music to which people, and especially children, are exposed, the level of general school education itself is dismal. American children spend fifteen hundred hours a year watching television, compared to nine hundred hours

★

at school. They are nineteenth in math and twenty-first in science out of the top twenty-five countries. In their final year of secondary school American students in math score just behind Lithuania but ahead of Cypress, way behind the students in western Europe and Japan. And the decline is continuous. The average number of words in the written language of a six-to-fourteen-year-old American child was less than half in 2000 than it was in 1945.[14] An amusing but basically horrible study showed that if our eighth graders continued to improve their basic math skills at the pace they have since 1973 it would take 125 years for them to catch up with their peers in Singapore.[15] But why spend money on education when it is more important to give additional tax relief to the wealthiest 2 percent of Americans?

Even the enlightened wealthy acknowledge this problem. A group of top technology executives, all Republicans, met with President George W. Bush shortly after his election and forcefully stated that, aside from short-term benefits such as tax cuts, they were mainly concerned with getting math and science education on a higher level into the classroom. Indeed, if it were not for the flood of foreigners—first refugees from Hitler and Mussolini, then Nazi post–World War II careerists, then those leaving the collapsed Soviet Union, and now a flood of Indians and Chinese—our vaunted technological research and new industries would falter. Economist Gary Becker, a Nobel laureate, reported that more than a third of the one million people employed in Silicon Valley are foreign-born.

Our politicians, scrounging for reelection money, ignore this most important issue. Education of the young is the future of a country. Raising our educational standards to confront the new technological revolution, enlarging such opportunities for the poor and the ethnic minorities, are far more important goals than the present approach, namely more and larger jails.

This is equally true for adults. The decline in educational standards goes back many decades. A study of the level of complexity of political discourse can illustrate this. In the Lincoln-Douglas debates right before the Civil War, Douglas's speeches tested at a nearly twelfth-grade reading level, those of Lincoln just above eleventh grade. In the first televised presidential debate of 1960, Nixon spoke above tenth grade while Kennedy was just slightly below. In the 1996 presidential election debates Clinton spoke at eighth grade level and Bob Dole was right for the sixth grade (eleven-year-olds). And in the first debate between Bush and Gore, Bush spoke at a level almost appropriate to a seventh grader (twelve-year-olds) while Gore, like Clinton, was appropriate for an eighth grader. It also should be mentioned that when Franklin D. Roosevelt declared war against the Japanese after Pearl Harbor, his speech was at the twelfth-grade level.[16] There seems to be a continuing contest among our present political leaders as to who might seem closer to cretins.

The average American is far ahead of Congress because he thinks rather than merely reacting like Pavlov's dogs to the monied interests. In a mid-1999 *Wall Street Journal*/NBC News poll only 9 percent stated tax relief should be the top priority; the largest group, 23 percent of those polled, favored improving public education.[17]

Voting among lower-income Americans has been declining as apathy and disgust replace hope. In 1990 almost 14 percent of the voters came from families with incomes under $15,000; in 1992 this declined to 11 percent; and in 1994, to less than 8 percent, a drop almost in half in four short years. The Republicans pitch their bid to the rich and upper-middle class, the group with the highest voting ratio and stock ownership. The Democrats, and even more so under President Clinton, portray themselves as the torchbearers for the middle class. Other than rhetoric, neither party is interested in the poor.

Many Americans are so terrified of their fellow compatriots that they stock guns at home as though they are dishware, and these are equally available to their children.[18] There are some 190 million guns in civilian hands, about 65 million of which are handguns, those most involved in killings. More than thirty thousand Americans die each year by gunfire, many of whom are children. There are more than four thousand gun shows annually where people can buy guns without a background check, and almost half of American households own them. Despite these oppressive facts—and, of course, influenced by large sums from the National Rifle Association for political campaigns—President Bush opposes licensing and regulation of firearms. In this matter, as in others, some states are ahead of the federal government. Eleven states—including Colorado and Oregon, considered "pro-gun" states—now require background checks at gun shows.[19]

One argument often used by the NRA is that regulatory laws would be ignored by a great majority with impunity. This is refuted by Canadian experience. In 1998 Canada passed a law whereby all guns are to be licensed by the end of 2002; handgun owners have been required to do so for years. Already one-fourth of Canadian gun owners have sold or surrendered their guns. Contrary to dire predictions, roughly 80 percent of gun owners had by the end of 2000 complied with this law.[20]

While these terrible problems eat at the roots of American society, the top generals and admirals are always calling for more money. More than a decade after the end of the Cold War, our country still spends more on the military than all of its NATO allies combined, and five to six times more than its rivals. The Pentagon's budget under President Clinton's last spending plan was projected to rise from $309 billion to $323 billion, with Congress calling for an additional $20-billion increase while the military leaders testified before Congress after Bush's inaugural that they needed $90 billion more than the largest previous projections. In the meantime our former greatest adversaries, Russia and China, are spending in the same period $64 billion at maximum in the former and $37 billion in the latter, with President Vladimir Putin of Russia demanding a greater reduction.

To make some comparisons, the National Park Service is budgeted at $1.4 billion; the FBI at $3 billion; the U.S. Border Patrol at $1 billion; Head Start at $5 billion; and aid for poor schoolchildren at $9 billion. These collectively add up to 1 percent of the federal budget. The expense of the National Endowment for the Arts, a perennial target of right-wingers, would finance the Pentagon for three hours. And foreign aid is another 1 percent of spending.[21]

A distorted solution for those with money is to turn away from these problems by creating what might be called the equivalent of twentieth-century moated castles, with private roads, gated areas, and twenty-four-hour security guards. It used to be commonplace to leave one's door open; that is now as obsolete as the Studebaker. Security alarm system companies are one of the great growth industries. There are even entire walled-in towns. The fastest-growing residential communities are private, with gates and guards, governed by a thicket of codes and restrictions. Nearly 4 million Americans live in these communities; another 28 million reside in areas governed by private community associations with similar restrictions. In Southern California a third of all new developments built in the last decade are regulated by private governments, and other areas moving in this direction are the suburbs outside Dallas, Phoenix, and Washington, D.C., as well as the major Florida cities. The number of such communities is supposed to double in the next decade.[22]

We are thus creating a balkanization of the nation with an absolute physical, as well as psychological, separation of the rich and poor. Obviously, to the degree this grows, the sense of community spirit declines. As almost all the people in these communities are middle- and upper-class whites, their sense of alienation from the changes in the U.S. population—the rise of Hispanics and Asians— grows as well. From indifference rises resentment and fear, which their children will hear from them, and this will breed even stronger efforts to elect candidates to pass legislation hindering newcomers from sharing in the American dream. But as Abraham Lincoln said during the Civil War, we cannot escape destiny—or bottle it. Minorities are now 26 percent of the population; by 2050 they will be almost half. And no gates, guards, or bought legislators can seal them from trying to enter the mainstream.

It would never occur to most of the very rich that it was mere accident that they were born white, healthy, with concerned parents, and in a favorable economic situation; and that to the contrary there are others born not white, not healthy, not in concerned families, and in a dismal economic situation. But these others are human beings who, as such, are entitled to respect and, when weak in mind or body, need help. "Nature is cruel and survival is competitive" will be one answer, but what distinguishes humankind from others in nature is a moral capacity to understand this difference and attempt to help the less fortunate. It is this moral value that separates the civilized from the savage and to the extent any belief in democracy implies this interpretation so should the fortunate recognize some responsibility for the unfortunate. A brief knowledge of history also shows that unless this is realized and acted upon to some degree, social tensions and wide economic disparity lead to class warfare.

President Calvin Coolidge said that the chief business of the American people is business. The United States, more than a nation, can be thought of as an enormous corporation bestriding a continent and exploiting its resources (as well as penetrating the rest of the world) for the benefit of its business executives and stockholders. Indeed, the analogy is far more than symbolic; the 2001 presidential election was the first in history in which a majority of voters were investors. Although almost everyone has the right to vote, many recent elections rarely bring out a majority; in the 1996 presidential election less than half the voters bothered; in off-year elections perhaps a third vote; and in 2000 barely a majority voted, with several million voters disqualified. The rest—the mass of the poor— through indifference or cynicism didn't show up.

Elections are usually won by a plurality of the voters and decided by a very small percent, though this is not often reflected in the Electoral College. The vote of the rich and upper-middle class is usually Republican but not decisive. It is the swing vote of the independents who, growing every year, decide the issue, and toward them the propaganda machine blasts. When business is good these voters almost always support the incumbent, in effect the national corporation executives. When business is bad the voters turn to the other major political party. And if and when the other party's candidates are elected they propose measures that hopefully will result in improved economic conditions, growth of stock values to shareholders, and greater tax relief for the monied class; that is, to the larger part of the ever-diminishing voting electorate.

The United States, as has been mentioned before, may be profitably compared to the Venetian Republic, whose stable government lasted over a thousand years because of a similar structure. There, too, the wealthy elite had created a system that worked efficiently and was supported by the class whose members benefited by its policy.

> For them the acquisition of wealth was the sole and necessary path to eminence and power. For them wealth and power and wealth and success became synonymous. They appreciated the fact that the prosperity of the individual merchant depended upon the welfare of the commercial class as a whole; and that for the benefit of the class everything else must be subordinated.[23]

Politically the United States is Procrustes' bed, cutting off the feet of those too long and stretching those too short. Whether Joseph McCarthy and Patrick Buchanan on the political right or Robert La Follette and Ralph Nader on the political left, the economic pressures shape or kill the politician. The perfect candidate is an Eisenhower, who goes through a shredding machine to come out bland and uniform. Indeed, the military, which has always produced the most popular candidates, is the perfect metaphor.

The system works for those who profit from its functioning, while those who do not are silent except in times of crisis, such as the 1930s and 1960s. Indeed, whether called a plutocracy, oligarchy, or oligopoly, a form of government where the most capable rise to the top (i.e., a meritocracy)—and which is increasingly open to the minority members of great ability and ambition—cannot easily be derided. It can be compared with some favor to the few feeble historical attempts at real democracy, that is, direct citizen participation without regard to status. Athens, following its loss to Sparta in the

★

Peloponnesian War in the very late fifth century B.C.E, collapsed into despotism. After its early experiment with democracy, France after the French Revolution turned to Napoleon. The moderate Kerensky government in Russia following the fall of Czar Nicholas II in 1917 ended in Bolshevik terrorism. Historically, those attempts at democracy resulted in tyranny in one form or other.

It is precisely because Americans have in the past fused the theoretical view of democracy with the actual rule by an elite that the country has attained such economic heights. The American upper class works for money and power and this has fueled our great material progress. It was so from the start. John Adams, our second president, stated in 1808, "We have one material which actually constitutes an aristocracy that governs the nation. That material is wealth. Talents, birth, virtues, services, sacrifices, are of little consideration with us." But a great advantage, unlike other plutocracies in history, is that our government is relatively flexible and, with money as the ultimate value, color, religion, and ethnic origin are becoming more and more subordinate to this supreme chase for personal wealth.

Focusing on the twentieth century, who did more for America? Our presidents, name who you will, or those inventive and hard-driving geniuses who stoked the country's forward economic march: men such as Henry Ford, Thomas C. Durant (General Motors), Henry J. Kaiser (steel and aluminum), Thomas J. Watson (IBM), Andrew Grove (Intel), and Bill Gates (Microsoft)? One can well state that these businessmen who created new industries and millions of new jobs were the real heroes of the United States rather than the presidential and legislative marionettes who capture the surface sound and light.[24]

It would seem that this line of thinking contradicts my thesis: namely, that the rich distort, and thus control, the country for their benefit. The thesis is still true. But the late twentieth century is marked by a technological revolution whose implications defy the most thinking person. New methods of mass production and product control have lowered prices on consumer goods such as refrigerators, stoves, washing machines, radios, and television sets

★

over recent years, testifying to the fact that even the poor now own VCRs, microwave ovens, and Sony Walkmans.

Our first man-to-the-moon expedition required room-sized computing monsters; the same controls are now reduced to finger-nail-sized chips. The data storage that by 2005 will fit into shoebox-sized devices would have required an area the size of Argentina in the technology of the 1950s. Storage prices are expected to drop (while profit increases) from almost forty cents a megabyte in 2001 to less than one cent in 2005, according to the company specializing in this field, EMC, making it cheaper for large companies to store information in centralized locations. It is calculated that by 2005 an individual will be able to have available a terrabyte (the equivalent of 250 million pages of text) of stored records, photos, and other data.

This is only the start. Within the next few decades our dependence on oil, coal, and gas will be greatly reduced. Wind velocity, ocean currents, tapping the earth's crust to exploit its molten interior, and fuel cells that will convert chemical energy without recharging are already on the horizon. Solar panels are already in use. Water shortage will be eliminated by an economical conversion of salt water to fresh water. Scientific advances in seeding will multiply crops many times, and the cultivation of fisheries will do the same for the supply of fish. The publishing of the entire human genome will make every cell a target for a drug, cutting back disease and increasing life expectancy in a healthy form. Robotic surgery is in its infancy. Copper wires will be obsolete, replaced by fiber, a strand of which can carry a hundred times more traffic. As a result, communication costs will be reduced; already, long-distance costs have dropped more than one-third since 1993, and cellular phone charges, even more. Chips, personal computers, and handheld data recorders in 2010 will be fifty times more powerful than today, and at the same price.

The digital revolution was unheard of only a few decades back, but it is omnipresent today. Digital cell phones can now simultaneously translate into sixteen languages, and video teleconferencing

★

may make business travel obsolete. Digital publishing will eliminate many publishers, and indeed bookstores as well. Digital texts will be distributed electronically, with copies reproduced on demand any-where—and in any language—either downloaded for a fee into an "e-book" or printed and bound for a few dollars a copy—the Internet will bypass both the middleman and physical book inven-tories. Already Xerox and IBM sell machines that in minutes can produce single bound copies of books in paper or hardcover.

The Internet is now engaged in new functions. Whole areas can be surveyed, with all pertinent details, for home buyers. Mortgages that cost up to 6 percent are now advertised at rates as low as 2 per-cent. And the bogeyman of abortion will be reduced to the same level as the medieval argument as to how many angels could stand on the head of a pin, for cheap, effective, and harmless birth-control pills to avoid pregnancy will be available everywhere. And then, for the first time in human history, worldwide increase in population will be attacked by rational means.

It has been estimated that Microsoft has made five thousand multimillionaires in the Seattle area, and that Cisco, Oracle, and Sun Microsystems, in the five hundred miles around Palo Alto, California, have as many as fifty thousand employees and investors worth more than $10 million each.★[25] A recent survey of about 320,000 compa-nies in the United States found there will be a demand for 1.6 mil-lion new technology jobs, many of which will go unfilled because of a lack of qualified applicants.[26]

These are some of the marvels before us. And new, enormous fortunes will be made—but only for a tiny few.

As liberty and equality are eternal enemies, so have been eco-nomics and morality. Indeed, all political life is a struggle between these two: the liberty to use human beings as mere factors in pro-duction for the benefit of the rich, and the vision of the spiritual equality of humankind. In the past, limited resources gave the laurel

---

★The recent sharp stock market technology decline has obviously altered these figures.

leaf to economics. Religions have attempted to modify these hard laws of nature by compassion. But, despite their striving, they have failed because with the shortage of available goods those persons with intelligence, drive, shrewdness, and a strong urge to power have always risen above the masses. We are reaching a new era in history where our technology can create unheard-of wealth. Should we use these new miracles to benefit increasingly only a small group of the rich—or extend this wealth, without unduly restricting opportunity, for the benefit of those less endowed by nature to triumph in the law of the jungle?

Did Louis Pasteur experiment for decades to develop a method to save the lives of millions of children only to obtain a patent on pasteurization? Did Andrew Carnegie give away his great fortune for libraries simply to have his name on buildings? Did Thomas A. Edison create his amazing inventions solely to see a Consolidated Edison sign? Even did John D. Rockefeller Sr., the prototype of the skinflint, endow majestic institutions of science and art simply because of his ego?

Yes, the ego invades all. Yes, the tax consequences are beneficial. But there is more. In all but an utterly selfish human being there exists a desire that may be simplified by the statement, "I would like to give back something of what I earned." To quote scripture, Luke 12:48, "Of those to whom much is given, much is required." Or at least *something* is required.

It is not only the most sensitive segment of the elite who think in these terms. The American people are among the most generous in history and do not begrudge wealth to those who earn it. But they feel something is wrong with a system where a man such as Bill Gates has such an enormous fortune while slum children don't get enough decent food to grow to be healthy adults. They sense something awry when the richly endowed United States is the only major industrial nation without a health plan to cover the poor, and has lower levels in educational standards than second-world countries. They feel, no matter how poorly it is expressed, that it is odd that the rich get richer while the real value of the wages of a good part of society decline. And they are puzzled when crooks in high places can go free through payoffs, while a young student who smokes a marijuana cigarette may sit in jail for years.

A nation that is capable of putting a man on the moon, that can transmit messages in a split second to every corner of the world, that can track the farthest reaches of the universe through super telescopes, that can conquer the most ravaging diseases and double the life span of ordinary people in a few decades, should be able to provide decent food for its hungry children, lodging for its aged and homeless, and medical attention for its poor.[27] With such tremendous wealth created through our new technological wizardry, this is not a utopian dream.

The means are there but the selfish interests of small groups, who buy our so-called leaders to enhance their great fortunes or plague them with outmoded values no longer relevant in our time, block the path. It is said a nation gets the kind of government it deserves; if so, we are an unworthy people. It lies within our hands to become more worthy.

# ———— APPENDIX ————

In every country, regardless of the form of government, there is an inner group that through early settlement, prestige, money, or tradition sets its stamp on that country's history. In our democracy such families exist. Usually called aristocrats, examples are the Adamses, Lees, Lodges, Roosevelts, Bushes, Tafts, Harrimans, and Kennedys.

Stephen Hess, author of *America's Political Dynasties: from Adams to Kennedy* (New York, 1966), compiled a list of high public offices held by such dynasties. The following is a resumé of most of these families, excluding those top figures mentioned in this book's text as well as some minor examples. Likewise eliminated are relatively less-important political positions. When an individual held a higher office after lesser ones, only the highest office is mentioned. Also eliminated are posts held before the American Revolution and the ratification of the U.S. Constitution. The web of intermarriages, a fascinating subject of itself, is likewise excluded. Note also that the list compiled stops at the date of the book's issuance, 1966.

*The Adams Family.* Seven such persons, including two presidents, a secretary of the navy, and a governor. In-laws and collateral relations include fourteen more, including a Supreme Court judge, one U.S. senator, and seven members of the U.S. House of Representatives.

*The Bayard Family.* One secretary of state, a minister to Great

★

Britain,★ and three U.S. Senators. In-laws and collateral relations included two members of the Supreme Court, two U.S. senators, two members of the U.S. House of Representatives, and two governors.

*The Breckinridge Family.* One vice president, one assistant secretary of war, one minister to Russia, one U.S. senator, and five members of the U.S. House of Representatives. In-laws and collateral relations included a secretary of state and a secretary of war, an assistant secretary of the treasury, a minister to Nicaragua, one U.S. Senator, and five members of the U.S. House of Representatives.

*The Frelinghuysen Family.* Four U.S. senators and one member of the U.S. House of Representatives. In-laws included a minister to Prussia.

*The Harrison Family.* Two presidents, two U.S. senators, four members of the U.S. House of Representatives, and one governor. In-laws and collateral relations included one U.S. senator and one member of the House of Representative.

*The Lee Family.* One attorney general, two U.S. senators, three members of the U.S. House of Representatives, and three governors. In-laws and collateral relations included one president, one chief justice of the Supreme Court, four U.S. Senators, three members of the U.S. House of Representatives, one governor, and one mayor.

*The Livingston Family.* One member of the Supreme Court (as well as secretary of the navy), one secretary of foreign affairs (as well as minister to France), one minister to Ecuador, one U.S. Senator, two members of the U.S. House of Representatives, two governors, and a lieutenant governor.

*The Long Family.* Two U.S. senators, three members of the U.S. House of Representatives, a governor, and a lieutenant governor.

*The Muhlenberg Family.* One U.S. senator and five members of the U.S. House of Representatives. In-laws and collateral relations included two members of the U.S. House of Representatives and two governors.

---

★Until 1893 the United States accredited abroad no higher diplomatic agent than ministers plenipotentiary.

*The Tucker Family.* One secretary of the treasury and three members of the U.S. House of Representatives. In-laws and collateral relations included one vice president, one secretary of the navy, a minister to Great Britain, three U.S. senators, and one member of the U.S. House of Representatives.

As of 1966, there had been some seven hundred families in which two or more members served in Congress, accounting for over 17 percent of all those elected to the federal legislature since 1774. Twenty-two families had four or more members of the same name elected to federal office. Sixteen of these families produced eight presidents, three vice presidents, thirty senators, twelve governors, fifty-six members of the U.S. House of Representatives, and nine cabinet ministers.

Eight of these families came to the United States before the eighteenth century; only two came after the American Revolution. All except the Kennedys were Protestants. As could be guessed, more than half of the families were millionaires. Very common has been intermarriage, creating a hereditary web to perpetuate their political dynasties.

A democracy?

---

★

---

# NOTES

---

★

---

## INTRODUCTION

1. In similar vein, John D. Rockefeller said, "God gave me my money." The Rockefellers' belief that money flowed to the virtuous gave rise to a famous remark of Martin Dooley (Finley Peter Dunne), the Irish American satirist, who wrote that it made them "a kind iv a society f'r th' previntion iv croolty to money." Justin Kaplan, *Mr. Clemens and Mark Twain* (New York, 1966), p. 323.

2. This, however, is becoming less true in the leading industrial European countries as politics bends to advanced technology and the service industries overtake, and indeed surpass in many cases, mining and manufacturing. International pressure from countries with low wages also forces an uneasy truce in common defense against cheap imports by capital and labor in high-wage countries.

3. On certain issues there are relative differences between the parties. Democrats tend to advocate environmental protection and gun control, for example. But even here there are no fixed positions. The Republican Theodore Roosevelt was a prime mover for national parks. Richard Nixon, though few realize it, was not only a strong supporter of environmental issues but also very sensitive to the plight of Native Americans. And, on the other hand, Democrats from the mining states are often tools of the mining companies.

4. Ambrose Bierce, "Politics," in *The Devil's Dictionary* (New York, 1993).

5. A survey taken by *Money* (October 1997) indicated that 61 percent of Americans are hostile to newcomers, believing that "too many immigrants want a free ride."

★

## CHAPTER ONE

1. In which 23 percent of West Point graduates opted for the Confederacy, including Robert E. Lee, Stonewall Jackson, Joseph Johnston, Jeb Stuart, and Jubal A. Early.

2. For this figure and those following see Dorothy B. Goebel and Julius Goebel Jr., *Generals in the White House* (New York, 1945).

3. Ibid., p. 269. The result was one of the biggest giveaway scandals in American history.

4. Jean H. Baker, *The Stevensons: A Biography of an American Family* (New York and London, 1996), pp. 252, 273.

5. Peter Lyon, *Eisenhower: Portrait of the Hero* (Boston and Toronto, 1974), pp. 364–80.

6. Roger Morris, *Richard Milhous Nixon: The Rise of an American Politician* (New York, 1990), p. 664.

7. Lyon, *Eisenhower*, p. 375.

8. Stephen E. Ambrose, *Eisenhower: Soldier, General of the Army, President-Elect, 1890–1952*, vol. 1 (New York, 1983), p. 437.

9. Ibid., p. 477.

10. Piers Brendon, *Ike: His Life and Times* (New York, 1986), p. 286.

11. Shelley Ross, *Fall from Grace: Sex, Scandal, and Corruption in American Politics from 1702 to the Present* (New York, 1988), p. 229.

12. Lyon, *Eisenhower*, p. 678.

13. Ibid, pp. 752–53. Herbert Brownell Jr., the chairman of the Republican National Committee who helped organize Eisenhower's nomination, was then appointed attorney general. A Nebraska native and a great supporter of civil rights, he resigned in 1957. Stephen A. Ambrose later wrote that Brownell was a political liability in the South because he was more insistent on integration than Eisenhower wanted him to be.

14. *Public Papers of the Presidents of the United States: Dwight D. Eisenhower* (Washington, D.C., 1960–61), p. 658.

15. Robert A. Divine, *Eisenhower and the Cold War* (New York, 1981), p. 51.

16. Robert J. Donovan, *Eisenhower: The Inside Story* (New York, 1965). Also Brendon, *Ike*, p. 303.

17. Morris, *Richard Milhous Nixon*, p. 666.

18. Arthur M. Schlesinger, "Our Presidents: A Rating by 75 Historians," *New York Times*, July 29, 1962, pp. 12, 40–41.

## CHAPTER TWO

1. Rexford G. Tugwell, *How They Became President: Thirty-Five Ways to the White House* (New York, 1964), p. 462. Tugwell, a professor of economics at Columbia University, served under President Franklin D. Roosevelt as governor of Puerto Rico.

2. Richard J. Whalen, "Joseph P. Kennedy: A Portrait of the Founder," *Fortune* (January, 1963): 117.

3. Apropos of the oligarchic strain in American politics, Jimmy Roosevelt ran, but was defeated by a more charismatic type, as the Democratic gubernatorial candidate in California in 1950. On the other hand, President Roosevelt's son Franklin D. Jr. was a member of the House of Representatives from New York from 1949 to 1955, and then an undersecretary of commerce in the Kennedy administration.

4. Playing behind a smokescreen as usual, early in the book he wrote, "I have no political ambitions for myself or for my children . . . "!

5. According to the late Tom Gillespie, then senior vice president of the Lumbermens Mutual Casualty Co., a division of Kemper Insurance of Chicago—and a close friend of the writer, to whom he told this personally—Marshall Field needed the approval of Washington to sell the Mart because of the tax loss involved. This was brought to the attention of President Roosevelt, who then alerted his friend Joseph Kennedy of the situation. For more specific details on the money making of Joe Kennedy, see John H. Davis, *The Kennedys: Dynasty and Disaster*, 1848–1983 (New York, 1984).

6. Richard J. Whalen, *The Founding Father: The Story of Joseph P. Kennedy* (New York, 1964), p. 427.

7. At least he didn't, like his younger brother Edward M. Kennedy, hire a classmate to take an examination in his stead, for which he was kicked out of Harvard in his first year. He was later readmitted. High connections are always very useful.

8. Barbara Gibson with Ted Schwarz, *The Kennedys: The Third Generation* (New York, 1993), p. 108.

9. Davis, *The Kennedys*, p. 120.

10. The chief suspect in the writing of this book, Ted Sorenson, has repeatedly denied his role. There is no question, however, that Professor Jules Davids of Georgetown University was hired to help John F. Kennedy; he was paid $700 for his writing or rewriting and indeed acknowledged in the book's preface as a material contributor.

11. Joe Kennedy arranged for John Hersey's account of the PT-boat episode, "Survival," to appear in the *Reader's Digest*. When JFK ran for Congress in 1946, his father had one hundred thousand copies reprinted, which were then distributed to every voter in his congressional district.

12. The Cabot Lodge oligarchy is the oldest in America. The first George Cabot was a friend and colleague of Washington and a political ally of Hamilton. He was elected a Massachusetts U.S. Senator in 1791 and became a leader of the Federalists. His granddaughter married John Lodge, a wealthy China trader, and the first Henry Cabot Lodge was their son. Boy Cabot Lodge, son of Henry and father of Henry II, married Elizabeth Davis, whose father was Judge John Davis, an assistant secretary of state, whose father was Hasbrouch Davis, a Union brigadier general in the Civil War. His father, in turn, was a Massachusetts governor and U.S. Senator in the early nineteenth century. The family has had money and power for the entire history of our country. The Venetian republic *redivivus*.

13. According to the official postelection report, Kennedy committees spent almost $350,000, while Lodge supporters spent $59,000. This did not include private family monies.

14. Gibson with Schwarz, *The Kennedys*, p. 140. In a footnote on this same page the authors state that JFK admitted to journalist Fletcher Knebel that the *Post*'s endorsement had been bought.

15. Davis, *The Kennedys*, p. 125.

16. Only 25,000 Democrats voted in the 1956 New Hampshire primary that set Kefauver on the path to national attention, which meant that 12,600 people could affect the nationwide election. Joe Kennedy observed and applied this technique for his son. To give a more startling example, in the 1980 Michigan primary only 16,048 Democrats voted, less than 1 percent of the Democrats who voted in that state in November. A sophisticated subclass of the state primary then developed, the "straw poll," whereby a tiny state group—often composed of fanatics on a single issue—can project for a candidate a false wave of popularity unrelated to

the reality of the general voting public within the state. Senator Dole, for example, in November 1995 won the Florida Republican straw vote with 1,104 votes; only 3,325 delegates voted. Newspaper headlines proclaimed, "Dole Wins."

17. Whalen, *The Founding Father*, pp. 480–83, n. 5.

18. Ibid., p. 487.

19. Ibid., p. 489.

20. Ibid., p. 490.

21. Ironically, New York Jews voted in greater proportion for Kennedy than did New York Irish Catholics.

22. Richard J. Whalen, "Joseph P. Kennedy: A Portrait of the Founder," *Fortune* (January, 1963): 168.

23. In 1959 JFK successfully pressured Joseph Dinneen to exclude from his book *The Kennedy Family* three paragraphs of an interview in which his father spoke in derision about Jews.

24. Whalen, "Joseph P. Kennedy: A Portrait of the Founder," p. 168.

25. For what might be considered murder if involving common folk, Ted Kennedy received a two months' suspended jail sentence in the Chappaquiddick incident.

26. Gibson with Schwarz, *The Kennedys*, p. 14. This was in the Eighth Congressional District held by his great-grandfather, John "Honey Fitz" Fitzgerald and then by his uncle John F. Kennedy.

27. The background on these events has been studied in two books: *"One Hell of a Gamble": Krushchev, Castro and Kennedy, 1958–1964*, by Alexandre Fursenko and Timothy Naftali (New York, 1997); and *The Kennedy Tapes: Inside the White House during the Cuban Missile Crisis*, edited by Ernest R. May and Philip D. Zelikow (Cambridge, Mass., 1997). A close reading of these books indicates how we are fodder to high-class fools and maniacs. In the height of this crisis, Dean Acheson, Douglas Dillon, General LeMay (head of the air force), General Wheeler (head of the army), Senator Richard Russell and even Senator William Fullbright, were for war; while only General Maxwell Taylor (chairman of the armed forces)—who strongly influenced Kennedy—rejected an immediate air attack. Bobby Kennedy, noted for his "dirty tricks" approach to Castro was particularly belligerent. Reading about Bobby's code-named Operation Mongoose, endorsed by the Joint Chiefs of Staff on March 13, 1962, makes one almost ashamed to be American.

28. Fursenko and Naftali, *"One Hell of a Gamble,"* p. 90.

## CHAPTER THREE

1. George Reedy, *Lyndon B. Johnson: A Memoir* (New York and Kansas City, 1982). Reedy was staff director of the Senate Democratic Policy Committee under Johnson when the latter was Senate Majority Leader and press secretary when Johnson was elected. He made this interesting psychological portrait after years of working with his boss.

2. Robert A. Caro, *The Years of Lyndon Johnson: Means of Ascent* (New York, 1990), pp. 48–51

3. William E. Leuchtenburg, *In the Shadow of FDR: From Harry Truman to Ronald Reagan* (Ithaca and London, 1989), rev. ed., p. 126. In the usual way of Washington, Johnson paid off FDR's son, Jimmy, appointing him a delegate to the UN after Jimmy served six terms as a congressman from California.

4. Caro, *The Years of Lyndon Johnson*, p. 399. As an admirer of Johnson's social legislation, though aware of these character defects, one is reminded of a slogan of the followers of Juan Perón in Argentina, when disclosures made evident Perón's preference for very young girls: *Aun degenerado, preferemos a Perón*—"Even though degenerate, we prefer Perón."

5. Eric F. Goldman, *The Tragedy of Lyndon Johnson* (New York, 1969), pp. 395–96 for quotations.

6. Ibid., p. 396.

7. Ronnie Dugger, *The Politician: The Life and Times of Lyndon Johnson* (New York and London, 1982), p. 371.

8. There never was a declaration of war in Vietnam or even a specific resolution of support from Congress. On the other hand, Congress could have, but never did, cut short the Vietnam conflict simply by withdrawing the money to support the war. The sustained bombing of North Vietnam was approved by Dean Rusk, Robert McNamara, McGeorge Bundy, Maxwell Taylor, General William Westmoreland, and General Earle Wheeler. As Doris Kearns remarked in *Lyndon Johnson and the American Dream* (New York, Hagerstown, San Francisco, and London, 1976), "The policy of escalation was advocated by every individual at the highest level of responsibility for actions relating to national security" (p. 261).

9. Caro, *The Years of Lyndon Johnson*, p. xxix.

10. There is such a flowing cornucopia regarding the lies, frauds, and deceits of LBJ one can only list the more prominent. Newspaper articles

include the following: *New York Times*, December 4, 1963; August 20, 1964; December 26, 1966; and December 9, 1969. *Wall Street Journal*, feature article, March 24, 1964. *International Herald Tribune*, October 31, 1969. Magazine articles most prominent are: *Life*, August 17, 1964; and *New Republic*, October 1, 1966, and December 17, 1966. Books are: Ferdinand Lundberg, *The Rich and the Super-Rich: A Study in the Power of Money Today* (New York, 1968), pp. 93, 518; Dugger, *The Politician*, pp. 266–68, 273; and, most detailed, Caro, *The Years of Lyndon Johnson*, pp. 80–118, 136.

11. *Wall Street Journal*, March 24, 1964. Feature article.

12. Caro, *The Years of Lyndon Johnson*, p. 136.

13. Ibid., pp. 16, 180, 273–75, and 339. Also Irwin Unger and Debi Unger, *LBJ: A Life* (New York, 1999), p. 73.

14. Unger and Unger, *LBJ: A Life*, p. 116.

15. Ibid., pp. 74–75.

16. See Caro, *The Years of Lyndon Johnson*, p. 273ff.

17. Dugger, *The Politiican*, p. 286.

18. This quotation and those following come from a series of articles *The New Republic* published as above stated in note 10.

19. With even more humor, the fabulous financier Warren Buffett wrote that the native Americans may have gotten the better deal. He pointed out that if the $24 had been invested at only 6 percent interest, it would have grown to a higher value than the multibillion dollar current real estate value of Manhattan.

20. See n. 10 for references to this particular deal.

21. Ibid.

22. *International Herald Tribune*, October 31, 1969.

23. Leuchtenburg, *In the Shadow of FDR*, p. 131.

24. Joseph A. Califano Jr., *The Triumph and Tragedy of Lyndon Johnson: The White House Years* (New York and London, 1991), p. 10. As a last point it may be mentioned that even the Machiavellian Johnson spawned a political dynasty of sorts, for his daughter married Chuck Robb, a U.S. Senator from Virginia.

## CHAPTER FOUR

1. Roger Morris, *Richard Milhous Nixon: The Rise of an American Politician* (New York, 1990), p. 131.

2. Frank Nixon, his father, was a supporter of Robert La Follette, the third-party Populist candidate for president in 1924.

3. Morris, *Richard Milhous Nixon*, p. 236.

4. The two quotations are from ibid., pp. 281, 283.

5. Jonathan Aitken, *Nixon: A Life* (Washington, D.C., 1993), p. 185. Aitken, whose biography is rather sympathetic toward his subject, states that Chotiner "could be described as the father of negative campaigning." Also see Anthony Summers, *Arrogance of Power: The Secret World of Richard Nixon* (New York, 2000), pp. 42–43.

6. Morris, *Richard Milhous Nixon*, p. 303.

7. Aitken, *Nixon*, pp. 130–31.

8. Morris, *Richard Milhous Nixon*, pp. 313–14.

9. Quotations from ibid., pp. 320–328.

10. At the end of the campaign a review indicated that Nixon had nearly 70 percent more advertising, more than twice the news stories, and thirty-eight favorable editorials compared to two for Voorhis. In the formal affidavits filed in Sacramento, Nixon spent eight times as much money as Voorhis. And three decades later, Nixon backers admitted that the actual comparison was twelve to one.

11. Morris, *Richard Milhous Nixon*, p. 341.

12. When he couldn't use these charges against John F. Kennedy because they were so obviously ridiculous, Nixon lost that election.

13. William B. Ewald, *Eisenhower the President: Crucial Days, 1951–1960* (Englewood Cliffs, N.J., 1981), p. 314.

14. J. Anthony Lukas, *Nightmare: The Underside of the Nixon Years* (New York, 1976), p. 26. For a more detailed analysis, see pp. 22–26.

15. Ibid., p. 68.

16. The best concise summary of these events is in Kenneth C. Davis, *Don't Know Much About History* (New York, 1990), pp. 396–405.

17. President John F. Kennedy did this before Nixon, as had Eisenhower and Johnson.

18. The men close to Nixon were very concerned that in his half-demented condition at the end, when he actually contemplated defying

the Supreme Court's backing of the legislative action (which indeed had a precedent in Andrew Jackson's spurning the Supreme Court's decision not to expel the Cherokee Indians from Georgia), he might try a coup d'état. Defense Secretary James R. Schlesinger indeed gave orders that the armed forces were to accept no commands from the White House without his countersignature. See Lukas, *Nightmare*, p. 559.

19. Senator Barry Goldwater defended Nixon to the last, unable to believe his hero could do such things. Later, disgusted at the duplicity, he called Nixon the greatest liar he had ever met. Many decent persons, including my own family, defended Nixon throughout.

20. The details of this wheeler-dealer purchase and sale, which gives one a good insight into the mentality of Richard Nixon, are hard to follow because they were deliberately buried. See the *New York Times* article of May 26, 1973. A later article in the issue of Aug. 31, 1973 showed somewhat different figures but came to the same conclusion, namely that Nixon, by these oblique methods, was left with the valuable waterfront property and house at no cost. The article then pointed out that the transaction, showing a profit, should have been reported on Nixon's 1970 federal income tax, which thus would explain the secrecy surrounding the details.

21. Thrown in was a new concrete shuffleboard court at Nixon's home in Key Biscayne. When Nixon lamely stated that the California improvements decreased the property value because of the masonry wall built to keep out intruders, Texas Representative Jack Brooks, chairman of the House committee investigation, wittily replied: "Anytime you want to desecrate my property with all that money you just come on down to Texas and do it."

22. Rebecca Larsen, *Richard Nixon: Rise and Fall of a President* (New York, 1991), p. 172.

23. The huge quantity of bombs dropped on suspected Khmer Rouge positions in Cambodia only swelled the Communist armies, as angry villagers flocked to avenge their dead families, thus ironically doing the reverse of what had been hoped for. Here again the American leadership failed to understand basic human motives.

24. Franz Schurmann, *The Foreign Politics of Nixon: the Great Design* (Berkeley, Calif., 1987), p. 118.

25. Nixon's public record in these matters is marred, however, by a taped conversation in which he referred to environmentalists as enemies of

★

the system; he also vetoed the 1972 Federal Water Pollution Control Act, a veto overridden by Congress.

26, Joan Hoff, *Nixon Reconsidered* (New York, 1994), pp. 67–68. Nixon thus alienated natural allies in his attempt to gather together all the strands of executive power and use them to subordinate the other two branches of government. One result, according to Hoff, was that many executive bureaucrats outside the small presidential clique became as hostile to Nixon as the liberals.

27. This was the newspaper that had been a major factor electing him at the start of his political career.

28. Both quotations from Stanley Kutler, *Abuse of Power: The New Nixon Tapes* (New York, 1997).

## CHAPTER FIVE

1. Jerald F. terHorst, *Gerald Ford and the Future of the Presidency* (New York, 1974), p. 67.

2. Ibid, p. 87.

3. Ibid, p. 101.

4. Ibid, p. 109.

5. James Cannon, *Time and Chance: Gerald Ford's Appointment with History* (New York, 1994), p. 101. Both terHorst and Cannon were close friends of Ford. TerHorst was appointed White House press secretary by Ford, but resigned a month later in protest over the pardon of Nixon.

6. terHorst, *Gerald Ford and the Future of the Presidency*, p. 218.

7. John Osborne, *White House Watch: The Ford Years* (Washington, D.C., 1977), p. 253.

8. Ibid., p. 424

9. Cannon, *Time and Chance*, p. 236.

10. Gerald R. Ford, *Humor and the Presidency* (New York, 1987), p. 125.

11. Cannon, *Time and Chance*, p. 411.

12. "Ford Believes G.O.P. Should Steer to Center," *New York Times*, July 27, 1998.

13. *Money* (July 1999): 90.

14. The series of previous remarks and quotations are from a long feature article by Francis X. Clines in the *New York Times*, September 19, 1996, the day following Agnew's death.

15. Ibid.

16. Ibid. Also Ronald Kessler, *Inside Congress* (New York, 1997) p. 233.

17. In the twentieth century a new Western Establishment is developing to challenge that more East. The Brown family is an example. Jerry Brown, who served as Democratic governor of California for two terms (1975–1983), was the son of Pat Brown, a previous Democratic governor of California from 1959 to 1967. Jerry ran for president in 1976, 1980, and 1992. Jerry's uncle, Harold C. Brown, long served as a California Appellate Court justice. Jerry's sister, Kathleen Brown Rice, was California State Treasurer (1990–1994), and ran without success for governor in 1994. And in a curious and unusual act, Jerry Brown in 1998 was elected mayor of the depressed city of Oakland, rather similar to the much older case of John Quincy Adams who, after his term as president was elected a U.S. congressman—one of the best members of Congress in U.S. history, one may add.

18. Michael Klepper and Robert Gunther, in *The Wealthy 100* (New York, 1996), proposed a system of valuing individual wealth as a ratio of the U.S. Gross Domestic Product (GDP). They estimated that John D. Rockefeller, who died in 1937, had a fortune equivalent to one sixty-fifth of the entire nation's GDP and was the richest American who ever lived. William Rockefeller, who died in 1922, was thirty-fifth on the list.

19. Nelson Rockefeller personally paid about one-fifth of the New York Republican State Committee's then $500,000 annual budget and also financed his own expensive campaigns. See the *New York Times* feature article by Maurice Carroll, June 19, 1977. The Rockefeller-Harriman contest was an earlier version of the 1996 U.S. Senate race in Massachusetts between John Kerry (married to a Roosevelt) and William F. Weld, where two rich members of the New England elite, with similar views—indeed, the contest was described as a polo match—battled with large sums to represent a potpourri state of recent immigrants.

20. Another Republican candidate for president in 1964 was U.S. Representative William E. Miller, who took money from Lockport Felt while in Congress, where he promoted regulations to benefit the company. Two weeks after leaving Congress he became a vice president of Lockport Felt.

## CHAPTER SIX

1. Betty Glad, *Jimmy Carter: In Search of the Great White House* (New York and London, 1980), p. 53.

2. Ibid., pp. 84–85.

3. As an aspiring politician he could hardly do otherwise for, as an example, Barry Goldwater won by a substantial majority in the national election of 1964 in both Sumter County and the entire state of Georgia. As Carter himself admitted, he did nothing "heroic or economically suicidal" on the race issue. See Kenneth E. Morris, *Jimmy Carter: American Moralist* (Athens, Ga., 1996), p. 119. As examples of this nonheroic position, he generally paid black tenants, who worked his family's land, less than whites, and wouldn't let blacks into his home except for a maid or sharecroppers, who could only stand in the hallway. It is doubtful whether even Lyndon Johnson, who practiced this same double standard, would use phrases like "ethnic purity" or "to inject black families into a white neighborhood," which Julian Bond said smacked of Nazi Germany.

4. Victor Lasky, *Jimmy Carter: The Man and the Myth* (New York, 1979), p. 74.

5. Ibid., p. 86.

6. Maddox and Harris were stunned after the election when Governor Carter declared at his inaugural that the time for social discrimination was over. This flip-flop was only a prelude to the many times Carter played both sides of the fence.

7. Lasky, *Jimmy Carter*, p. 23.

8. Carter was defeated in the Democratic primary in his first run for governor of Georgia in 1966. Dejected, he became a born-again Christian. The change only whetted his political ambitions and he declared, "I believe God wants me to be the best politician I can possibly be." Glad, *Jimmy Carter*, p. 119.

9. Ibid., p. 155. The reference was to business leaders but sprang from his own knowledge of how politics works.

10. Ibid., p. 157.

11. Ibid., p. 141.

12. Ibid., p. 206.

13. McGovern chose Sargent Shriver, a Kennedy in-law, instead, another example of the politically incestuous relations on the highest levels.

14. Glad, *Jimmy Carter*, p. 211.

15. ". . . Carter was not even the first choice of those who supported him. Polls generally indicated that, had Hubert Humphrey entered the primaries, he would have defeated Carter. Even without Humphrey, had Udall just increased his vote by as little as one percentage point in two or three primaries—or had Brown and Church entered earlier—Carter would have been denied the nomination." Morris, *Jimmy Carter*, p. 228.

16. Glad, *Jimmy Carter*, p. 267.

17. Ibid., p. 280.

18. William E. Leuchtenburg, *In the Shadow of FDR: From Harry Truman to Ronald Reagan* (Ithaca, N.Y., 1989), rev. ed., p. 194.

19. Bert Lance, *The Truth of the Matter: My Life in and out of Politics* (New York, 1991), p. 31.

20. Ibid., p. 30.

21. Clark R. Mollenhoff, in *The President Who Failed: Carter out of Control* (New York, 1980), has written the most detailed analysis of the wheeling and dealing of Bert Lance. See pp. 47–68, 189–200, and 240. The Lance deceit is touched on in Glad, *Jimmy Carter*, p. 439; as well as Bruce Mazlish and Edwin Diamond, *Jimmy Carter: A Character Portrait* (New York, 1979), p. 74.

22. Mollenhoff, *The President Who Failed*, p. 66.

23. Ibid., p. 188.

24. Ibid., p. 190.

25. It is interesting how the adoring Carterite Peter G. Bourne, in *Jimmy Carter: A Comprehensive Biography from Plains to Post-presidency* (New York, 1997), p. 412, disposes of this evidence: "In the sweltering dog days of summer in Washington during non-election years, new stories that would pass largely unnoticed at any other time take on a life and tenacity of their own. Such was the case with the so-called 'Lance Affair.' "

26. These are the usual figures quoted. Part of this was due to the doubling of crude oil prices, which, of course, was beyond Carter's control. Lou Cannon, *President Reagan: The Role of a Lifetime* (New York, London, etc., 1991), p. 20, gives somewhat lower figures: 15.26 percent prime interest rate and 12.5 percent inflation.

27. Carter's weakness over the Iranian hostage crisis was contemptible in certain ways but grounded in truth: namely, that he was facing a religious fanatic capable of anything, and Carter tried not to provoke such actions. In

effect, Carter—like Nixon—was attempting to adjust to new world realities. Ironically, his reasonable caution greatly decreased his popularity.

28. *Money* (July 1999): 90.


## CHAPTER SEVEN

1. Reagan stated that Humphrey's opponent was "the banner carrier for Wall Street." Quoted by William E. Leuchtenburg, *In the Shadow of FDR: From Harry Truman to Ronald Reagan* (Ithaca, N.Y., 1989), rev. ed., p. 216.

2. Bill Boyarsky, *The Rise of Ronald Reagan* (New York, 1968), p. 101.

3. Ibid., pp. 209, 211.

4. Theodore H. White, *America in Search of Itself: The Making of the President 1956–1980* (New York, 1982), p. 426.

5. Quoted by Senator Daniel Patrick Moynihan in *Came the Revolution: Argument in the Reagan Era* (San Diego, New York, and London, 1988), p. 322.

6. "Goodbye to the Gipper," *Newsweek*, January 9, 1989.

7. *Wall Street Journal*, October 8, 1981.

8. Lou Cannon, *President Reagan: The Role of a Lifetime* (New York and London, 1991), p. 120.

9. It is unfortunate that Julius Caesar could not avail himself, sending a monthly check, as did Nancy Reagan, to ask Madame Zorba about the Ides of March.

10. In the spring of 1976 Reagan told an interviewer: "Fascism was really the basis for the New Deal." Leuchtenburg, *In the Shadow of FDR*, p. 219.

11. Bob Schieffer and Cary Paul Gates, *The Acting President* (New York, 1989), p. 179.

12. Reagan had so little interest in his appointees that in a famous incident he didn't even recognize Samuel Pierce, his own cabinet member.

13. Two of his more inflammatory remarks can be cited. The first was dividing Americans into two categories: "Liberals and Americans." The second was describing a panel as consisting of "a black, a woman, two Jews, and a cripple."

14. Dubbed thus by Colorado Congresswoman Patricia Schroeder for his uncanny ability to keep controversial issues from sticking to him.

15. The story of these land purchases and sales come from two feature articles, one in the *Wall Street Journal*, August 1, 1980; the other in the *New York Times*, October 6, 1980. Small details vary but the substance of the two articles is the same.

16. Cannon, *President Reagan*, pp. 102–107; also Boyarsky, *The Rise of Ronald Reagan*, pp. 104–106.

17. *Wall Street Journal* article above mentioned.

18. Reagan sold these 771 acres in late 1976 for $850,000, more than doubling his money.

19. See n. 15.

20. Cannon, *President Reagan*, pp. 354–57.

21. Ronald Reagan, *An American Life* (New York, 1990), p. 505. Certain details in this account differ from those written by Schieffer and Gates in *The Acting President*, and Jane Mayer and Doyle McManus in *Landslide* (Boston, 1988). I am following the account of Lou Cannon, the acknowledged expert on Reagan. Because of the death of William J. Casey at the time of the later investigation, there are probably aspects of the Iran-contra story that will never be revealed.

22. North was not a profiteer in these deals; his sole concern was diverting money to pay the contras in Nicaragua. He was, however, later convicted for accepting an illegal gratuity to install a security system in his Virginia home. The contras, however, were involved in the drug trade for profit. The CIA long ignored charges during the Reagan administration that anti-Sandinista rebels on their payroll were head-over-heels in drugs. In 1997, however, an internal investigation reported that such allegations involved fifty-eight contras, including fourteen pilots who flew the drugs into protected U.S. airports. (*New York Times*, October 10, 1998).

23. *Report of the Congressional Committees*, p. 197.

24. Cannon, *President Reagan*, p. 630.

25. Ibid., quoting the Reagan diary, p. 638. Also Mayer and McManus, *Landslide*, p. 188.

26. Mayer and McManus, *Landslide*, p. 299.

27. Cannon, *President Reagan*, p. 684.

28. Sidey, "An Interview with the President," quoted in ibid., p. 703.

29. Ibid., p. 714.

30. When Reagan met Gorbachev over a modus vivendi on nuclear missiles, McFarlane at the meeting was startled how alert he was, "almost

★

unique in his ability to sustain a conversation for more than five minutes."
Interview with McFarlane, September 11, 1990, noted in ibid., p. 751.

31. When the Cold War ended in 1989, there were at least sixty thousand nuclear warheads stockpiled in the United States and the USSR, enough to kill everyone on earth many times over.

32. Cannon, *President Reagan*, p. 791.

33. Bob Schieffer and Gary Paul Gates, *The Acting President* (New York, 1989), pp. 376–77.

34. Ibid., p. 277.


## CHAPTER EIGHT

1. Herbert S. Parmet, *George Bush: The Life of a Lone Star Yankee* (New York, 1997), p. 28.

2. Ibid., p. 41.

3. Ibid., p. 65.

4. Ibid., p. 68.

5. Ibid., pp. 74–75.

6. A lesson that his son noted. While in Congress, he took an affirmative stand on abortion; later, on the national scene, where the Roman Catholic vote became more important than in Texas, he opposed it.

7. Parmet, *George Bush*, p. 83.

8. Ibid., pp. 80–86.

9. Arnold Forster and Benjamin Epstein, *Danger on the Right* (New York, 1964), p. 40.

10. Parmet, *George Bush*, p. 96.

11. *Houston Chronicle*, October 28, 1964.

12. A factor in Bush's defeat was the revelation that he was "a substantial stockholder" in Seacat Off-Shore Drilling Company, which operated as a British company without paying American taxes. Bush's profits from this operation in 1963 alone, according to the figures presented, were over $1 million. Parmet, *George Bush*, p. 111.

13. Fitzhugh Green, *George Bush: An Intimate Portrait* (New York, 1991), p. 91.

14. Parmet, *George Bush*, pp. 118–19.

15. *Houston Chronicle*, January 7, 1968.

16. Parmet, *George Bush*, p. 141.

17. Richard Ben Cramer, *What It Takes: The Way to the White House* (New York, 1992), pp. 612–13.

18. George Bush to James A. Baker III, Public Service Archives, Series 4, Box 7, Woodson Research Center, Rice University, Texas.

19. Ibid. Notes for August 5, 1974. Courtesy of George Bush, Parmet, *George Bush*, p. 165.

20. Bush was the favorite of the more conservative Republicans, who distrusted the moderate wing led by Nelson Rockefeller. However, *Newsweek* on August 26, 1974, revealed that in the Bush Senatorial campaign of 1970 $40,000 had never been reported, as required by the Corrupt Practices Act. Though later denied by Ford, it was claimed that the new president, sensitive to public opinion so shortly after Watergate, preferred a man not tarred by such allegations, whether true or false.

21. Green, *George Bush*, p. 153.

22. Hearings followed confirming much of this information. *Hearings Before the Committee on Armed Services*, U.S. Senate, 94th Congress (Washington, D.C., 1975), p. 70.

23. Parmet, *George Bush*, p. 208.

24. Ibid., p. 209.

25. Ibid., p. 257.

26. Randall Rothenberg, "In Search of George Bush," *New York Times Magazine*, March 6, 1988, p. 48.

27. George P. Shultz, *Turmoil and Triumph: My Years as Secretary of State* (New York, 1993), pp. 639, 625–26.

28. Noriega interview with Lally Waymouth of the *Washington Post* in 1983, cited in Parmet, *George Bush*, p. 289.

29. Former Secretary of Defense Caspar Weinberger's records, revealed in court proceedings right before Bush's election as president, indicated that Bush had lied. See also Parmet, *George Bush*, pp. 307, 322; and Stanley G. Hilton, *Senator for Sale: An Unauthorized Biography of Senator Bob Dole* (New York, 1995), p. 182.

30. Fred Barnes, "On the Supply Side: Bush comes down in the Corporate Camp," *Business Month* (September 1988).

31. "TRB from Washington," *New Republic*, October 15, 1984.

32. The program was originally initiated by a former Republican governor, but clumsy Dukakis forgot to use this point until too late. Another

curious fact is that Al Gore, running in the Democratic primary, was the first political figure to use the Horton issue against Dukakis. It may be mentioned that in the Republican primaries, fighting both Bush and Dole, was another prototypical upper-class figure, Pierre (Pete) DuPont, former governor of Delaware. DuPont had two of the legs of the tripod on which power sits, money and name, but lacked the political finesse of Bush.

33. Jack Mitchell, *How to Get Elected* (New York, 1992), pp. 197–98. Also Parmet, *George Bush*, p. 336. Lee Atwater came from a religious background. Struck by an incurable brain tumor in 1990 when only thirty-nine, at the end he felt God had punished him for his dirty tricks and implored forgiveness.

34. Bush diaries, February 23, 1989, Office of George Bush, Houston.

35. Sununu was a man so consumed by vanity that he made mistakes a fifteen-year-old would have avoided. Called a bull in a china shop, he was described as unbearable, impatient, rude, condescending, and arrogant. He insulted Democrats to their face but, worse, also did this to Republicans. In one famous incident he dismissed powerful Republican Senator Trent Lott, later Senate majority leader, as "flat-out inconsequential." Sununu used U.S. military planes and government-chauffeured limousines for personal trips to ski resorts, football games, and even stamp shows. Bush, with his usual loyalty, hung on but in the mounting storm finally asked him to step down.

36. The Cold War was over but Bush's budget requests were only 4 percent below the all-time record spending at the height of the Cold War. "The influence of a conservative and powerful military-industrial complex that lobbies persistently for large budgets, and is generous with campaign contributions, is undeniable. On a more personal level, President Bush prospered in the oil industry and unfailingly supported political and economic policies favorable to big oil. Five oil companies rank among the top 100 U.S. military contractors." Rear Admiral Eugene J. Carroll Jr. (Ret.), "Military Spending," in *Eyes on the President, George Bush: History in Essays & Cartoons* (Occidental, Calif., 1993), p. 68.

37. Texas A & M speech of May 12, 1989, Bush Presidential Materials Project, Bush Presidential Library, College Station, Texas.

38. The United States had hitherto tilted toward Iraq and supplied it with war material, considering Iran, three times larger in population than Iraq, a greater danger. There is some indication from published diplomatic memoirs that Iraq had hinted at its aggressive intentions but misinterpreted

U.S. silence as assent to invade; we do know that our ambassador to Bagdad had failed to warn Saddam Hussein that an attack on Kuwait would bring American reprisal.

39. *New York Times*, editorial, March 1, 1995.

40. Parmet, *George Bush*, p. 111.

41. Ibid., p. 299.

42. Ibid., p. 368.

43. *New York Times*, May 23, 2001, p. A1.

44. "For members of Congress, it would also mean alienating thrift owners who had become valued Congressional campaign contributors." Stephen P. Pizzo, "Savings and Loan Scandal," in *Eyes on the President, George Bush*, p. 232. This went right to the top. Michael Wise of Silverado was chairman of a 1987 Republican dinner in Denver that raised $300,000 for Bush's presidential campaign.

45. Already by 1985 Silverado's questionable practices were known to David Paul, head S & L regulator for the state of Colorado, who wanted to close it down. He reported that Silverado was insolvent and losing millions of dollars each day. Paul testified later before Congress that he was told by Washington regulators to hold off closing Silverado. It was during this period that Michael Wise, chairman of Silverado, asked Neil Bush to become a director.

46. Parmet, *George Bush*, pp. 395–96.

47. *New York Times*, January 19, 1990, feature article by Thomas C. Hayes; ibid., May 17, 1992, feature article by Martin Tolchin; "A Crisis in the First Family," *Newsweek*, July 23, 1990, p. 18.

48. Parmet, *George Bush*, p. 396.

49. As a summary of the activities of Neil Bush, this material is condensed from a series of investigative articles in the *New York Times*, dated May 23, 1990; July 21, 1990; September 12, 1990; September 24, 1990; April 19, 1991; April 19, 1992; and September 11, 1992. Also in the issue of March 26, 1993, L. William Seidman, former chairman of the FDIC, was quoted as stating that a top White House official under President Bush intervened in the Silverado government investigation, trying to move the case to what was considered a more lenient agency.

50. Hilton, *Senator for Sale*, p. 114

## CHAPTER NINE

1. Robert E. Levin, *Bill Clinton: The Inside Story* (New York, 1992), states that in an interview with his old high school principal, she remarked it was necessary to put a cap on the number of organizations any one student could belong to or Clinton would have been president of them all.

2. In an odd and rather ironic way, the early development and academic prestige of Bill Clinton is quite similar to that of the young Richard Nixon.

3. It was in this period that Roger Clinton, Bill's younger brother, was arrested as a cocaine user and distributor. Despite the great adverse publicity, Bill Clinton's hold on the electorate was so great—it was said half jokingly that he knew every person in Arkansas by first name—he was reelected governor in the next election. In Roger Clinton's autobiography, written with Jim Moore, *Growing Up Clinton: the Lives, Times and Tragedies of America's Presidential Family* (Arlington, Tx., 1995), the support given him, and Roger's love and respect for his older brother, is refreshing. Those fundamental Christians who hate Bill Clinton should read this book to see the compassion that grew out of the president's religious belief, without cant at this early point.

4. Kenneth E. Morris, *Jimmy Carter, American Moralist* (Athens, Ga., 1996).

5. Where people feel voting makes a difference they vote. Eighty to 90 percent of Israelis vote in national elections. In the 1999 presidential election to replace Nelson Mandela in South Africa, citizens stood patiently for miles waiting their turn to vote.

6. Bob Reich's *Locked in the Cabinet* (New York, 1997), is a most illuminating and amusing account of the Clinton administration.

7. George Stephanopoulos, *All Too Human: A Political Education* (Boston, 1999), p. 289.

8. NAFTA was actually voted against by the majority of the Democratic legislators.

9. Clinton's first two budgets reduced the federal deficit from 5 percent of the gross domestic product at the end of the Reagan–Bush years to 2.5 percent. His emphasis on cutting the deficit and balancing the budget, so attacked by liberals who saw other priorities as more important, was hardly a betrayal: In his election campaign Clinton had promised to

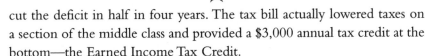

cut the deficit in half in four years. The tax bill actually lowered taxes on a section of the middle class and provided a $3,000 annual tax credit at the bottom—the Earned Income Tax Credit.

10. Article on October 7, 1994.

11. Under President Eisenhower, a Republican, the top ordinary tax rate was 90 percent. From 1972 (except a period in the 1980s) the top capital gains bracket fluctuated between 35 percent and 28 percent—mainly under Republicans. Settled at 28 percent under Clinton, elected as a liberal Democrat, the top capital gains bracket was then further reduced, with his assent, to 20 percent. To be fair to Gingrich, a fan of technology, however, he believed that certain new technological developments, especially in communications and biomedical science, could transform society. By increasing economic incentives, such as a capital gains reduction, society as a whole would thus benefit. The stock market boom, based mainly on such companies exploiting these scientific advances, proved his point up to spring of 2000. Whether it would have done so without such tax breaks, both personal and business, is an open question.

12. Elizabeth Drew, *Showdown: The Struggle Between the Gingrich Congress and the Clinton White House* (New York and London 1996), p. 63.

13. "In endorsing the Republicans' bill [welfare reform], Mr. Clinton was acquiescing in the most sweeping reversal of domestic policy since the New Deal—and in a remarkable retreat from the vision of welfare that be had outlined in 1992." Peter T. Kilborn and Sam Howe Vernovek, "The Clinton Record," *New York Times*, August 2, 1996. The bill cut more than $50 billion out of federal programs for the poor and allowed states to cut an additional $40 billion over six years. Three assistant secretaries resigned on principle because it had been calculated that the bill would throw more than a million children into poverty.

14. Dale was indicted but acquitted on charges of misusing travel office money. Republicans charged that the requested files were an attempt to build a case against him. Among the files obtained by Clinton aides was a dossier on former Secretary of State James A. Baker III.

15. The United States had already spent some $55 billion, to no avail, trying to develop a workable weapon.

16. Articles in the *New York Times*, June 10, 1996; June 15, 1996; March 29, 1997; October 22, 1998; December 4, 1998; January 2, 1999; and January 7, 1999.

## The World's Biggest Military Powers

Comparison of the 14 countries that spend more than $10 billion a year on their armed forces.

### By Total Spending[1]

Total 1998 defense budget in billions

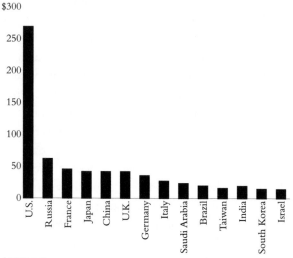

[1]1997 dollars
*Wall Street Journal*, November 12, 1999.

It should be added that in late November 1999 the Senate sent President Clinton a budget that included more for the military than in 1998, a part devoted to pay increases. Even more exaggerated than these differences in the civilian business world, as of January 2000 sergeants will get $120 more a year, while four-star generals will get $10,000 more, a differential ratio of 1 to 833.

17. To many of these congressmen, especially southerners, Ambrose Bierce's sardonic definition of "African" (now called African American) in his *The Devil's Dictionary* is still valid: "A nigger that votes our way."

18. Richard Nixon resigned before the House vote on impeachment.

19. Shelley Ross, *Fall from Grace: Sex, Scandal, and Corruption in American Politics from 1702 to the Present* (New York, 1988), pp. 22–28.

20. He was hardly alone in this matter. When young Andy Jackson, later President Jackson, moved west, among the first things he did was to buy a very young slave girl; presumably this was to wash his laundry.

21. Enzo Biagi, *Un Uomo in Griglio alla Casa Bianca* (Rome, n.d.), p. 107.

22. Ross, *Fall from Grace*, pp. 158, 160–64.

23. Ibid., pp. 172–74.

24. Ted Morgan, *FDR: A Biography* (New York, 1985), p. 453.

25. Ross, *Fall from Grace*, pp. 187–90.

26. Ibid., pp. 198–201.

27. Ibid., pp. 220–24. For readers wishing to read further on these various revelations regarding the presidents mentioned, the reference section on pp. 299–314 lists sources.

28. Ron Nessen, *It Sure Looks Different from the Inside* (Chicago, 1978), pp. 24–26.

29. Bruce Shapiro, "We, the Jury," *Nation*, November 30, 1998. These activities are nothing new. In *The Devil's Dictionary*, Ambrose Bierce defined the U.S. Senate as a body of elderly gentlemen charged with high duties and misdemeanors. When Edward Everett served as chaplain of the U.S. Senate, he was asked if he prayed for the senators. "No," he said, "I look at the senators and pray for the country." Mark Twain was even sharper. "Congress," he wrote, "is America's only genuine criminal class." And when Congress voted in June 1999 to post the Ten Commandments in public schools, it would have been wiser to have them posted in the congressional chamber.

30. The various above statements regarding House Republicans are quoted from two sources: Stanley G. Hilton and Anne-Renee Testa, *Glass Houses: Shocking Profiles of Congressional Sex Scandals and Other Unofficial Misconduct* (New York, 1998); and Shapiro, "We, the Jury." In every case except that of Helen Chenoweth (where the item was published in the book but not in the *Nation*), the same facts are reported in both sources. Page numbers therefore all come from the book: Hyde, pp. 9, 24, 241; Burton, pp. 10, 77–78; Chenoweth, p. 10; Barr, p. 31; Watts, pp. 10, 235; Calvert, pp. 10, 82, 85; Armey, pp. 44–45; and Petersen, pp. 10, 190–92.

31. "Clinton Accuser's '94 Deposition Comes Under Attack as Untruthful," *New York Times*, February 6, 1999. DeLay is so reactionary he denounces evolution.

32. Hilton and Testa, *Glass Houses*, pp. 8, 115.

33. Compare the Clinton impeachment with the slap on the wrist that House Republicans gave Speaker Newt Gingrich after he was caught lying about violating House ethics rules. Instead of expelling him from

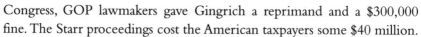

Congress, GOP lawmakers gave Gingrich a reprimand and a $300,000 fine. The Starr proceedings cost the American taxpayers some $40 million.

34. Nearly half of those who voted for Clinton in his first election told pollsters after voting that they thought he was a liar. Roger Morris, *Partners in Power: The Clintons and Their America* (New York, 1996), p. 6.

35. The United States refused to turn over any evidence justifying its position in the Khartoum (Sudan) bombings and rejected a request at the United Nations to send inspectors to search the building rubble for such evidence. Clinton then accused Osama bin Laden of plotting to kill the pope and President Hasni Mubarek of Egypt, again without proof. Not unrelated, three days earlier Clinton had just completed his grand-jury appearance in the Monica Lewinsky matter; like Reagan, there is a strong suspicion that he used military action to deflect public criticism of his other mistakes.

36. Steven Erlanger, *New York Times*, January 14, 2001, p. 6.

37. Christopher de Bellaigue, "Justice and the Kurds," *New York Review of Books*, June 24, 1999, p. 19.

38. The most recent survey in the Basque country indicated that only 10 percent of the population identifies itself as Spanish. *New York Times*, August 11, 2000, p. A3. The French, however, have learned from the mess in Kosovo. France, which struggled for decades against Corsican separatist violence, gave Corsica autonomy in July 2000.

39. That brush wars are considered good business may be shown by the fact that the stock market rose rather than declined when the Kosovo assaults started. Americans as a people are becoming so used to war without declaration that, if no Americans are killed, life goes on as though the televised explosions and photo horrors are happenings in a phantasy or are mere science fiction. This numbing of feeling is the spiritual degrada-tion that has resulted from our constant military actions. The level of cal-lous dehumanity can be summarized by one news quote. Bombers destroyed the home of Slobodon Milosevic, president of Serbia. "Although NATO sent a missile into Mr. Milosevic's bedroom, officials insisted that it was nothing personal." *New York Times*, April 23, 1999, page A11.

40. *Greenwich Post*, April 30, 1999, p. 10.

41. October 28, 1992. Quoted by Paul Greenberg, *No Surprises: Two Decades of Clinton-Watching* (Washington and London, 1996), p. xiv.

42. It is often forgotten that Clinton supported the death penalty,

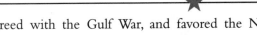
agreed with the Gulf War, and favored the Nicaraguan contras in the 1980s. George Stephanopoulos defined him as a southern conservative before his first Democratic nominating convention.

43. Dick Morris, Clinton's brilliant pollster—who rather oddly came to the president through the advice of his wife—formerly worked for the election of Senator Jesse Helms of North Carolina, considered by many to be the most reactionary man in the U.S. Senate. Morris's idol was Lee Atwater, who conducted George Bush's smear campaign against Michael Dukakis.

Bob Reich, in *Locked in the Cabinet*, describes a conversation with Dick Morris shortly before Clinton's reelection:

> "You've got to understand," Morris explained to me one day in the main corridor of the West Wing . . . "Clinton tacks to the right when the wind is blowing right. Then he tacks to the left when it's blowing left. Now it's blowing right, so that's where he's heading. But he always knows his ultimate destination."
>
> "Where's *that*, Dick?" I asked him.
>
> "Back to the White House for another four years," he said, without so much as a smile. (p. 331)

44. In the American people's judgment of a president, what counts for the poor is jobs, for the middle class inflation, and for the upper class lower general and capital gains taxes. When all goes well, a president—any president—is popular regardless of such pressure groups as the leaders of labor or Christian fundamentalists. For six straight years Clinton led the Gallup poll list of the men most Americans admired, indeed receiving a higher percentage of the vote after the impeachment proceeding than the previous years.

45. Stanley G. Hilton, *Senator for Sale: An Unauthorized Biography of Senator Bob Dole* (New York, 1995), p. 152. Hilton was former Senate counsel and aide to Dole.

46. In July 1999 Michael Andreas, son of Dwayne Andreas and heir apparent at Archer Daniels Midland, was sentenced to a short prison term and a fine of $350,000 for conspiracy to fix prices on the price of the feed additive lysine.

47. All the examples and questions above written come from Hilton, *Senator for Sale*; Ross, *Fall from Grace*; and the *New York Times*, April 16, 1996, and September 5, 1996.

★

## CHAPTER TEN

1. Bill Minutaglio, *First Son: George W. Bush and the Bush Family Dynasty* (New York, 1999), pp. 99, 101–102, 113.

2. Joe Conason, "Notes on a Native Son. I. The George W. Bush Success Story," *Harper's* (February 2000): 40. Molly Ivins and Lou Dubose in *Shrub: The Short but Happy Political Life of George W. Bush* (New York, 2000), state the sum of $4.7 million on p. 23.

3. Conason, "Notes on a Native Son," p. 41.

4. Ibid., p. 42. Again there is a difference. Ivins and Dubose, in *Shrub*, state $83 million on p. 36.

5. Conason, "Notes on a Native Son," p. 43. Ivins and Dubose, *Shrub*, p. 41. Elizabeth Mitchell, *W. Revenge of the Bush Dynasty* (New York, 2000), pp. 259–60.

6. The usual reported figure. Ivins and Dubose, *Shrub*, p. 41, state the sum of $15.4 million.

7. *New York Times*, April 13, 2001, as reported by David Cay Johnston.

8. Michael Isikoff, "A Bush Mystery in Alabama," *Newsweek*, July 17, 2000. Also Joe Thomas, "Bush's Guard Attendance is Questioned and Defended," *New York Times*, November 3, 2000,

9. Ivins and Dubose, *Shrub*, p. 4.

10. Ibid., p. 7.

11. Myra MacPherson, *Long Time Passing: Vietnam and the Haunted Generation* (New York, 1984), p. 141.

12. Michael Murphy, *Technology Investing* (August 2000).

13. Ivins and Dubose, *Shrub*, p. 14.

14. Ibid., p. 44.

15. Ibid., pp. 142–44.

16. Ibid., pp. 94–96.

17. Ibid., p. 107.

18. Ibid., pp. 110–11.

19. Ibid., p. 115.

20. *New York Times*, November 6, 2000, p. A35.

21. Ibid., January 13, 2001, p. A7.

22. Ibid., December 13, 2000. Feature article by Linda Greenhouse.

23. James Carney and John T. Dickerson, "How Bush Decided," *Time*, August 17, 2000, pp. 27–28.

24. Robert S. McIntyre, "Dick Cheney, Fiscal Conservative?" *New York Times*, July 28, 2000; Bob Herbert, "Smiles All Around," *New York Times*, August 10, 2000.

25. Leslie Wayne, "Two Reaped Profit on Texas Soil," *New York Times*, July 26, 2000.

26. *New York Times*, July 27, 2000.

27. *New York Times*, August 3, 2000, feature article by Charles Lewis.

28. Diana B. Henriques, "The 2000 Campaign: Running Mates," *New York Times*, August 24, 2000, has a long feature titled "Cheney Has Mixed Record in Business Executive Role," discussing the financial background of Dick Cheney at Halliburton.

29. *New York Times*, September 6, 2000.

30. *New York Times*, September 9, 2000, quoting the *Dallas Morning News*.

31. *New York Times*, August 12, 2000; August 24, 2000; and September 2, 2000.

32. As a summary review of the Cheney-Halliburton relation, all the quotations and most of the Cheney material appeared in a series of articles published by the *New York Times*, dates (all in 2000), July 25, 26, 27, and 28; August 8, 10, 12, and 24; and September 2 and 6. Also Carney and Dickerson, "How Bush Decided"; and Ronald Dvorkin, "A Badly Flawed Election," *New York Review of Books*, January 11, 2001.

33. "Harper's Index," *Harper's* (June 2001).

34. Even if some part of the estate tax remains, there is a new option. A Florida so-called Dynasty Trust now permits assets to remain in trust up to 360 years without being subject to tax upon the death of each generation. The trust can also be used to protect assets from invasion by a greedy family individual so that the future line within that family will be shielded. Washington has a similar trust limited, however, to 150 years. There are other variants: see John Turrettini, "Providing for the Year 3000," *Forbes*, June 11, 2001. These are a reversion to the feudal European past where they achieve the same purpose as entailment, outlawed by the American Revolution.

35. Buffett's criticism was very sharp and to the point: "Without the estate tax, you in effect will have an aristocracy of wealth, which means you pass down the ability to command the resources of the nation based on heredity rather than merit." David Cay Johnston, "Dozen of Rich

Americans Join in Fight to Retain the Estate Tax," *New York Times*, February 14, 2001.


## CHAPTER ELEVEN

1. The social programs in Britain since the early 1920s have brought down the richest 1 percent of the population from 59 percent to 18 percent of the total national wealth. David Cay Johnston, "Gap between Rich and Poor Found Substantially Wider," *New York Times*, September 5, 1999, p. 16.

2. The above figures, with minor variations, have been published many times. See Edward N. Wolff, *Top Heavy: The Increasing Inequality of Wealth in America and What Can Be Done about It* (New York, 1996); Peter Brimelow, "Who's Got the Bucks," *Forbes*, July 5, 1999; *Forbes*, September 4, 2000, p. 86; *Money*, December 2000, p. 110; Lars-Erik Nelson, "Watch Out, Democrats!" *New York Review of Books*, July 20, 2000; and the following articles from the *New York Times*: April 21, 1995; August 17, 1995; October 27, 1995; September 5, 1999; June 14, 2000; August 2, 2000; August 31, 2000; September 3, 2000; February 26, 2001.

3. *Forbes*, January 22, 2001. Also see issues dated July 3 and October 9, 2000. It should be understood that with the gyrations of the stock market and real estate these figures jump up and down considerably.

4. Keith Bradsher, "Gap in Wealth in U.S. Called Widest in West," *New York Times*, April 17, 1995.

5. Reed Abelson, "Chief Executive Compensation Rose 16% Last Year over '99," *New York Times*, February 15, 2001. The value of some of these stock options has greatly declined in the telecommunications depression running from late 2000 to late 2001.

6. "The Top Paid CEOs," *Forbes*, May 15, 2000.

7. John K. Galbraith, *Annals of an Abiding Liberal* (Boston,1979), p. 79.

8. Quoted by David Sheff in *Worth*, June, 1999. We are back to what has been called the Age of the Robber Barons, the period from the end of the Civil War to Teddy Roosevelt. J. P. Morgan smugly remarked, "America is good enough for me." Democratic presidential candidate William Jennings Bryan, the champion of the underdog, answered, "Whenever he doesn't like it, he can give it back to us."

9. The day after each national election, thus covering the election of congresspeople, senators, and presidents, the *New York Times* publishes a state-by-state review, including thumbnail sketches of the candidates—the losers as well as the victors—and the monies spent in campaigning. The following sketches of senatorial races are taken from these issues. The extraordinary victory of Maria Cantwell by just two thousand votes in Washington was covered in a feature article in the issue of November 23, 2000, p. A24.

10. It does not follow that money automatically wins elections. Huffington and North lost. Former Governor John B. Connally of Texas spent $13 million in the Republican presidential primaries in 1980 and won just one delegate. Senator Phil Gramm, also of Texas, uselessly spent $20 million seeking the same prize in 1996. In that same year Steve Forbes spent almost $38 million in his vain attempt to become the Republican presidential candidate. The candidate must have some charisma as well as money. But studies have shown that candidates who raise the most money in primaries almost always get the nomination. And once elected, because of name recognition and the flow of lobbyist monies, they are almost sure of a strong leg towards reelection.

11. *New York Times*, September 8, 1999.

12. The extraordinary coarse purchase of a senatorial seat by the super-rich Jon S. Corzine was electrifying national news. The *New York Times* alone devoted eleven articles following this purchase. The facts noted come from these articles, all written in 2000 on the following dates: May 3, May 26, May 27, June 7, July 16, September 3, September 30, October 14, October 18, November 3, and November 8.

13. Leslie Wayne, "Gingrich's Race Was Costliest for the House," *New York Times*, January 3, 1997.

14. Regarding the differing positions of the two political parties, see the articles in the following dates in the *New York Times*: July 31, August 1, August 3, and August 14, 2000.

15. *New York Times*, January 18, 2001. It is interesting that General Powell, who was over our military forces under President Bush, has over $1 million invested in General Dynamics, the weapons, aviation, and shipbuilding giant.

16. *New York Times*, July 22, 2000.

17. *New York Times*, July 6, 1999, p. A12.

---

## CHAPTER TWELVE

1. Britain outlawed the sale of all handguns after an elementary-school massacre in 1996. Twenty-nine countries have severely restricted gun ownership in the past five years. By 1997 more than half of the two million handguns supplied to the U.S. market were either imported or produced locally by foreign countries. The leading American corporation making these guns is Smith & Wesson which, ironically, was purchased in 1986 by a British company. Foreign interests are shooting our American children. More than 75,000 children were killed and 375,000 wounded by firearms in a little over the last two decades. Texans own 80 million guns, close to five times the state's population.

2. *The New York Times,* June 13, 2000. Feature article by Leslie Wayne, p. A 6. When pushing for NATO expansion (which meant additional business supplying arms to the newly admitted countries of Eastern Europe), American arms manufacturers in 1996 and 1997 spent $51 million on lobbying. *New York Times,* March 30, 1998.

3. Leslie Wayne, "Lobbyists' Gifts to Politicians Reap Benefits, Study Shows," *New York Times,* January 23, 1997.

4. Jeff Gerth Stolberg and Sheryl Gay Stolberg, "With Quiet, Unseen Ties, Drug Makers Sway Debate," *New York Times,* October 5, 2000; also *Technology Investing,* August 2000.

5. Lars-Erik Nelson, "Democracy for Sale," *New York Review of Books,* December 3, 1998.

6. Tim Weiner, "Senate Riders Put Some on the Inside Track," *New York Times,* July 7, 1999.

7. Robert Pear, "Insider Bemoans What He Wished For," *New York Times,* May 20, 1999.

8. Robert Pear, "Unlikely Lobbyist Will Lead HMOs into Battle," *New York Times,* July 12, 1999.

9. "Can't 'the Coach' Change Tactics?" *New York Times,* December 22, 1998.

10. Kevin Sack, "For the South G.O.P. Secures Defense Bounty," *New York Times,* December 8, 1997. Also September 27, 1999.

11. Joel Brinkley, "Microsoft Covered Cost of Ads Backing It in an Antitrust Suit," *New York Times,* September 18, 1999.

12. Nelson, "Democracy for Sale."

13. Martin L. Gross, *The Political Racket: Deceit, Self-Interest and Corruption in American Politics* (New York, 1996), p. 42. However, money is free of prejudice. In 1994, with the Republican sweep of Congress, the firm of Goldman, Sachs & Company, which had previously favored Democratic contributions, switched horses and tilted to the Republicans.

14. *New York Times*, August 8, 2000. Feature article by John M. Broder and Don Van Natts Jr.

15. Timothy Egan, "Failing Farmers Learn to Profit from Federal Aid," *New York Times*, December 24, 2000. Yet these farmers, despite benefiting from what can be accurately described as a socialist-type system, consistently vote Republican.

16. Elizabeth Becker, "Some Who Vote on Farm Subsidies Get Them As Well," *New York Times*, September 1, 2001, p. A10.

17. Roh Tae Woo, former president of South Korea, was arrested with a possible sentence of life in prison, on the possession of soliciting corporate donations to create a political slush fund in return for favors. Almost all of our elected representatives would have to go to jail if such a rule were enforced in the United States.

18. David Cay Johnston, "Study finds that Many Large Companies Pay No Taxes," *New York Times*, October 20, 2000, p. C2.

19. Jeffrey H. Birnbaum, *Madhouse: The Private Turmoil of Working for the President* (New York, 1996).

20. Leslie Wayne, "Trading on Their Names: Turning Government Experience into Corporate Advice," *New York Times*, May 23, 2001.

21. Leslie Wayne, "Lucrative Lobbying Jobs Await Many Leaving Government Service," *New York Times*, December 16, 2000.

22. David D. Kirkpatrick, "Ex-Regulator Hired to Advise Bertelsmann," *New York Times*, February 1, 2001.

23. Bryan Gruley, "Government Work Has Its Rewards—After You've Left," *New York Times*, September 13, 1999.

24. *New York Times*, March 6, 2001.

25. Matthew L. Weld, "FAA to Skip Bids on Traffic System," *New York Times*, March 6, 2000.

26. For a review of these perks, see Gross, *The Political Racket*.

27. Byrd's pork-barrel achievements include the Robert C. Byrd Bridge, Robert C. Byrd Institute for Flexible Manufacturing, Robert C. Byrd High School, Robert C. Byrd Freeway, Robert C. Byrd Highway,

Robert C. Byrd Expressway, Robert C. Byrd Lane, Robert C. Byrd Education and Resource Center, as well as two dozen other projects. Serving some forty-three years in the Senate, this vestigial octogenarian, a former Ku Klux Klan member with an ego larger than a dirigible, is a rather awe-inspiring relic of another age.

28. See Gross, *The Political Racket.*

29. Quoted by Gerald A. Ford in *Humor and the Presidency* (New York, 1987), p. 184.

30. Kessler, *Inside Congress*, p. 242.

## CHAPTER THIRTEEN

1. When it looked like Al Gore might win a recount in Florida, several Republican state legislators actually suggested this possibility.

2. Under some state laws, electors who violate a pledge to vote for a particular candidate may be subject to a fine, but there is not a single recorded case where this was enforced.

3. It is interesting to note that in 1969 the House of Representatives overwhelmingly approved a proposed constitutional amendment to abolish the Electoral College; President Nixon endorsed the measure and urged the Senate to adopt it. But the bill was killed by senators from the small states and the South. President Eisenhower also believed in term limits, a twelve-year limit for members of Congress and twenty years for federal judges. Gabor S. Boritt, "Ike Liked Term Limits," *New York Times*, November 8, 1994.

4. Alex Keyssar, "It Pays to Win the Small States," *New York Times*, November 20, 2000.

5. *U.S. News & World Report* (December 25, 2000–January 1, 2001): 37.

6. The figures on the cost of various machines come from John Hendren, "Armed to Send Chads Into Voting Oblivion," *New York Times*, December 17, 2000. In spring of 2001 a bipartisan senatorial effort to revive a voting overhaul took the form of a bill to offer $2.5 billion over five years to help state and local governments buy new machines in time for the 2002 elections.

7. Even the papacy forbids cardinals over eighty to vote for the new pope.

8. Martin L. Gross, *The Political Racket: Deceit, Self-Interest and Corruption in American Politics* (New York, 1996), p. 87.

9. Thomas Patterson, "Point of Agreement: We're Glad It's Over," *New York Times*, November 8, 2000.

## CONCLUSION

1. Roger Morris, *Partners in Power: The Clintons and Their America* (New York, 1996), p. 302.

2. Theda Skocpol, *The Missing Middle: Working Families and the Future of American Social Policy* (New York and London, 2000), pp. 104–105. Also *New York Times*, August 11, 2000. Feature article by Don Terry.

3. Robert Pear, "A Million Patients Lost Medicaid, Study Shows," *New York Times*, June 20, 2000.

4. *New York Times*, June 5, 20, and 21, 2000, feature articles by Barbara Crossette, Robert Pear, and Philip J. Hilts.

5. *New York Times*, September 29, 2000. Feature article by Robert Pear, p. A 16.

6. "Health Fitness," *New York Times*, December 26, 2000, p. F5. Also "Diabetes Looming Epidemic," *New York Times*, January 30, 2001, p. F8.

7. *New York Times*, July 27, 2000.

8. Richard Rosenfeld, "Patterns in Adult Homicide: 1980–1995," in *The Crime Drop in America*, ed. Alfred Blumstein and Joel Wallman, p. 151. Also John J. DiIulie Jr., "Prisons Are a Bargain," *New York Times*, January 16, 1996.

9. *New York Times*, August 10, 1995.

10. *Forbes*, October 2, 2000. Feature article by Dan Seligman.

11. *Greenwich Post*, September 10, 1999, article by Col. David Hackworth.

12. Daniel Akst, "The Culture of Money," *New York Times*, March 7, 1999.

13. David Rosenbaum, "Panel Documents How Violent Fare Is Aimed at Youth," *New York Times*, September 12, 2000.

14. "Harper's Index," *Harper's* (August 2000).

15. Jodi Wilgoren, "Glacial School Improvement," *New York Times*, September 10, 2000.

16. David D. Kirkpatrick, "Why the Mind Shrivels for the Body Politic," *New York Times*, October 16, 2000, p. C 16.

17. *New York Times*, July 1, 1999, p. A6.

18. *New York Times*, September 5, 2000.

19. *New York Times*, November 14, 2000.

20. *New York Times*, December 26, 2000.

21. Matthew Miller, "The Big Federal Freeze," *New York Times Magazine*, October 15, 2000.

22. Timothy Egan, "Many Seek Security in Private Communities," *New York Times*, September 3, 1995.

23. George B. McClellan, *The Oligarchy of Venice* (Boston and New York, 1904).

24. *Life*, an American magazine and thus naturally tilted by nationalism, in a 1999 "Millennium" issue picked the hundred most eminent men of the last thousand years. Not one twentieth-century American president was listed, but those chosen included Thomas Edison, Henry Ford, Orville and Wilbur Wright, Alexander Graham Bell, Samuel Morse, John D. Rockefeller, and Walt Disney.

25. Rich Karlgaard, "Digital Rules," *Forbes*, October 30, 2000.

26. Source: Information Technology Association of America. Since these figures were published in mid-2000, they are surely less valid now, given the sharp drop in the prices of technology stocks.

27. Merely to mention one approach, a flat surcharge of 10 percent beyond ordinary tax rates on $10 billion or more on the richest Americans would yield over $7.5 billion (figures based as of December 2000), a good start toward solving these problems. It would hardly leave these multibillionaires poverty stricken, despite President Bush's desire to reduce further their taxes.

Gates indeed has funded a tremendously rich charitable foundation, but only $1 billion of the total $22 billion is planned for education and children's health in the United States. At the same time Congress is trying to cut $20 billion a year devoted to these aims in order to give more money to the military.

# INDEX

★

★

★

★

★

★

★